# The Theology of Colin Gunton

# The Theology of Colin Gunton

Edited by

Lincoln Harvey

t & t clark

Published by T&T Clark International
*A Continuum Imprint*
The Tower Building, 11 York Road, London SE1 7NX
80 Maiden Lane, Suite 704, New York NY 10038

www.continuumbooks.com

First published 2010
Paperback edition first published 2012

British Library Cataloguing-in-Publication Data
A catalogue record for this book is available from the British Library

ISBN: 978-0-5673-3752-8 (Hardback)
ISBN: 978-0-5672-3119-2 (Paperback)

Typeset by Pindar NZ, Auckland, New Zealand
Printed and bound in Great Britain

# CONTENTS

# ACKNOWLEDGMENTS

Three of the essays to be found in this collection were originally presented at a day conference on the theology of Colin E. Gunton held at Spurgeon's College, London in 2007. The vision and hard work of Douglas H. Knight and Terry J. Wright made the day conference possible. Their persistent encouragement helped to produce this book.

Thanks also to Nick Townsend and Alan Spence for their advice and counsel during the process, and to Graham McFarlane for all his help over the years. And many thanks to Tom Kraft, Associate Publisher at T&T Clark, for his enthusiastic support from start to finish.

This book is for Tereza, with love.

# Contributors

## *In Order of Appearance*

DOUGLAS FARROW is Professor of Christian Thought at McGill University in Montreal, Canada. He has written numerous books and articles, including *Ascension and Eccelsia* (T&T Clark, 1999).

LINCOLN HARVEY is Tutor in Theology at St Mellitus College in London. He was previously Tutor for Christian Doctrine at The South East for Theological Education (SEITE). He is ordained in the Church of England, serving his curacy at St John-at-Hackney. He was one of Colin Gunton's last research student.

ROBERT W. JENSON was the Senior Scholar for Research at the Center of Theological Enquiry, Princeton, New Jersey, USA, until his retirement. Previously, he taught at Luther College, Iowa, Lutheran Theological Seminary at Gettysburg, the University of Oxford and St. Olaf College, Northfield, Minnesota, USA. He co-founded the journal *Pro Ecclesia*, as well as The Center for Catholic and Evangelical Theology. He is the author of numerous books and articles, including the two-volume *Systematic Theology* (Oxford University Press, 1997, 1999).

JOHN WEBSTER is Professor of Systematic Theology at the University of Aberdeen, Scotland. He has held previous posts at the University of Oxford, the University of Toronto, Canada and Durham University, England. He is the author of numerous books and articles, including *Barth's Ethics of Reconciliation* (Cambridge University Press, 1995). In addition, he co-edits the *International Journal of Systematic Theology*.

STEPHEN R. HOLMES is Senior Lecturer in Systematic Theology at the University of St Andrews, Scotland. He previously taught at King's College London. He is author of a number of books and articles, as well as being co-editor of the *International Journal of Systematic Theology*.

ALAN SPENCE is the minister of a United Reformed Church in Northampton, England. He has written a number of books and articles, including *Christology: A Guide for the Perplexed* (T&T Clark, 2008) and *The Promise and Peace: A Unified Theory of Atonement* (T&T Clark, 2006).

PAUL CUMIN was one of Colin Gunton's last research students, earning his PhD in Christian Doctrine at King's College London and completing it at Heidelberg University, Germany. He is currently pastor of Pemberton Christian Fellowship in British Columbia, Canada.

JOHN E. COLWELL is now Minister of Budleigh Salterton Baptist Church and is Senior Research Fellow at Spurgeon's College, London, where he was formerly Tutor in Christian Doctrine and Ethics. He has written a number of books and articles, including *Living the Christian Story* (T&T Clark, 2002), *Promise and Presence* (Paternoster, 2006) and *The Rhythm of Doctrine* (Paternoster, 2007).

PARASKEVÈ (EVE) TIBBS holds a PhD in Systematic Theology from Fuller Theological Seminary, Pasadena, California, USA, where she presently serves as Adjunct Assistant Professor of Systematic Theology. She is Chair of the Eastern Orthodox Studies Group of the American Academy of Religion.

JUSTYN TERRY is Dean and President of Trinity School for Ministry, Ambridge, Pennsylvania, USA, having been Associate Professor of Systematic Theology there. He is ordained in the Church of England and was Vicar of St Helen's Church, North Kensington, London, prior to moving to the USA. He has an interest in contemporary theology and received his PhD from King's College, London under the supervision of Colin Gunton. He recently published *The Justifying Judgment of God* (Paternoster, 2007).

TERRY J. WRIGHT is an Associate Research Fellow at Spurgeon's College, London. He won the inaugural Colin Gunton Memorial Essay Prize in 2004, which was subsequently published in the *International Journal of Systematic Theology* (2005). He is author of *Providence Made Flesh* (Paternoster, 2009).

BRAD GREEN teaches theology at Union University in Jackson, Tennessee, USA. His essays and reviews have appeared in the *International Journal of Systematic Theology* and *Touchstone*, and he is author of *Understanding and the Cross: Toward the Recovery of a Christian Mind* (Crossway, forthcoming) and editor of *Shapers of Orthodox Theology: Thinking Theologically with the Ancient and Medieval Theologians* (IVP, forthcoming). His dissertation examined the theology of Colin Gunton in light of Augustine.

CHRISTOPH SCHWÖBEL was Lecturer in Systematic Theology at King's College London from 1986 to 1993. In 1988 he founded the

Research Institute in Systematic Theology and became its first Director. After returning to Germany he has held chairs in the University of Kiel and Heidelberg University and is now Professor of Systematic Theology and Philosophy of Religion in the Protestant Theological Faculty at the University of Tübingen, Germany. His recent books include *Gott in Beziehung* (Mohr Siebeck, 2002), *Christlicher Glaube im Pluralismus* (Mohr Siebeck, 2003) and *Die Religion des Zauberers* (Mohr Siebeck, 2008).

# FOREWORD

Colin Gunton's theological garden was an exceptionally fertile one. Its trinitarian lines and Christological contours gave it shape and definition, generating space and perspective. It was not slavishly cultivated, however, but allowed for the harbouring of a rich variety of insights into the world God made for humanity to inhabit. History, philosophy, science, music, art, politics, and gardening too – all interested him, both as a man and as a theologian. *People* interested him, not merely ideas, and in his little plot at King's College, beside the Thames, grew many young theologians who, like me, were pleasantly surprised to find themselves planted there, watered and pruned as needed, until they were ready to be replanted somewhere else. Some have written here, and we should be grateful to them – as to Lincoln Harvey – for beginning this process of reflection on his work. Though the gardener is gone, the garden is still being tended.

The tending is no simple matter. Colin Gunton, who stood in the very front ranks of English-speaking theologians, understood theology as a communal activity whose participants should be 'dedicated to thinking in as orderly a way as possible'; but that order, he believed, could not be determined in advance or controlled by anything less dynamic than the gospel itself. It must be a 'free and open' order, responsive both to history and to the Lord of history, for the task of theology lies in thinking 'from the Christian gospel and to the situation in which it is set, rather than in the construction of systems'.[1] Otherwise put, he thought theology systematic in so far as it is evangelical, and evangelical in so far as it bears the gospel from the heart of the Church to the heart of the culture. To toil with him in his garden requires us to adopt the same point of view and to do what he himself did.

Colin Gunton, like the soon-to-be beatified Newman – though Newman was not among those whom he read with the greatest empathy or sensitivity – thought a lot about the culture in which we live, about its ancient roots and modern branches, about what it owes to the gospel and what it does not, about what it has treasured of the gospel and what it has squandered. He thought it to have squandered much, in particular the respect for the particular that it had begun to learn from the incarnation of the Son of God. The gospel he wanted to bring to the culture is a gospel capable of renewing that respect. The theology at which he laboured – including the systematics that he was sketching at Princeton just before his death – was devoted to bringing out in fresh ways the specificity of the persons of the Trinity and of the incarnate Son as the proper basis for grasping the specificity or concreteness of creaturely reality itself. His Bampton lectures suggest that he saw himself as one who was helping thus 'to lay the intellectual basis for the liberation of the many from the submersion in the one that is so much the reality and the threat of modern life'.[2]

I mention this, not to anticipate things that will be said in the present book or to make up any deficiency in it, but to remind its readers that doing theology with Colin Gunton was and is an evangelical task in that sense. It is not a matter of finding him more or less congenial because of his Reformed or Barthian leanings, or because one is interested, as he was interested, in Irenaeus, say, or in Coleridge and Irving, or perhaps in John Zizioulas (whose frequent presence in the seminars on the Strand added considerably to their allure). It is not a matter of attending to him because, as was already evident with the publication of *Yesterday and Today*,[3] he has so many interesting things to say on so many important dogmatic loci. It is not even a matter of siding with him because he is robustly Nicene, or because he does not confuse the Spirit of God with the spirit of the age. Doing theology with Colin Gunton is a matter of embracing his enthusiasm for a gospel capable of liberating modern man, and of perfecting the discipline necessary to see where and how it may do so.

That, to be sure, was not always appreciated by theologians who were less critically, hence less constructively, 'modern' and who often found themselves scandalized by his vigorous credal orthodoxy. 'Believing in the Trinity is like believing in pixies', one of his elder colleagues was rumoured to have said, shortly before retiring. But theology itself was in danger of being retired, even at the Society for the Study of Theology, until Colin began, in his rather pixie-like way, to unsettle the prevailing liberalism and to combat the torpor into which it naturally declines. He did believe in the Trinity, and hence in what Barth called the happy science. The cheerfulness with which he undertook that science, which was to him art as much as science – the art 'of finite and sinful people whose achievements come as gift'[4] – was a gift to us all. In a civilization seemingly in steep decline, where the threat of submersion he perceived is increasingly the reality, it is a gift to be the more greatly treasured and, as it is here, shared.

*Douglas Farrow*
Professor of Christian Thought
McGill University

## *Notes*

1  Colin E. Gunton, *Intellect and Action. Elucidations on Christian Theology and the Life of Faith* (Edinburgh: T&T Clark, 2000), p. 44; cf. Colin E. Gunton, *Theology Through the Theologians. Selected Essays 1972–1995* (Edinburgh: T & T Clark, 1996) p. 8.
2  Colin E. Gunton, *The One, the Three, and the Many. God, Creation and the Culture of Modernity* (Cambridge: Cambridge University Press, 1993), pp. 190f.
3  Colin E. Gunton, *Yesterday and Today. Studies of Continuities in Christology* (London: Darton, Longman & Todd / Grand Rapids: Eerdmans, 1983).
4  Gunton, *Intellect and Action*, p. 45.

# INTRODUCTION

## Lincoln Harvey

Colin Gunton helped to rekindle the discipline of systematic theology in England. He was a prolific writer, authoring over 20 books and dozens of essays and articles, as well as contributing regularly to academic conferences around the world.[1] He also established a vital space at King's College London for the enjoyment of theology. Energetic, excited and confident in the truth of the gospel, Gunton invited friends, colleagues and students to think through the central questions of God and creation in Jesus Christ.

With Gunton, the theological task was to be undertaken on its own terms. Theological speech is first and foremost a response to the action of the triune God in which God gives himself to be known in relation to the creature. Seeking to respond to God's gift within the life of the Church, Gunton attempted to re-present the gospel today on the basis of the gospel given. Confident that God accompanies the theologian in this work, Gunton encouraged a process of vigilant reception and faithful Christian confession. With Gunton, theology was in no way captive to culture.

Nevertheless, Gunton was always on the front foot. He was keen to mine the history of ideas, both theological and philosophical, identifying dead-ends, righting wrong turns and correcting mistakes in the unshaken belief that the gospel can open new vistas for thought. He believed that the theological community must immerse itself in culture – the culture to which it is sent, the culture to which it witnesses – because good theology is a gift from the Church to the world. At King's, theology was in no way a ghetto.

And from his base at King's, Gunton faithfully set about the dogmatic task. He believed that God has generously given the creature its own relative self-standing in Christ and the Spirit, not because God needs to remain aloof from a messed-up world – ontological distance forcing cold disinterest and consequent 'autonomy' – but because God values the creature *as* creature, something genuinely other than himself and with which to share the eternal fellowship of Father, Son and Spirit. As Gunton understood it, the triune God has not abandoned the creature, nor has he overwhelmed the creature; instead – through the ontological *taxis* of his own eternal being – God mediates himself freely in relation to the world he has made.

For Gunton, communion and mediation nicely dovetail: because God is who he is, he relates as he relates; unity and distinction; the 'one' and the 'many'. By systematically linking triune communion to economic mediation in this way, Gunton set about developing his neo-Irenaean theology of creation in which the Son and the Spirit were presented afresh as the 'two hands' of the Father, God himself graciously holding the world close-yet-at-a-distance. Linking the humanity of Christ to the economy of the Spirit, Gunton sketched the priestly vocation of the human creature within creation's projected journey from the protological Garden of Eden to its eschatological city, the new Jerusalem. Gunton kept the big picture in view.

This collection of essays celebrates Gunton's expansive vision. The 12 contributors include a number of Gunton's close friends, professional colleagues and former students from King's College, as well as several contributors who began to engage with his thinking during the course of their postgraduate studies. On reading these essays, the reader will get to grips with Gunton's constructive proposals as the focus shifts from the overarching texture – Trinity, Christology, pneumatology and creation – in towards some of the finer details. Critical in form, and positive in purpose, the various contributors pick out key decisions, developments and trajectories within Gunton's thought, thereby identifying areas of promise, as well as flagging up potential problems. In this sense, the essays together bear witness to the dynamic scope of Gunton's theology, and to the unfinished nature of his work. They are in no way exhaustive – being offered only as a small step towards evaluating his contribution – but it is hoped that they will assist the ongoing process of critical reception by drawing together loose threads, connecting ideas and teasing out the architectural structure of Gunton's thought.

In the first essay, Robert Jenson examines a number of decisions that Gunton made through the course of his career. Clearing a straight path from Gunton's early doctoral work right through to the unfinished (and unpublished) dogmatics, Jenson evaluates Gunton's approach to the doctrine of God, thereby highlighting the way in which Gunton was able to wrestle himself free from the restrictive accounts of divine simplicity by allowing the gospel story to determine his thinking about who God is in himself. Through the course of his essay, Jenson examines Gunton's critique of Augustine, as well as his promotion of a Cappadocian and Irenaean alternative to the established doctrine of God – taking a few moments along the way to refute those who critique the 'Augustine-bashers'. In charting Gunton's faithfulness to the gospel story, and underlining the 'hyper-cyrillian' Christology which was eventually to emerge, Jenson finishes with a question: do Gunton's dogmatic decisions in fact undermine our understanding of the genuine presence of Jesus in the Church today? Leaving the question open-ended, Jenson reminds his reader that they – like Gunton – must make their own 'lively' decisions in these matters.

In the second chapter, John Webster likewise journeys the length of Gunton's career, this time examining the influence of Karl Barth in the development of his thought. Webster shows how Barth informed Gunton's early theology decisively, particularly in respect to the intellectual beauty of the gospel and the need to present it on its own terms. Webster details the way in which Gunton learned to link God's being to creaturely history, thereby overturning an inherited dualism between eternity and time. Though Barth influenced Gunton's pursuit of a genuinely gospel-shaped ontology, Webster shows the way in which they differed, thereby highlighting Gunton's eventual criticisms of Barth. For Gunton, it is Barth's overestimation of divine transcendence that leads to an inadequate pneumatology and an insufficient role for the humanity of Christ in the triune economy. In defending Barth against Gunton's charge, Webster quickly turns the tables, arguing that Gunton's attempt to promote the humanity of Christ in conjunction with a strong pneumatology means that Gunton himself fails to offer a properly worked out theology of *the Son*. By downgrading the Son's action in the way that he does, Webster asks whether or not Gunton is in danger of removing an important barrier against adoptionist and exemplarist Christologies.

In the third chapter, Stephen Holmes identifies some important developments in Gunton's doctrine of the Trinity. At first functioning as an interpretative tool with which to unravel philosophical problems, the doctrine of the Trinity eventually becomes the basis for Gunton's understanding of the ontological priority of persons and relations. In charting the vital shift from hermeneutics to ontology, Holmes spots the key influences which shaped Gunton's theology, showing the way in which these various authorities helped Gunton in his attempt to settle the problem of referral in theological language. By examining Gunton's account of persons in relation and the univocal use of language in Christology, Holmes maintains – though with some critical qualifications – that Gunton's theological ontology is properly Trinitarian because it is first and foremost properly Christological. Though Holmes flags up problems in the ascription of univocal meaning to persons and relations, Gunton's work is judged to be a valuable source of inspiration in the ongoing theological task.

In the fourth chapter, Alan Spence takes a look at Gunton's Christology. Spence highlights Gunton's desire to get behind the Nicene and

Chalcedonian formulas to reach an almost neo-Irenaean naïveté. Spence evaluates Gunton's attempt to avoid classic theological debates concerning natures and wills, notably his decision to posit only *one* internal will in Christ (with the second will being ascribed to the Father). While applauding Gunton's wish to bring the doctrine of the Holy Spirit into Christological discussion, Spence argues that Gunton's failure to develop an active ministry for the Son raises a number of difficulties. To counter these, Spence invites the reader to reconfigure Gunton's proposal, thereby seeing Christ as one person in whom *the Son* (not the Father) acts on the humanity of Christ through the mediation of the Spirit. As Spence sees it, this proposal retains the strength of Gunton's position but avoids its weaknesses.

In the work of Paul Cumin, the reader is shown how Gunton's doctrine of God is shaped by the twofold promotion of Christ's humanity and the economy of the Spirit. Cumin argues that Gunton can prioritize divine persons over divine communion because God's being 'ends', so to speak, just as much with the personal Spirit as it 'begins' with the Father. This allows Cumin to conclude that the twofold mediation of the God–world relation has its source in the 'completion' of the divine life, a claim anchored within Gunton's renewed Christology in which unity and distinction are maintained through the ongoing activity of the two hands, the Son and Spirit. As Cumin sees it, the systematic cohesion to Gunton's work and its faithfulness to the gospel story together mean that Gunton is an invaluable contributor to the Church's ongoing theological task of properly describing the God–world relation in light of Jesus Christ.

In the sixth essay, I examine the importance of Christology for Gunton's theological method. The essay first details the way in which Gunton's doctrine of creation rules out natural theology, with the positive nature of Gunton's subsequent claims being justified Christologically. Having examined Gunton's justification for reading the doctrine of God out of the Christological economy, I show that Gunton switches the direction of thought, linking the revelation of God in Jesus Christ to knowledge of the world as well. I also argue that Gunton's two-way train of thought is anchored precisely and exclusively in the person of Jesus Christ, thereby showing the methodological importance of Christology for a proper theology of nature as well as for the doctrine of God. It is only because Jesus is of one being with the Father *and* of one being with humanity – the double *homoousion* – that the theologian can speak of God and the world with genuine validity.

In the seventh chapter, John Colwell explores a different aspect to Gunton's project, this time critically examining his theology of the Church. Picking out an 'occasionalist' pattern within Gunton's ecclesiology, Colwell argues that Gunton struggles to link his Christology and pneumatology to an adequate ecclesial ontology. Therein highlighting Gunton's indeterminate conception of divine freedom, Colwell looks to develop a brief theology of the sacraments in conversation with Gunton. Colwell's proposal is shaped by Christological confession, which allows him to conclude that the Spirit is genuinely present to the Church as *promise*, anticipating its fulfillment, and through whom the Church is united with Christ. Colwell contends that God, in his freedom, does not turn up 'from time to time' but instead commits himself to particular practices as *directed promise*. God's freedom is determinate.

In the eighth chapter, Paraskevè Tibbs examines Gunton's relational anthropology, especially how it is shaped by a strong Christological conception of the doctrine of the image of God. Tibbs argues that Gunton's concept of the human being – though properly relational in its ontology – underplays the 'vertical' dimension to human life. As Tibbs sees it, Gunton focuses too much on the constitution of humans in relation to other creatures, which is to the detriment of their vertical relation to God. As a result, Gunton's account fails to see the priority of worship within the *imago Dei*. Tibbs concludes that Gunton's analysis of the project of creation – especially creation's origin in a garden – needs to be extended beyond the priesthood of Christ to include the priestly function of all believers. In so doing, the importance of worship for true human *being* will be recognized more clearly.

In the ninth chapter, Justyn Terry examines Gunton's handling of the doctrine of atonement. Terry argues that Gunton frees the discussion from its captivity to modern polarities by rehabilitating metaphor as the primary way to speak of divine action. According to Terry, this move frees the biblical portrayal from a narrow rationalism into an expansive and flexible mosaic of necessary-but-insufficient descriptions of ongoing divine action linked to creation, eschatology and the Church. By rehabilitating metaphor in service to the doctrine of atonement, Gunton's theology, according to Terry, deserves to become a primary text in the ongoing study of soteriology.

In the tenth chapter, Terry Wright examines the way in which Gunton subtly – yet significantly – reframes the doctrine of providence. Through a close reading of two texts, Wright shows that Gunton avoids crude determinism and instead promotes creaturely freedom by recasting divine providence within an account of God's triune action in relation to creatures. Wright argues that providence, for Gunton, is the action of God *as* faithful fellowship with the creature – witnessed to in Scripture by the election of particular people – as God draws his creation towards its eschatological perfection. Though Wright believes Gunton's account to be somewhat underdeveloped and piecemeal, he maintains that it does provide the theological community with a vital resource with which to construct a trinitarian account of providence, one in which the ontological distinction between God and the world is upheld, the faithful presence of God celebrated and a zero-sum conception of God's will and human freedom avoided.

In the penultimate chapter, Brad Green takes Gunton to task for his reading of modernity. The essay first highlights how generous Gunton is in his reading of Western history, especially in his contention that modernity is in part caused by poor theology. Green argues that Gunton's thesis therefore implies that the best way to overcome the entrenched patterns of modern life is to offer good theology as an antidote, with trinitarian theology re-establishing the particularity of the 'many' against the homogenizing forces of the 'one'. However, as Green reads it, modernity is not in fact the product of bad theology but instead stems from the corruption of the human will in the Fall. As a result, Green believes that Gunton is in some sense Pelagian in both diagnosis and remedy – 'we caused it and can fix it' – because he does not offer a strong enough account of human disobedience and the fallen desire to be as God. As Green concludes, modern thinking is part of the gospel story too: it needs to be put to death and brought to life, not simply corrected by good theology (as important as that is!).

The final essay is written by Christoph Schwöbel. Schwöbel offers a grand exposition of Gunton's theology, one in which the mutual conditioning of the economic and immanent Trinities is traced through the course of Gunton's career. Schwöbel expertly guides the reader through a number of Gunton's publications, taking care at all times to detail important developments in his thought as well as underlining the way in which his constructive proposals are presented in relation to God. As Schwöbel understands it, the twofold process of God identifying himself *and* interpreting himself renders theology inherently provisional and 'open' because the ongoing discovery of who God is – in his active difference – shapes our thinking. In effect, God's action provides an 'open frame' in which the whole is seen and re-imagined because *God* is genuinely present with us as himself. As a result, the 'shape' of Gunton's theology is properly dynamic: God does not stand in a spatial relation to us but instead relates as mediated creator, which includes – but is not reduced to – the height, length and depth of the ongoing theological task.

As these brief summaries suggest, the 12 essays cover a wide range of themes. Some telescope in to particulars, while others detail the panoramic scope of Gunton's work. Contributors sometimes agree, sometimes differ and sometimes overlap, with a number of recurring themes emerging. A coherent synthesis of these themes would require a supplementary essay, however, with the decision *not* to include one being based on the belief that the slightly unruly and open-ended nature of the collection is somewhat fitting because Gunton worked at pace. His thinking is dynamic, energetic and transparently excited by the theological task. Usually theologians get the details of their argument right – the historical niceties, the small things

– but they often get the big things wrong; their whole orientation.[2] With Gunton, however – working at speed, energized by the gospel, enlivened by his vision – the reverse is in fact the case. His overall direction is right, the details sometimes wrong, the arguments seldom watertight, the small things somewhat scruffy. And, with that in mind, the open-ended nature of these essays is intended to help the reader begin to evaluate Gunton's dynamic orientation towards the gospel, an orientation mediated here – to speak appropriately! – through the theological community he loved to serve.

## Notes

1 For a detailed bibliography of Gunton's published works, see the work of Paul Brazier in Colin E. Gunton, *The Barth Lectures*, ed. P.H. Brazier (London: T&T Clark, 2007) or Colin E. Gunton, *Revelation and Reason: Prolegomena to Systematic Theology*, ed. P.H. Brazier (London: T&T Clark, 2009).
2 For this way of putting things, I am indebted to James Griffin, *Value Judgement: Improving Our Ethical Beliefs* (Oxford: Clarendon Press, 1996), p. 2.

Chapter 1

# A Decision Tree of Colin Gunton's Thinking

Robert W. Jenson

I have organized the following as a decision tree that displays partings of some theological ways that presented themselves to Colin Gunton, and, at each such parting, marks the way Gunton chose. This seems appropriate to the way I know his theology. It has also the advantage of keeping this chapter from being purely historical, since the choices he made are lively choices also for us.

The first thing I did in preparation for this chapter was to reread parts of Gunton's Oxford dissertation, begun under my supervision and published as *Becoming and Being*.[1] I do not remember exactly how Gunton came to me in the first place – the *reason*, anyway, was that he wanted to write on a systematic subject, with reference to modern theologians, and that devotees of either were not then numerous in the Oxford theological faculty. After a bit, I suggested he might compare the differently revisionist doctrines of God represented by Charles Hartshorne and Karl Barth. I knew little about Hartshorne, and like many a dissertation adviser thought Gunton could usefully read him for me, instead of my having to do it. I thought I could use my knowledge of Barth as a control on his scholarly accuracy. So Gunton went to work, with his usual obsessive diligence.

When I reread *Becoming and Being* I was taken aback by the way in which abiding determinants of Gunton's thinking were full-blown and decisive already in his dissertation, indeed in its opening pages. The dissertation displays with all possible clarity a first parting of Gunton's way from another way, represented or even dominant in the tradition, a way that he then called 'classical theism'. The phrase was Hartshorne's, and indeed Gunton adopted much of Hartshorne's critique of this theological syndrome. At the time, Gunton characterized classical theism with three notions: it is supernaturalistic; it thinks of God as timeless; and it construes a hierarchy of being.

Classical theism is, according to Gunton, supernaturalistic in that this doctrine of God construes deity by negating what he at that time called 'nature'. Gunton then used 'nature' as a label for the whole of what we 'naturally' experience. Thus the God of classical theism has no parts, as all the entities of our ordinary experience do; this God is not temporal, as we are; this God does not speak any human language; etc.

Gunton's distinction between nature and supernature is perhaps not altogether clear, and does not quite track with the ways that distinction has been used in the tradition. I think, indeed, that we have to probe a bit to discern what exactly he rejected under the label 'supernaturalism'. I suggest that what he rejected was any foundational apophaticism, any notion that we achieve knowledge of God merely by negating aspects of his creation. The way to God – in concepts or in experience – does not, according to Gunton then or later, lead *away* from the world as it presents itself to us. We often, of course, do and must say that God is not this or not that, and so did Gunton; what he would not do was allow any epistemologically special and normative place to such propositions.

One aspect of nature negated by theistic 'supernaturalism' is especially significant for Gunton: *time* is alien to the God of classical theism. On Gunton's list of classical theism's sins, this one bit of 'supernaturalism' got a rubric of its own and it will remain a staple of Guntonian polemics: the characterization of God by the notion of timelessness – imported from the Greeks – must finally make every decisive assertion of the gospel oxymoronic. Centrally, if to be God is simply to be timeless, then a man with a mother and an executioner simply cannot be full-fledged and full-time God, chop the logic as we may. Some readers may have noticed that I just slipped into my own language – since on this I do indeed agree with Gunton.

Finally, classical theism locates God at the top of a vertical chain of being, following the Neoplatonic strain in Western thought generally. In this case there is something visceral in Gunton's rejection. He saw reflections of this ontology all over the churchly and civil landscape; and it is hard to know which way the animus runs, whether he distrusted the English establishment because it reflects a Neoplatonic vision, or rejected Neoplatonism because it looks like a model for the English establishment. For example, midway through a nice evening, Blanche Jenson once asked Colin if he could, for the sake of the unity of Christ's Church, belong to a church governed by bishops in historical succession. Gunton thought for a bit, then slapped the table and said only 'I am a dissenter!'

In his Oxford dissertation, Gunton – fairly or not – fathers the classical theism of Western Christian theology on Thomas Aquinas, as Aquinas is a great thinker and a chief shaper of the tradition. This view of Aquinas will remain – it was always hard to get a good word for Aquinas out of Gunton.

But gradually, Augustine would replace Aquinas as the one chiefly blamed for those aspects of the theological tradition that Gunton, at the time of the dissertation, labelled classical theism, and against which he never ceased to argue.

As time would go on, the polemic initiated in Gunton's dissertation would come to circle ever more tightly around one feature of Augustinianism: its commitment to an abstract doctrine of divine simplicity. And it is of course the case: for the Greeks, and then for Augustine and his followers, the world of quotidian experience is many – a vast plurality of different items. This is what ails it. Therefore, if there is deity in which to find refuge from our ills, deity must be one precisely in the abstract sense of *not* being 'many'.

The incompatibility of this doctrine with the Scriptural portrayal of God never ceased to agitate Gunton. It is the doctrine of the Trinity that is at issue. As Gunton saw it, if God is simple in this unqualified and fundamentally negative sense, then his immanent triunity, the triunity of his own inner reality, becomes a mystery about which we can say nothing ontological at all, and which in consequence we can put to no theological or spiritual use. If truly there can be no plurality of any sort in God, then the 'and' in Father and Son and Spirit does no epistemic or ontological work. Now one can, like some recent writers on Augustine, regard this epistemic ascesis as a virtue; Gunton did not – and neither do I.

In the existing draft of a first volume of his planned dogmatic theology (which is lamentably still unpublished), Gunton brings his critique of Augustine together in one formula: 'Augustine's chief weakness is that he asked the wrong question . . . about how to reconcile the absolute simplicity of God with the apparent plurality of the persons, rather than [seeking] a concept of divine unity on the basis of the economy', that is, on the basis of Scripture's portrayal of the works and relations of Father, Son and Spirit as they appear in saving history.[2] From his doctoral research, Gunton knew that Hartshorne's way out of classical theism was the incorporation of God into the temporal whole, but this move is still very much on the pattern of Plato or Aristotle – which Gunton does not fail to point out. Gunton instead chose Barth's way – as I was sure he would when I suggested the topic. Like Barth, Gunton would make precisely the *triunity* of God the founding beginning of his reflections. Only a triune God, he said at the beginning and at the end, could allow a creature that is truly other than he, and yet could be intimately related to him. That is, only a triune God would not be a supernatural entity, at the top of some hierarchy or other. The otherness of the three, one from another, is the possibility of a creation that is other than God; and their constituting relations to each other, their intrinsic relationality, is the possibility of an intimate relation of the creation to God.

We thus come to another fork in the road, for there are different sorts of Trinitarian thinking. After his work on Barth, Gunton discusses three: Augustine's, that of the Cappadocians and – the chosen way – that of Irenaeus.

Augustine is the negative foil. According to Gunton, Augustine is driven by his uncritically assumed doctrine of divine simplicity to cut the cognitive and ontological links between the economic Trinity – that is, the triplicity displayed in God's history with us, as recorded in Scripture – and the immanent Trinity – that is, the triplicity of God himself that trinitarian doctrine posits as the possibility of his triplicity in our history. For if God is in himself utterly simple, there cannot be anything in him that could *be* the possibility of the tumultuously dramatic history of Father, Son and Spirit with us.

Gunton's great case in point is the Augustinian doctrine that it could have been the Father or the Spirit that became incarnate. Augustine and the following tradition do of course say that it is in some sense 'appropriate' for the Son to be incarnate rather than the Father – and so try to accommodate the language Scripture in fact uses – but according to them there is nothing in God or his relation to us that would have prevented the Father from being incarnated rather than the Son. In my own way of putting it, this made the doctrine of Trinity into a conceptual puzzle, rather than a saving mystery, and into a liturgical flourish rather than the enabling structure of our worship.

Gunton was not alone in his critique of Augustine, and especially of Augustine on the Trinity. Karl Rahner was of course a pioneer of the later twentieth-century's critique. I did my share; Wolfhart Pannenberg had his complaints; etc. Now in the history of scholarship, every polemic provokes a counter-polemic, and bashing the Augustine-bashers has lately become a popular scholarly exercise – the very journal Gunton co-founded just carried a defence of Augustine against his objections, though, to be sure, a much more cautious and polite defence than some.[3]

Did Gunton overdo it? Probably. Maybe I did too – once or twice. But was Gunton just wrong? I think not, and for an understanding of Gunton's theological choices, it is important to see that he was not wrong. Let me, therefore, insert a general comment on the current polemics against those who criticize Augustine's Trinitarianism. Whether long books or short articles, all display the same pattern: 'But just look at these other things that Augustine said about God's triunity, and look at this way in which trinitarian language shaped his preaching and catechetics, and acknowledge that he was a great Trinitarian both in his pastoral practice and his personal piety.' To all of which one must simply say: 'Well – sure – of course he was – no one ever doubted it – he did say all that good stuff too, and preach and teach brilliantly to a trinitarian pattern – one can indeed construct a praiseworthy Trinitarianism from the whole body of Augustine's many utterances.'

What is *not* done by those who bash us Augustine-bashers is to face up to the truly disastrous propositions Augustine did in fact emphatically and insistently lay down, propositions that became maxims of subsequent Western theology. He *did* in fact say that the Cappadocian distinction of *ousia/hypostasis* – the very distinction that enabled the creedal doctrine of the Trinity – could be no more than a purely linguistic device, that it could tell us nothing about the reality of God. He did treat the works of God in the economy, in the history of God's saving work, as 'indivisible', in the sense that any of them *could* have been done by any of the three, thereby destroying the whole basis on which an immanent triunity could be affirmed in the first place. He did say that it is absurd, as violating the divine simplicity, to think that the Father could not be what he is apart from the Son, and vice versa – thereby rejecting a foundational proposition of trinitarian thought and worship from Tertullian on. Augustine, alas, did in fact say these things, and they have been a curse on Western theology ever since. Augustine on the whole has of course been far more a blessing than a curse – which can be said of very few theologians. And while we are at it, one should always be suspicious when theologoumena, Augustine's or others', are justified by saying that they 'guard the Mystery' or something of the sort; the true mystery of God does not need our guarding; our menial task is to try to think in the face of the mystery.

In the draft first volume to Gunton's projected dogmatics, the righting of Augustinian errors meant moving chronologically backwards from Augustine.[4] In Gunton's estimate, the Cappadocians had gotten much more of it right than Augustine did. Their great achievement had been precisely the philosophically new ideas that Augustine dismissed. Their achievement was to give ontological weight to the notion of person, and to the notion of relations. With the two notions together the Cappadocians created a new understanding of what we are saying when we say that God 'is', and by analogy a new understanding of what we are saying when we say that creatures 'are'. The Cappadocians – at least the Cappadocians according to Gunton – understood the being of God as *communion*, established in the mutual relations of persons, and so understood also the being of created persons as communion. Gunton cites with satisfaction a letter usually attributed to Basil of Caesarea: God *is* 'a sort of continuous and indivisible community'.[5] How much of this Gunton took from his sometime colleague at King's, John Zizioulas, and how much of it he would have come to in any case, is probably impossible to determine – and of course it makes no important difference.

Nevertheless, also the Cappadocians sometimes – according to Gunton – too often shared the habit of theologians from Origen on, of deriving and describing triune communion otherwise than by reference to the actual lively communion of Father, Son and Spirit in their history with us in the economy. Historically and properly, the immanent Trinity is the foundation in God of his communion with us as the economic Trinity, and so can be properly construed only by keeping that economy always in mind. In its own way also, the Eastern Trinitarianism that developed from the Cappadocians' thinking turned out to be alienated from the doctrine of the Trinity's soteriological roots. Thus Gregory Palamas, 'the Thomas Aquinas of the East', distinguished in God's reality between that in which creatures could participate and that in which they could not; and located the three persons themselves on the far side of the line, in his own way making the actual Trinity a blank mystery.

Jumping backwards again – and some readers will know where we will land – for Gunton, Irenaeus of Lyons did have it almost entirely right, before any of these distortions developed. For Irenaeus, the very function of trinitarian talk about God is rightly to construe the economy, the history of creation, redemption and consummation. From beginning to end of Gunton's writings on the Trinity, he insists that precisely this must be the founding and continuing concern of all trinitarian teaching. Even the new ontology he cherishes in the Cappadocians is good just because the God it adumbrates is the God who can have the economy of which the rule of faith and Scripture tell us.

Gunton affirms also Irenaeus' particular construal of the economy. The history of creation, redemption and consummation is one history, *the* history of creation, redemption and consummation, because it is all finally the work of one person, the Father. The Son and the Spirit, says Irenaeus, are the Father's 'two hands', *by* whom he does all that he does.

In general, Irenaeus speaks very simply of the Son doing this and the Spirit doing that and of the Father doing these things by them. It is nevertheless clear that Irenaeus is no modalist: the God at work is not a fourth behind Father, Son and Spirit. And it is clear that neither is Irenaeus a subordinationist: that the Son and the Spirit do the economic works of the Father in no way degrades their deity, which Irenaeus finds affirmed by the rule of faith and Scripture. Carrying on in his own voice, Gunton will teach that the Son's divinity, far from being denigrated by his obedience to the Father – that would indeed be subordination – is in fact the expression of his divinity. The Son's divinity is demonstrated, not denied, by his humiliation.

As Gunton notes, Irenaeus does not much worry about the ontological status of the Son and the Spirit. This, in Gunton's view, is how it ought always to have been. Irenaeus can relax in this fashion because the alien philosophical notion of divine simplicity had not yet intruded to make plurality simply as such a problem. And since history did not, and perhaps could not, remain with Irenaean simplicity, we have to be extremely cautious and conceptually creative as we pick our way through subsequent complications, always asking, 'But how does this derive from and illuminate Scripture's account of the economy?'

Gunton's reception of Irenaeus brings him and us to yet another fork in the road. A key part of Irenaeus' fidelity to the economy is that he never speaks of the eternal Son as other than that Son who is the man Jesus. In his unpublished dogmatics, Gunton refers to what he calls 'the strange logic' of a key passage: '[God's] only-begotten Word, who is always present with the human race, united to and mingled with his own creation . . . and who became flesh, is himself Jesus Christ . . . .'[6] When is the Word Jesus? Only after he 'became flesh'? Apparently not, since the subject of the proposition 'is himself Jesus' is 'the only-begotten Word who is always present . . .'. Dealing with the strange logic of Irenaeus' way of speaking posed to Gunton yet another choice.

One way to cut the knot of Irenaeus' strange logic is of course to say, with the apologists from Justin to Origen, that for all eternity the Son/Logos was unincarnate, a *Logos asarkos*, and that when Mary got pregnant this Logos became Jesus. Gunton chose instead to stick precisely to the oddity of Irenaeus' way of speaking, and he went very far with that way of speaking. Let me give some examples from the unpublished work.[7]

'Jesus is to be understood as the one whose human career was perfected by the Father through the eternal Spirit. It is *as such* that he is to be understood also as the divine Son of God . . . who as a result of his work is placed in the center of the divine economy of creation and salvation.' Indeed, 'the man Jesus Christ, the mediator of salvation, is first of all mediator of creation, so that finally he might be eschatological mediator, recapitulating . . . all things in himself'. And even more startling, '. . . we must not divorce our conception of the Son's office as the Logos, as the basis of all rationality and truth, from his material humanity'.[8]

It is a very risky branch that Gunton has gone out on. Perched out there, one move would be simply to eschew the concept of a *Logos asarkos* – which is what I recommend, untraditional though it may be. But Gunton is unwilling to do that, for the sake of 'the historical newness marked by Jesus' birth to Mary': if the Logos is not somehow other after the birth than he was before, what is the point of the birth?

The question, of course, is what exactly can be meant by 'historical newness' in this connection, or 'before' and 'after'. There is obviously a timeline on which Mary comes after, say, Nebuchadnezzar. But is this a line on which we can lay out in sequence the eternal begetting of the Son by the

Father and Mary's pregnancy? Be that as it may, according to Gunton, 'we have to say two things which appear to be contradictory: that he is Son quite apart from and in advance of being Jesus of Nazareth – for Jesus of Nazareth has a begetting in time – and yet he is not Son apart from being Jesus'.

When I ask why Gunton wouldn't take my good advice here, it seems to me that the answer is that he was and wanted to remain a Reformed theologian, and Reformed theology is always on guard against too undialectical an identification of events in time with events in God. The issue is Christological, and so we come to the last fork that I have time to locate on Gunton's path.

One Christology that could enable the kind of talk about the man Jesus that Gunton thinks essential – that he is the agent of creation, etc. – would be a very strong version of the ancient doctrine of the communion of attributes, a sort of hyper-Cyrillianism, the sort of thing in which the Lutherans indulged. According to such teaching, the man Jesus is indeed the Creator simply because in his identity with the Son he fully shares the Son's predicates and actions. For the sake of his Reformed heritage, Gunton will not take that way either. But what then?

Gunton found a starting point in the Christology of Oliver Cromwell's sometime chaplain, John Owen. According to Owen, the hypostatic union of the Son and the man Jesus is so sheerly a *meta*physical reality that it has no consequences at all on the 'physical' level; that is, it makes no difference for either the divine nature of the Son or the human nature of Jesus. The man Jesus is indeed precisely as himself one of the Trinity. But being one of the Trinity does not itself constitute his ability to do all those divine things that Jesus does – forgiving sins, raising the dead, interpreting Scripture as if he had written it, etc. Indeed, being one of the Trinity does not in itself establish anything about either the Son or Jesus *except* that you cannot refer to one without referring to the other. But how then is the man Jesus able to be our savior? According to Owen, the man Jesus' divine capabilities are gifts of the Spirit to him.

I do not know if Gunton worried about the way in which this Christology repristinates that of late medieval theology. But I cannot end without noting that late medieval theology left Jesus' presence in the life of the Church Christologically unfounded; if the risen Jesus does not have the eternal Son's transcendence of time and space, how does he get to be in First Presbyterian of a Sunday morning? The medieval Church filled that gap with a promise to those ordained, that God would make their words invoking his presence – such as 'This is the body of Christ' – true when and because they said them. The Reformers by and large found no such promise in Scripture. What then? It does not seem to me that created gifts of the Spirit to the human nature of Jesus will carry the weight. Or anyway will not unless you much lighten the weight with a fully Zwinglian doctrine of Christ's relation to the gathered community – which Gunton did not want. I think if he had lived, he would have had to move differently at the end of the path I have traced – but that is a guess.

I have not of course made a complete map of Gunton's thinking – that covers just about everything. I have simply traced one road on that map, one I think interesting and challenging. And now I ask you to look back on that road: it is a real *theological* road. Gunton was into the genuine stuff.

### Notes

1 Colin E. Gunton, *Becoming and Being. The Doctrine of God in Charles Hartshorne and Karl Barth* (Oxford: Oxford University Press, 1978).
2 Colin E. Gunton, *A Christian Dogmatic Theology. Volume One: The Triune God. A Doctrine of the Trinity as Though Jesus Makes a Difference*, 2003, unpublished typescript, chapter 5.
3 Brad Green, 'The protomodern Augustine? Colin Gunton and the failure of Augustine', *International Journal of Systematic Theology* 9.3 (2007), pp. 328–41.
4 Gunton, *A Christian Dogmatic Theology*.
5 Colin E. Gunton, *The Promise of Trinitarian Theology*, 2nd edn. (London and New York: T&T Clark, 2003), p. 94.
6 Irenaeus, *Against the Heresies*, 3.16.6.
7 Gunton, *A Christian Dogmatic Theology*.
8 See also the recent volume for which Gunton and I jointly wrote an article on the import for our understanding of reason itself, of the circumstance that a first-century Jew is the universal Logos. Colin E. Gunton and Robert W. Jenson, 'The *Logos Ensarkos* and Reason' in Paul J. Griffiths and Reinhard Hütter, eds, *Reason and the Reasons of Faith* (London: T & T Clark, 2005), pp. 78–85.

# Chapter 2

## GUNTON AND BARTH[1]

### John Webster

Karl Barth was an enormously important figure in Gunton's intellectual formation, and a reference point in nearly all his mature work; even when he felt duty bound to part company with Barth (which was increasingly often as the years went by), he usually did so with due acknowledgment of the magisterial character of Barth's achievement. What Barth offered to Gunton (and to a significant handful of other young English theologians) in the 1960s was an alternative to the dismal business of doctrinal criticism, then at its height in British theology, with its half-guilty, half-self-congratulatory naturalism, and its assumption that almost the only interesting question to ask about a Christian doctrine was why we can no longer believe it. Barth helped Gunton – already a nonconformist in the Oxford Anglican establishment – to swim against the stream. 'Where Barth is concerned', he once remarked, 'a frequent English reaction is one of puzzlement that someone should commit intellectual suicide in so spectacular a fashion'.[2] By contrast, Gunton was early convinced that Barth exemplified both a lack of anxiety about the intellectual integrity of Christian theology and a willingness to see what happens when the explanatory and critical power of Christian dogmatics is let loose. Barth did what the doctrinal criticism school assumed could not be done: inhabit the modern world with Christian intellectual freedom.[3]

Gunton's Barth was basically the Barth of the *Church Dogmatics*, with some of the earlier writings, above all the second edition of *Romans*, thrown in as a contrast to the mature Barth. His views on Barth, shaped in the course of his doctoral work on Barth and Hartshorne, were therefore settled before the publication of the Barth *Gesamtausgabe* changed the landscape of Barth studies. Thirty-five years after Barth's death, the Barth corpus looks very different and much fuller, and requires both a more complex account of Barth's theological development and a greater alertness to the fact that the *Church Dogmatics* cannot be read in isolation. In giving us much more of Barth, the materials in the *Gesamtausgabe* have served to bring into relief what was already there in the *Dogmatics*, especially its exegetical, historical and ethical dimensions, without which the character of its dogmatic content may be missed. Gunton's primary immersion in Barth's work preceded this shift, however, and though his views were later modified, most commonly in a more critical direction, his map of the Barth corpus remained by and large that of conventional Anglo-American reception: *Romans*, a few occasional pieces from the 1920s, the Anselm book, the *Church Dogmatics*.[4] His reading of Barth was shaped by the dominant figures of Barth interpretation in the 1950s and 1960s: Torrance and Jenson in English; Jüngel, Balthasar and Barth's Lutheran and Roman Catholic critics among the continentals. All, it should be noted, took strong constructive interests to the interpretation of Barth. One of the things that Gunton learned from such readers, even when they disputed what Barth had to say, was the sheer conceptual prowess of the *Church Dogmatics*, a capacity unsurpassed by any modern theologian, to give a commanding account of the Christian gospel on its own terms.

Gunton had no ambitions to be a specialist on Barth or any other thinker: he was primarily a constructive theologian, and though he published a good deal on theological issues approached 'through the theologians', his work as commentator was ancillary to the central enterprise of giving a rational articulation of the Christian confession.[5] 'Our doctrinal past is best understood if its representatives are taken seriously as living voices with whom we enter into theological conversation',[6] he once wrote – hence his fondness for Barth's grand *Protestant Theology in the Nineteenth Century*, because it is 'an exercise in the history of ideas which is yet resolutely theological . . . a history of theology which uses theological criteria for all the varied judgements that it makes'.[7] Gunton read widely in historical theology but by no means exhaustively; he was not often harassed by scruples about making sure he had got to the bottom of the literature; and he had loves (Irenaeus, the Cappadocians via Zizioulas, Owen, Coleridge) and hates (that dreadful North African bishop, that Dominican who never read the Bible). Even though his judgements were sometimes tendentious (breathtakingly so on Augustine), he could, however, be a perceptive reader of texts, precisely because his intense engagement in constructive dogmatics made his instincts very alert. As an interpreter he was especially concerned to observe the arrangement of, and relations between, the different parts of the dogmatic corpus. 'Systematic theology is not so much a matter of the organising of doctrines into systems, as of weighting and balance in the ways doctrinal matters are placed into relation with one another.'[8] The critical judgements which Gunton himself reached about what he called

Barth's 'unique and prophetic theological achievement'[9] were almost always of this kind: worries that the vast bulk of the *Church Dogmatics* contains imbalances, overweighting some doctrines at the expense of others, using the wrong doctrine to accomplish a particular task, acceding too readily to the inherited shape of the account of the gospel found in the theological traditions of the West.

Alongside this preoccupation with dogmatics, however, Gunton had a more consistent interest in the general metaphysical entailments of the Christian gospel than did Barth. Certainly Barth was a shrewd interpreter of philosophy and could write vigorously on, for example, the conflict between idealism and realism in metaphysics; and he never cherished the illusion that dogmatics is a philosophy-free zone. But his interests in philosophy are by and large extramural. He was nervous that over-investment in philosophy might lead to a '*mixophilosophicotheologia*',[10] and he usually stuck to the task of dogmatic description, leaving readers to draw any philosophical inferences. In this matter, Gunton was freer. He was, of course, in no doubt that the philosophical theologian is a *theologian*, and from his early critique of Hartshorne onwards, he was as clear as Barth ever was that the Church's confession must govern what theologians say on metaphysical matters. But this did not inhibit him from addressing such questions (most boldly in *The One, the Three and the Many*[11]), precisely so as to work out answers more fittingly governed by the Christian gospel than those which had found their way into the mainstream Christian West. He once described his work in trinitarian theology as 'a quest for ontology',[12] because 'it is only through an understanding of the kind of being that God is that we can come to learn what kind of beings we are and what kind of world we inhabit'.[13] One of Gunton's worries was that Barth restricted the range of what Christian doctrine might achieve in interpreting the world, in part because his doctrine of God, oriented as it is to election and reconciliation, does not press him outwards into engagement with the being of the creaturely world. There is a real difference here: where Barth was intensely (to some, compulsively) focused, Gunton, especially in his later work, was an associative thinker more concerned to trace the ramifications of the gospel for the material and cultural world. He did so as a corollary and application of a tenaciously held set of doctrinal convictions, at whose heart lay Trinitarian and especially pneumatological teaching developed partly in critical conversation with what he saw as Barth's unfinished and not wholly successful attempt to extricate Reformed theology from the deficiencies of the Augustinian heritage.

The central question to ask of any theology according to Gunton is this: 'How does it relate eternal God to temporal creation, and does it do so in such a way as to preserve at once the sovereignty and priority of divine action and the proper *Selbständigkeit* – relative independence – of the world? On an answer to this question hangs, if not the law and the prophets, at least the proper weighting of the different elements of a dogmatic theology of salvation.'[14] The question was first formulated in response to Barth in Gunton's doctoral thesis, later published as *Becoming and Being*. In it, Gunton learned his trade by taking on two big thinkers – Hartshorne and Barth – on a big topic – the doctrine of God (few doctoral supervisors would run the risk of turning loose even a stellar student on such vast territory). The book's proposal, worked out with greater rigour than anything he wrote subsequently, is that Barth's doctrine of God, with its inseparability of God's aseity and God's action in the economy, offers an alternative (though in important respects a flawed one) to both classical theism and Hartshorne's neoclassical replacement. Like Eberhard Jüngel earlier in the decade,[15] Gunton found that Barth's doctrine of God's free becoming offered a way of escape from the paralysing effects of a false polarity: either static, unrelated divine transcendence or the subsuming of the divine into a general ontology of flux. Much of Gunton's mature work was an attempt to articulate a non-competitive view of divine transcendence: this is a major preoccupation in *The One, the Three and the Many*, in *Act and Being*[16] and in many of his essays.[17] But the basic shape of both the problem and its resolution was learned early from Barth: attention to the internal structure of the Christian doctrine of God effects its separation from theism and its critics.

Yet even at this stage, Gunton was not without his worries, urged on him, perhaps, by his first *Doktorvater*.[18] The worries had their first outing in an article from 1972 (the year the thesis was defended) on 'The development of Christian doctrine'.[19] Here Gunton was troubled by Barth's equivocation between a 'static' and an 'eschatological' model of the history of Christian thought: is Barth perhaps trapped by 'an excessively backwards-looking view of the development of doctrine', one in which 'everything significant has already happened'?[20] He was not reassured by what he regarded as Barth's muted account of the Spirit as 'the one who moves the Church through history';[21] and so although Barth's 'stress on the freedom of God has pointed the way to a historical and eschatological understanding of the movement of the Church's teaching . . . the question remains whether God is free enough on this understanding'.[22] The criticism was given fuller articulation with the publication of a revision of the thesis. There Barth's project in the *Church Dogmatics* was read as an extraordinarily cogent yet incomplete reworking of the Christian doctrine of God, one whose intention – a non-contrastive understanding of God's relation to creaturely history – is not fully realized. Barth 'moves towards a concept of eternity in which it is seen not in opposition to or negation of time, but both as its affirmation and fulfilment and as its judge'.[23] Yet a shadow remains: a failure to maintain 'the full temporal reality of the revelation event', or 'a persistent tendency . . . to contaminate the temporality of revelation with a conception of revelation as a timeless theophany'.[24] Gunton mapped out a number of corollaries: historically, an orientation to the past which means that there can be 'no significant future divine history';[25] pneumatologically, 'neglect of the third appropriation of the triune God';[26] Christologically, a lack of interest in the human history of Jesus. Most of these worries will surface in later reflections; indeed, *Becoming and Being* already set the agenda of Gunton's reception of Barth's work, as well as indicating something of what were to become the major motifs of his own constructive work. We turn to look more systematically at Gunton's analysis of Barth's imperfections and at his counter-suggestions.

One way of bringing together Gunton's various hesitations about Barth's work would be to say that he feared that Barth lacked an adequate theology of mediation. In his later work, the concept of mediation (and often the term itself) played a central role in articulation of what he regarded as a properly ordered theology of the relation of the eternal Trinity and the temporal creation. Gunton never gave the concept of mediation the kind of comprehensive exposition and analysis for which we might have hoped;[27] he relied, instead, on appealing to the notion in the course of examining other doctrinal matters, as a kind of summary term for a gospel-governed understanding of the triune God's active relation to created reality. A characteristic formulation can be found in his last monograph, *Act and Being*, a ground-clearing exercise in respect of the theology of the divine attributes: 'all of God's acts take their beginning in the Father, are put into effect through the Son, and reach their completion in the Spirit. Put otherwise, God's actions are *mediated*: he brings about his purposes towards and in the world by the mediating actions of the Son and the Spirit, his "two hands".'[28] At its simplest, that is, 'mediation' indicates that the Father operates in the world through the agency of the Son and the Spirit. Furthermore, the acts of the Son and the Spirit are not to be conceived as purely interruptive or vertical, intruding upon the creation *ab extra*. For 'the Son is the focus of God the Father's immanent action, his involvement within the structures of the world',[29] while 'the Spirit, as the one by whose agency the Father makes the creation perfect in his Son, is the focus of transcendent, eschatological action, pulling things forward to that for which God has made them'.[30] Son and Spirit mediate the Father's action, and do so from within the structures of creation and not simply extrinsically or at a distance.

Such convictions were never far from the surface of Gunton's mature thought, above all in its magnetic attraction to two doctrines: creation and pneumatology. By these convictions, Gunton announced his refusal of what he saw as a basic error in the Western traditions of theology and philosophy, namely 'the platonizing tendency to distinguish sharply between the world of sense and the world of intellect'.[31] Of this tendency the paradigmatic theological instance is Augustine who bequeathed to Western Christianity the instinct 'to locate the weight of ontological and epistemological interests in the realm of the timeless eternal'.[32] Gunton frequently polemicized against the signs of the presence of this inheritance: an ontology centred on 'the relation of time and eternity',[33] a doctrine of God not as 'communal dynamism' but as a 'static fixity over against the moving world',[34] and much else. Its most problematic feature is its unease with talking of the real yet indirect character of God's relation to creation. The unease can take the form either of unrestricted transcendence or of unrestricted immanence, both being modes of dualism which make impossible a notion of the creaturely as the medium of divine presence and action, and both of which assume that God is to be considered a single causal agent. 'Mediation' attempts to counter this by offering a depiction of God's mediating acts in Son and Spirit, acts that enable the world to be itself in relation to God.

What of Barth? 'The significance of Barth as a Western thinker', Gunton wrote, 'is that he refused to think in terms of these dualisms, but attempted theologically to construe them in ways that transcend both Augustinianism and its rebellious but true child, the Enlightenment'.[35] Particularly in his later theology, Barth began to develop 'a new ontology, deeply Christological and Trinitarian, in which the relation of eternal God and temporal creation was rethought in a thoroughgoing way'.[36] Yet – and here is the crucial qualification – the rethinking was 'perhaps not adequately completed'.[37] Though – as *Becoming and Being* had laboured to demonstrate – Barth's achievement was to evade both the polarization of God's being and history and their collapse into one another, he retained vestiges of an uncorrected concept of divine transcendence. And when wedded to an immensely potent doctrine of eternal election, to an undeveloped sense of the personal differentiations of the godhead, to a characteristically Reformed understanding of the hypostatic union, and to an almost exclusively applicatory conception of the Spirit's work, the result is that, *malgré tout*, Barth's theology cannot completely shake itself free from the separation of God and creaturely time.

As these thoughts on Barth unfolded throughout Gunton's work, it was pneumatological considerations which more often than not provided the focus. Gunton always considered Barth's treatment of the doctrine of the Spirit to be 'far more conventional than his contributions to other dogmatic loci',[38] the point at which this otherwise astonishingly free thinker was still in the thrall of the tradition of the West, a tradition which he often depicted as 'beginning with Augustine and culminating in Barth'.[39] In a comment on Barth's doctrine of revelation, Gunton noted that there is built into the fabric of the doctrine is an attraction to the notion of 'revelatory immediacy',[40] and suggested that there is 'something suspicious' about this idea of 'direct communication with God',[41] namely a lack of awareness of 'the mediatedness of revelation'.[42] Why is this a problem? Because it fails 'to give due place and function to the Holy Spirit' by reducing the Spirit simply to 'internal Word'.[43] Thus: Gunton *was* suspicious, deeply so, fearing that Barth's conventionally Reformed account simply repeats a set of moves which filled him with dismay. In mapping Barth's pneumatological antecedents, he usually started with Augustine, the *fons iniquitorum*, from whose balefully inadequate Trinitarianism Barth never really managed to extricate himself; for counter-examples he looked usually to Owen and Edward Irving. Thus in 'God the Holy Spirit: Augustine and his successors', he laid out his objections (which are themselves, it ought to be noted, rather conventional) as follows: 'the effective *ontological* subordination of the Spirit to the Son' which 'militates against an identification of the Spirit's specific *persona*';[44] insufficient on 'the activity of the Spirit as the life-giving power of God in and towards his creation'[45] both in Christology and in the doctrine of creation; an undertow which drags Christian doctrine back to the past and so inhibits the Spirit's eschatological role as 'the perfecting cause of the creation'.[46] There are a number of issues here that are worthy of comment.

On the question of the personhood of the Spirit, Gunton was consistently critical of Barth's preference for the term '*Seinsweise*' rather than 'person' in trinitarian theology. This choice, which Barth was led to make as a way of resisting the importation of modern notions of individual personality into trinitarian theology, was nevertheless read by Gunton as achieving the opposite, and therefore as symptomatic of a deep-seated difficulty, namely the undermining of the irreducibility of the personal in a Christian theological account of God's relation to the world. He tried to set the record straight in the occasionally grumpy 'Epilogue' to the second edition of *Becoming and Being*: 'Trinitarian theology is in part devoted to the preservation of the ultimacy of the person in the purposes of God for the world. To define the person in terms of something else is to suggest that there is something logically or – more important – ontologically more primitive in terms of which persons can be defined. But if the world is created by a personal God in such a way that aspects of its destiny are entrusted to those who are created in his image – and therefore also personal – should the personal not be that *in terms of which* other things are understood?'[47] Barth would not let such a phrase as 'the ultimacy of the person' go unchallenged, fearing the unheralded arrival of a general metaphysic.[48] But what drove such a statement were some very basic principles about which Gunton was not open to negotiation: a highly differentiated presentation of the triune persons according to which 'it is necessary that the particularity of the persons can be established as *beings*, centres of distinctive kinds of action';[49] a disapproval of the principle *opera trinitatis ad extra indivisa sunt*; a maximal commitment to the principle that *opera trinitatis ad intra divisa sunt*; determination to ferret out any attempts to associate divine personhood with divine unity. And all this on the basis of the fact that, as Gunton put it in one of his less qualified *dicta*, 'the truly creative achievement of all trinitarian thought was that of the trinitarian ontology provided by the Cappadocians'.[50] That being the case, Barth can scarcely pass muster: his explication of the triunity of God in tandem with the threefold character of revelation is too abstract; he apparently loads the dice from the beginning by starting from unity and making threefoldness derivative; and the idiom of the being of God as 'event' is particularly problematic. In the first edition of *Becoming and Being*, Gunton found Barth's event-ontology of the divine to be of real service in responding to process pantheism; but after 20 years of developing an ontology centred on personal action and relation, he was no longer convinced. Such talk, he feared, calls attention away from 'the priority of persons in the being of God';[51] like the notion of 'substance', which it is supposed to replace, it conceives of being as *underlying* the act and communion of persons; and in terms of pneumatology it can result in 'an essentially introverted conception of the Trinity' in which, as the bond of union between Father and Son, the Spirit 'closes the circle' of God's life rather than opening that life to creaturely reality.[52]

Gunton said often enough that none of this means that Barth is a modalist. But the grounds for his reticence to press the point home remain obscure, and in the last decade of his writing, as the theology of mediation and Spirit came to exercise a real hold over his mind, he was quite seriously at loggerheads with Barth's pneumatology, both over the place of the Holy Spirit in the immanent Trinity and over the role of the Spirit in the economy of creation and redemption. We have already indicated something of the first matter; what of the second? This takes us to the heart of Gunton's later pneumatology.

In his mature work, Gunton used 'Spirit' as a designation for the one who brings things to perfection by constituting their particularity. The Spirit 'perfects the creation',[53] or is 'the perfecting cause of the creation';[54] the presence of the Spirit is 'the presence of one enabling the world to be and become truly itself', so that 'where God the Son is the (personal) principle of the world's unity and coherence, the Holy Spirit, through that same Son, becomes the focus of the particularity of things, their becoming "perfect" – complete – as distinctly themselves'.[55] The most ambitious (and arguably the most problematic) statement of this kind of pneumatology is found in Gunton's Bampton lectures, *The One, the Three and the Many*. There he expounded a theologically derived metaphysic of spirit as a transcendental

or what he called a 'Coleridgean idea':[56] 'that which is or has spirit is able
to be open to that which is other than itself, to move dynamically into
relation with the other.'[57] Far from being a mere Christological addendum
concerned with the *distributio beneficia salutis*, language of spirit is of wide
and illuminating significance. 'Theologically, it is a way of speaking of the
personal agency of God towards and in the world; anthropologically a way
of speaking of human responsiveness to God and to others; cosmologically
a way of speaking of human openness to the world and the world's openness
to human knowledge, action and art.'[58] Both in the eternal relations of the
godhead and in the ordered relational life of the creation, spirit brings 'to
completion that for which each person and each thing is created';[59] and so
'we can understand the Spirit's distinctive mode of action as the one who
maintains the particularity, distinctiveness, uniqueness, through the Son, of
each within the unity'.[60]

What again of Barth? The internal dynamic of Barth's trinitarian and
pneumatological thought simply prohibits him from moving in the direction which Gunton believed necessary if some of the compulsions of the
Augustinian tradition are to be avoided. Gunton often illustrated this
point with reference to Barth's treatment of the humanity of Christ, an
aspect of the *Church Dogmatics* that gave him increasing trouble, because
he believed it to signal the inadequate coordination of Christology and
pneumatology. His argument ran along these lines. In Barth (Gunton has
in mind *Church Dogmatics* IV/2) the Spirit's relation to Jesus is 'more causal
compulsion than liberation for action';[61] there is too limited a presentation
of the role of the Spirit in the sending of the Son, and, in particular, in the
constitution and maintenance of Jesus' humanity. One symptom of this is
Barth's distinct preference for the godlike features of Jesus' ministry, such
that 'one has to search hard for any real interest in Jesus' action as free
human action'[62] (an extraordinary judgement, I have to say, and one which
surely cannot be sustained from a reading of the doctrine of reconciliation).
But connected with this are two deeper deficiencies in Barth's account of
incarnation and salvation: his handling of the virgin birth and his treatment
of Jesus' human priesthood. Both bring to the fore the dialectic of unity
and distinction between the Word and the humanity of Christ which Barth
always considered essential to an orderly doctrine of the incarnation but
which Gunton believed corrosive of the saving import of Jesus' Spirit-
directed humanity.

In respect of the virgin birth, Gunton criticized Barth for, in effect,
blocking Jesus' undiminished participation in our humanity by so stressing
the miraculous, interceptive act of Jesus' conception that the Spirit's role of
enabling Jesus' integral humanity is neglected. 'The divine action *towards*
the creation' is emphasized 'at the expense of this action *within* the structure

of time and space'.[63] Similarly, in Barth's hands Jesus' priesthood 'is ordered to the divinity of Christ', with the result that 'what is lost is the priesthood exercised by Christ in his humanity'.[64] In both cases, Barth – on Gunton's reading – allows his Christology to be dominated by the efficient causality of the Word, thereby eclipsing Jesus' humanity as an historical enactment, grounding it in advance in its unity with the divine Word and so, in effect, undermining it as an achievement in time. Once again, this weakness is to be traced to an impotent pneumatology. Barth compacts divine action and the humanity of Christ together, so that 'incarnation' becomes 'immanence', with the result that Jesus' freedom and identity as agent in space and time are compromised. 'A conception of the relation of God to the world which ties it too closely to God's (Christologically conceived) immanence is in danger of making the world too much a function of God's presence to it, too little its own autonomous reality.'[65] This is a considerably foreshortened account of Barth which ought not to go unchallenged;[66] here we need simply note that it is the outworking of a set of misgivings about Barth which had been present to Gunton's mind since *Becoming and Being* – that Jesus may become merely a temporal signifier of what has taken place in pre-temporal eternity; and that protology outbids pneumatology (the perfecting Spirit) and hence eschatology (the creature whose perfection is enabled by the Spirit).

The corollary of this Christological line of criticism is that Gunton was ill at ease with Barth's account of creation, and especially with his orientation of the doctrine to the notion of covenant. In Barth's hands, of course, the motif of 'covenant' is intended to indicate the mutuality between God and creatures, which constitutes the beginning and end of God's works and ways. For Gunton, however, 'covenant' cannot be detached from what he took to be a rather sinister notion of eternal election. 'The historical, temporal, covenant is the outcome of God's eternal choice to elect Jesus Christ and in him the whole human race. On this account salvation means the working out of the divine purpose, which precedes the creation in the divine intention, to come into reconciled relation with humankind.'[67] That is, it is *pre-temporal determination* rather than *fellowship* which is central to Barth's thought, 'the logic of eternity'[68] rather than the directedness of God's ways to life with the creature. 'The chief weakness of this way of relating creation and redemption is the way in which Barth conceives "God's decision and plan".'[69] In short: for Gunton, both Barth's doctrine of creation and aspects of his Christology and soteriology remain caught in the briars of Neoplatonism and its divorce of the eternal from the temporal. The only means of release is a more consistently trinitarian, and especially pneumatological, doctrine of God's relation to the history of creatures.

What are we to make of all this? Early on in his career, Gunton asked whether Barth 'rightly criticized the idea of the theologian as a kind of bank manager, jealous guard of his charge . . . only to replace him with a theological archaeologist, burrowing around for something he already knows to be there'.[70] It is a sour and uninformed judgement: no one could possibly think that about Barth after reading what Barth has to say, for example, about the nature of confession and the distinctive confessional attitude of Reformed theology. But however ill-judged, the remark does indicate a good deal of Gunton's self-conception as a theologian: he valued openness, freedom, range; he listened usually carefully but not too long to his masters and then made up his own mind; he never evaded theological responsibility by hiding in the skirts of a tradition. Barth would have enjoyed that kind of feisty Christian independence.

What did Gunton take from Barth? Above all, a conviction that the doctrine of God will do things: the resolution of a number of central theological questions concerning God's relation to the world requires a non-oppositional account of God's transcendence of creaturely time, and such an account is to be won by following the logic of what the Christian confession indicates of the being of God and of God's work in the economy. But he thought that Barth's theology ran aground before completing its journey, lacking as it did the trinitarian and pneumatological materials required to hold together God's freedom and the creation's freedom.

I remain unpersuaded, partly because I do not (sometimes cannot) follow Gunton's criticisms, partly because I do not share the dogmatic judgements which undergird them. His reading of Barth, though generally well-informed, was more of a presentation of the *grandes lignes*. There is a distinct advantage to such an approach, namely that it can often perceive the overall structure and implications more clearly than does myopic exegesis. The disadvantage is criticism by generalization, and, as Gunton said in one of his more self-subverting moments, 'all generalisations are dangerous'.[71] He was too respectful a reader and too aware of his debts to Barth to fall into the transports of interpretative rage which sometimes afflict those who make up their minds that Barth is a Platonist. In the end, however, I fear his case not proven. A number of hints might be offered along these lines.

Gunton seriously underestimated the significance which human time and history held for Barth. That he did so was largely because he extracted what Barth had to say about the freedom of God's eternal decision from Barth's equal emphasis on the direction of that freedom to fellowship with the creature. What Gunton sought to maintain by speaking of the Spirit as constituting creaturely particularity, Barth maintained precisely by his doctrine of election as God's self-election to life in partnership with the creature in the creature's own active life of obedience. Unless we see this, then the single line of argument that holds together the being, perfections, election and command of God in *Church Dogmatics* II will be lost on us. Oddly enough, in one essay on Barth, Gunton did stumble into this, commenting that '[e]lection is election to a particular kind of life';[72] but he never gave enough serious attention to the moral and political theology over which Barth laboured in the *Church Dogmatics* and elsewhere, and did not allow it to call into question his reading of Barth's doctrine of election. In part, this was because Gunton misperceived the tradition from which Barth was coming. He associated Barth rather too quickly with what he took to be the features of Augustine's theology, and did not do anything like justice to Barth's fascination with the Reformed tradition, especially in the 1920s when he was lecturing extensively on Reformed historical theology and confessional texts. What Barth created out of that engagement was a version of the Reformed faith that emphasized the strictly non-reversible yet utterly real relation of God and God's active human creatures. As Barth's exegetical, historical and dogmatic work developed, he was able to fill out what he had learned from the Reformed tradition, and it remained one of the most powerful strands of the theology of covenantal fellowship in the *Church Dogmatics*. If Barth was ever tempted to associate God's freedom with pure transcendence (I am not convinced that he was, even in the second edition of *Romans*) he learned the perils of doing so very early, poring over Calvin's theology of the Christian life and the Christology of the Reformed confessions.

Gunton was seriously sceptical about aspects of classical Reformed Christology, disliking what he took to be its docetic tendencies, its prioritising of the divine nature of the incarnate one, and the absence from it of an operative pneumatology. My own judgement is that his criticisms of Barth in this matter are in large part misplaced, and rest on a separation of Word and Spirit which gives little room to the Word's continuing activity in the history of the incarnate one. It is worth adding that, though Barth mounted a lively – though extraordinarily subtle and by no means uncritical – defence of the Christological thought of the early Reformed tradition, particularly the *extra Calvinisticum*, he did not consider this to endanger the genuine and permanent humanity of Jesus. 'It is one thing to speak of the humanity of God and another to speak of the humanity of Jesus Christ.'[73] But for Barth it *isn't*; and to think that it is is to be beguiled into believing that Jesus' humanity needs somehow to be protected from the determination of the Word if it is to have integrity. There are adoptionist and exemplarist affirmations of the integrity of Jesus' humanity into which Gunton would never fall; but his capacity to resist them was surely weakened by one of the oddest lacunae in his thought, namely a full-dress treatment of the theology of the Son of God.[74]

Systematic theology owes Gunton an immense debt. He gave intellectual and rhetorical weight to the task of constructive Christian theology in Britain at a time when the majority believed it to be redundant. He was animated by the momentous ideas of Christian dogmatics; though sometimes in his writing they were clumsily or hurriedly expressed, he loved to let them loose and watch what happened. He edified students and colleagues in the academy and the church by restless intellectual energy, by cheerful partisanship, by his catholic range of interests, above all, by his conviction that the gospel is a grand matter for the mind. And he was fortified in these matters by his engagement with Barth, on whom his most important dictum was: 'Read the man himself!'[75]

## *Notes*

1   A revised version of a paper presented at a meeting of the Karl Barth Society of North America in November, 2003.

2   Colin E. Gunton, 'The knowledge of God. "No other foundation" – one Englishman's reading of *Church Dogmatics* chapter V', in *Theology Through the Theologians. Selected Essays 1972–1995* (Edinburgh: T&T Clark, 1996), p. 50. In the posthumously published transcripts of his lectures on Barth (*The Barth Lectures* [ed. P.H. Brazier] [London: T&T Clark, 2007]), Gunton notes how the assertive Barth usually proves too much for 'mild-mannered establishment Anglicans' (p. 66) – though it is unclear where this leaves Sir Edwyn Hoskyns, the translator of the *Römerbrief*.

3   Further on the context of Gunton's early work, see his remarks in the 'Epilogue' to *Becoming and Being. The Doctrine of God in Charles Hartshorne and Karl Barth*, 2nd edn. (London: SCM Press, 2001), p. 226.

4   The survey of Barth in *The Barth Lectures* bears this out: little attention is given to Barth's academic writings from the 1920s, especially the *Göttingen Dogmatics* and the *Ethics*, and there is little evidence of acquaintance with the exegetical and historical works from the period.

5   The book on Barth that Gunton considered writing in retirement never, of course, saw the light of day. *The Barth Lectures* may give a glimpse of what the book might have looked like, though their value lies not so much in their analysis of and judgements on Barth as in what they convey of his intensity as a teacher.

6   Colin E. Gunton, 'Historical and systematic theology', in Colin E. Gunton, ed., *The Cambridge Companion to Christian Doctrine* (Cambridge: Cambridge University Press, 1997), pp. 5f.

7   Colin E. Gunton, 'Preface' to K. Barth, *Protestant Theology in the Nineteenth Century* (London: SCM Press, 2001), p. xv.

8   Colin E. Gunton, 'A systematic triangle. Hegel, Kierkegaard, Barth and the question of ethics', in *Intellect and Action. Elucidations on Christian Theology and the Life of Faith* (Edinburgh: T&T Clark, 2000), p. 79.

9   Gunton, *Becoming and Being*, p. 245.

10  K. Barth, *Evangelical Theology* (London: Weidenfeld and Nicolson, 1963), p. v.

11 Colin E. Gunton, *The One, the Three and the Many. God, Creation and the Culture of Modernity* (Cambridge: Cambridge University Press, 1993).

12 Colin E. Gunton, *The Promise of Trinitarian Theology* (Edinburgh: T&T Clark, 1991), p. vii.

13 Ibid.

14 Colin E. Gunton, 'Salvation', in J. Webster, ed., *The Cambridge Companion to Karl Barth* (Cambridge: Cambridge University Press, 2000), p. 155.

15 E. Jüngel, *Gottes Sein ist im Werden* (Tübingen: Mohr, 1965).

16 Colin E. Gunton, *Act and Being. Towards a Theology of the Divine Attributes* (London: SCM Press, 2002).

17 For just two examples: 'Transcendence, metaphor, and the knowability of God', *Journal of Theological Studies* 31 (1980), pp. 501–16; 'The triune God and the freedom of the creature', in S.W. Sykes, ed., *Karl Barth. Centenary Essays* (Cambridge: Cambridge University Press, 1986), pp. 46–68.

18 See Robert W. Jenson, *Alpha and Omega. A Study in the Theology of Karl Barth* (New York: Nelson, 1963); idem., *God After God. The God of the Past and the God of the Future as Seen in the Work of Karl Barth* (Indianapolis: Bobbs-Merrill, 1969). Gunton explains his indebtedness to Jenson in 'Creation (1). Creation and mediation in the theology of Robert Jenson. An encounter and a convergence', in *Father, Son and Holy Spirit. Essays Toward a Fully Trinitarian Theology* (London: T&T Clark, 2003), pp. 93–106; in 'Salvation', p. 155, he is a little more wary of the argument presented in Jenson's *Alpha and Omega*.

19 Revised as 'The development of Christian doctrine. Karl Barth's understanding of the theological task', in *Theology Through the Theologians*, pp. 34–49.

20 Gunton, 'The development of Christian doctrine', p. 42.

21 Gunton, 'The development of Christian doctrine', p. 44.

22 Gunton, 'The development of Christian doctrine', p. 45.

23 Gunton, *Becoming and Being*, p. 179.

24 Gunton, *Becoming and Being*, p. 181.

25 Gunton, *Becoming and Being*, p. 182.

26 Gunton, *Becoming and Being*, p. 185.

27 For some initial materials, see *The Triune Creator. A Historical and Systematic Study* (Edinburgh: Edinburgh University Press, 1998), pp. 41–64; *The Christian Faith. An Introduction to Christian Doctrine* (Oxford: Blackwell, 2002), pp. 3–19; *Father, Son and Holy Spirit*, pp. 164–80.

28 Gunton, *Act and Being*, p. 77. It would, presumably, be better to speak of 'the Father's actions', not of 'God's actions'.

29 Gunton, *Act and Being*, pp. 77f.

30 Gunton, *Act and Being*, p. 78. 'Transcendent' and 'eschatological', it should be noted, are not used here to suggest remoteness, but to refer to the fact that the Spirit's acts do not supplant those of creaturely realities, but enable the creation to be itself in its integrity.

31 Colin E. Gunton, 'Karl Barth and the Western intellectual tradition. Towards a theology after Christendom', in J. Thompson, ed., *Theology Beyond Christendom. Essays on the Centenary of the Birth of Karl Barth* (Allison Park: Pickwick, 1986), p. 285.

32 Gunton, 'Karl Barth and the Western intellectual tradition', p. 286.

33 Ibid.

34 Gunton, 'Karl Barth and the Western intellectual tradition', p. 287.

35 Gunton, 'Karl Barth and the Western intellectual tradition', p. 289.

36 Gunton, 'Karl Barth and the Western intellectual tradition', p. 300.

37 Gunton, 'Karl Barth and the Western intellectual tradition', p. 299.

38 Colin E. Gunton, 'God the Holy Spirit. Augustine and his successors', in *Theology Through the Theologians*, p. 106.

39 Colin E. Gunton, *Christ and Creation* (Grand Rapids: Eerdmans, 1992), p. 50.

40 Colin E. Gunton, *A Brief Theology of Revelation* (Edinburgh: T&T Clark, 1995), p. 4.

41 Gunton, *A Brief Theology of Revelation*, p. 10.

42 Gunton, *A Brief Theology of Revelation*, p. 5.

43 Gunton, *A Brief Theology of Revelation*, p. 119.

44 Gunton, 'God the Holy Spirit', p. 116.

45 Gunton, 'God the Holy Spirit', p. 114.

46 Gunton, 'God the Holy Spirit', p. 120.

47 Gunton, *Becoming and Being*, p. 228.

48 See the comment by Paul Molnar in *Divine Freedom and the Doctrine of the Immanent Trinity. In Dialogue with Karl Barth and Contemporary Theologians* (London: T&T Clark, 2002): 'Gunton appears at times to imply that relationality is the subject while God's act becomes the predicate' (p. 294; cf. p. 310).

49 Gunton, *Becoming and Being*, p. 228.

50 Gunton, *Becoming and Being*, p. 232.

51 Gunton, *Becoming and Being*, p. 238.

52 Gunton, *Becoming and Being*, p. 239.

53 Gunton, *A Brief Theology of Revelation*, p. 120.

54 Gunton, 'God the Holy Spirit', p. 120.

55 Gunton, *The Triune Creator*, p. 143.

56 Gunton, *The One, the Three and the Many*, p. 184.

57 Gunton, *The One, the Three and the Many*, p. 185.

58 Gunton, *The One, the Three and the Many*, p. 187.

59 Gunton, *The One, the Three and the Many*, p. 189.

60 Gunton, *The One, the Three and the Many*, p. 206.

61 Gunton, 'A systematic triangle', p. 78.

62 Gunton, 'A systematic triangle', p. 79; cf. 'Salvation', pp. 152f.

63 Gunton, *Christ and Creation*, p. 51.

64 Gunton, 'Salvation', p. 157.

65 Gunton, 'The triune God and the freedom of the creature', p. 63.

66 The challenge has been ably mounted by Paul Molnar in *Divine Freedom and the Doctrine of the Immanent Trinity*, pp. 294–96.

67 Gunton, *The Triune Creator*, p. 162.

68 Gunton, *The Triune Creator*, p. 163.

69 Gunton, *The Triune Creator*, p. 165.

70 Gunton, 'The development of Christian doctrine', p. 45.

71 Gunton, 'A rose by any other name? From "Christian Doctrine" to "Systematic Theology"', in *Intellect and Action*, p. 22.

72 Gunton, 'The triune God and the freedom of the creature', p. 51.

73 Gunton, 'Salvation', p. 157.

74 The nearest we come (apart from the brief survey 'Gott der Sohn' in *Religion in Geschichte und Gegewart 4. Auflage*, II, 310–19) is *Christ and Creation* and *The Christian Faith*, pp. 78–116.

75 Gunton, *The Barth Lectures*, p. 9.

## Chapter 3

## Towards the *Analogia Personae et Relationis*: Developments in Gunton's Trinitarian Thinking[1]

### Stephen R. Holmes

Probably no locus of theology is more associated with Colin Gunton's name than the doctrine of the Trinity. In surveying Gunton's corpus, however, it is evident that his interest in the Trinity, although ever-present in the published works, changes in shape and focus through his career. I want to spend most of this chapter tracing the development of Gunton's interest in, conception of and use of, the doctrine of the Trinity throughout his writing.

We can begin, and almost end, with the published version of Gunton's doctoral thesis, *Becoming and Being: The Doctrine of God in Charles Hartshorne and Karl Barth*.[2] First published in 1978, six years after Gunton's earliest published work,[3] this nonetheless contained and summed up almost everything that appeared earlier, excluding the occasional review.[4] In 2001, two years before Gunton's death, a new edition appeared, with an added epilogue. The index of this second edition is revealing: under 'trinity, doctrine of' we find eight brief references, an indication that one chapter of the work, the shortest, has the doctrine of the Trinity as its focus, and then 'epilogue, *passim*'. In the 23 intervening years, the Trinity had become ubiquitous.

The earlier work begins with simple acceptance of what Gunton perceived as a shared critique Hartshorne and Barth offered of the 'classical' doctrine of God, identified with the doctrine taught by St Thomas in the *Summa Theologiae*.[5] The recent critique of theistic belief, we are told, is directed at this classical doctrine and is compelling: the tradition had defined the divine in terms of opposition to nature, and located God primarily as that which is timeless, unchanging, immaterial and at the top of a chain of being. It was built on an uneasy, and ultimately unstable, marriage of rational argument derived from Ancient Greece and biblical revelation. With the collapse of this approach, two roads to recovery are open: a rational doctrine of God, developed with no more than polite interest in any account of revelation – this is found in Hartshorne and process theology for Gunton – or a doctrine of God built solely on revelation, which Gunton finds in Barth. From this unquestioned starting point, the book is split almost equally into a reading of Hartshorne's doctrine of God and a reading of Barth's doctrine of God, in fairly constant conversation with Hartshorne. It is not a great surprise to find little on the Trinity in the exposition of Hartshorne; the exposition of Barth, however, is entitled 'Barth's Trinitarian Theology'.[6] The section consists of an introductory chapter on Barth's theological method, in conversation largely with Barth's *Anselm: Fides Quaerens Intellectum*,[7] followed by two close expositions of sections of the *Church Dogmatics*: on the Trinitarian structuring of revelation in I/1 and on the divine perfections in II/1.[8] The latter makes no mention at all of the Trinity; the reading of the trinitarian material in I/1 is explicitly dependent on Eberhard Jüngel and Robert Jenson. Jüngel is used for an interpretation of relationality and Jenson is mined for an interpretation of temporality – both themes that are needed to bring Barth into useful conversation with Hartshorne, of course. Barth's rejection of the language of person for the three hypostases is noted, without very much by way of comment, as is his insistence that it is the one God who is properly called 'personal'. Claude Welch and Jüngel are cited for the idea that Barth is doing something fairly radical in developing a dynamic and relational account of God's existence, but God's relationality here is used only as a way of speaking of God as essentially relational without falling into Hartshorne's trap of making God's existence dependent on the world. A revealing section on 'the meaning of the doctrine of the Trinity' suggests that the doctrine serves to name the identity of the one God the Church worships.

Now, this is all offered by Gunton by way of exposition of Barth, and the exposition is penetrating, close to the text and essentially faithful. My own suspicion is that Jüngel puts a slightly Hegelian or Lutheran spin on Barth, finding a closer identity between God's transcendent identity and God's economic action than Barth may have intended. (Although the placement of the doctrine of election within the doctrine of God, rather than as the first of the works of God, does invite such a reading.) Although the section on Barth stands under the title 'Barth's Trinitarian Theology', it is the reading of Anselm, and the discovery of method there, which controls the whole. The doctrine of the Trinity, that is to say, is used as the way to speak of God's relationality under the Anselmian condition of rational discourse governed by the faith of the Church. 'Its function', to use Gunton's own words, 'is at least in part hermeneutical'.[9]

When Gunton revisited the book in 2001, the 20-page 'Epilogue' reflecting on the earlier work was almost entirely taken up with criticism of

Barth's Trinitarian theology,[10] under two main heads: the concept of 'person'; and the lack of pneumatology. On personhood, the discussion leads to a simple celebration of the conclusions of John Zizioulas,[11] of whom more later; on pneumatology, the criticism is drawn from a less subtle Orthodox theologian, Vladimir Lossky (mediated in part through an early study by the present Archbishop of Canterbury, Rowan Williams), and centres on a suggestion that Barth's embracing of the *filioque* is pneumatologically, and indeed theologically, disastrous.[12] Augustine is, unsurprisingly, cited repeatedly and disparagingly in both discussions;[13] equally unsurprisingly he is contrasted repeatedly with the success of the Cappadocian Fathers, whose achievement is understood to be exactly what Zizioulas has claimed it to be.

An assessment of the Trinitarian theology of the epilogue should wait, as should the equally interesting comparison of the reading of Barth here with that offered in the published lecture transcripts that Paul Brazier has edited.[14] I hope, however, that I have indicated enough of the flavour and content of the 1978 work to demonstrate that Gunton's doctrine of the Trinity did indeed develop quite radically from this point. In content – the *filioque*; the centrality of hypostatic personhood – and in deployment, his later work is rather different from anything we find here. What there is, though, is an awareness that the Trinity matters to Christian doctrine, unusual enough in 1970s English-language theology.

For the decade after the publication of *Becoming and Being*, Gunton's major published works seem almost to ignore the Trinity. Christology comes to the fore first, with a series of papers leading to the publication of *Yesterday and Today* in 1983,[15] and then a series of discussions of questions surrounding metaphor and the atonement which coalesce into the 1988 work *The Actuality of Atonement*.[16] Neither of these books, nor the various papers leading up to them, are untrinitarian, of course, but their focus is elsewhere.

*Yesterday and Today* has also been republished with a revealing epilogue.[17] Its major theme was the claim that classical Christology remains relevant to any attempt to do theology in a post-Enlightenment world; it hardly needs saying that this argument was carried with conviction and great skill. The doctrine of the Trinity cannot, of course, be absent from a book on orthodox Christology, but in some ways it is remarkable how much it remains in the background to this one. (In the 'Epilogue' to the second edition, and indeed in a later book on Christology, *Christ and Creation*, Gunton comments that Geoffrey Nuttall wrote to him after the book was published noting that it was odd for a book on Christology to have quite so little to say about the Holy Spirit.[18]) In a 'Christology from above', we are told in a quotation from Wolfhart Pannenberg, 'the Trinity is presupposed',[19] although Gunton himself disagrees with this point, suggesting that the mere confession 'Jesus is Lord' is adequate to develop both Christology and Trinity.[20] Otherwise, there are, I think, only two explicit mentions of the Trinity: a note about Hegel's attempt to demythologize the doctrine and a slightly longer discussion of the issue behind the disagreement with Pannenberg, of the relation of Christology to Trinity.[21]

This last is interesting, although covering little more than two pages. '[C]onfessions of Jesus of Nazareth's temporal-eternal significance do not presuppose the doctrine of the Trinity', we read, but 'they do inevitably lead to it, for they presuppose the reality of a God who is able to become spatio-temporal without loss of his divinity'.[22] Charles Norris Cochrane is quoted to the effect that the point of this is an 'assault on classicism's absolute dualism of time and eternity'.[23] Gunton suggests that the danger in the Western tradition has been the replacement of this dualism with another, just as corrosive, between transcendent Father and immanent Son. The correlation of Trinity and ontology is here hinted at for the first time, although the hint remains undeveloped. A second hint, undeveloped here but that will come to flower in Gunton's later theology, is the suggestion that in the doctrine of the Trinity is the assertion that 'God is . . . orientated from all eternity to what happened in Jesus of Nazareth . . .'.[24] This is just Barth's doctrine of election, of course, but Barth's Trinitarian theology has been developed prior to his doctrine of election, and letting this account of God's eternal orientation shape a doctrine of the Trinity is going to become important before my chapter is over.

*The Actuality of Atonement,* by contrast, has a chapter devoted to trinitarian themes, entitled 'The Atonement and the Triune God'.[25] Up to this point, the book has been centred around the concept of metaphor, developing that concept and applying it to the various 'theories' of atonement bequeathed to us by the tradition. Two points have been made in the discussion on metaphor that are of interest to what follows. The first is a subtly different version of the point I have just found in *Yesterday and Today*; to quote: 'in what sense, if any, is it possible to speak of God as he is in himself, apart from and as the basis of his articulation in narrative? (That is, of course, the question of the nature of God as triune.)'[26] The second is the suggestion that all language, particularly all theological language, is to some extent metaphorical: we simply cannot speak of God in ways that literally refer.

Let me dwell on the first of these for a moment because the comparison with the Christology book raises an issue that seems to me to be important. I stress that here I am picking up on two passing comments, one occupying a paragraph, the other merely parentheses. However, by the end of Gunton's writing career the distinction between them will be rather central. The question is, to use language I have used before, is the gospel story *definitive* of God's triune life, or merely *revelatory* of it? In *Actuality of Atonement*, the meaning is clearly the second of these: God lives behind and before the narrative, and it is precisely the task of theology to find ways of speaking about God's eternal life that accept that it is repeated or mirrored or lived out in the economy. In *Yesterday and Today*, however, the language at least suggests the first of my options: 'God is from all eternity oriented towards' the gospel story; it is through the events of gospel narrative that God defines who he is.

Now, I do not suppose that Gunton meant anything quite so blunt as this; indeed, I suppose that his lifelong commitment to doing theology in a specifically Reformed tradition meant he could not have. The *extra Calvinisticum* and the *communicatio* alike make such a move impossible. In the twentieth century though, various Reformed theologians have strained against these boundaries in their eagerness to reconnect God and the gospel: Barth in *Church Dogmatics* II/2; Bruce McCormack in many of his recent writings; and, I will suggest before the end of this chapter, Gunton himself. More on this later, though.

After this initial exploration of the nature of metaphor, *Actuality of Atonement* discusses three metaphors of the atonement, before turning to how these might be incorporated into theology proper. The sixth chapter begins with a suggestion that what binds the various metaphors together is a concept of 'relationship': the relationship of God with creation, and with the human creation in particular, and how that might be conceived and renewed. As the chapter develops, there is less about the Trinity than the heading might suggest, but the concept of relationship remains key. Two things need to be said about this: first, the 'relationship' in question is entirely the relationship of God to his creation. The climax of the chapter is an assertion of a trinitarian economy ('*to be part of the creation means to be related to the Father through the Son and in the Spirit*'[27]), but there is no attempt at all to link this economic account to any account of the eternal relations in God, however surprising this might be to readers of Gunton's later theology. Second, it is not clear, at least to me, how this language of 'relation' relates to the earlier strictures about the inescapably trophic nature of all theological language. We are told that 'what the metaphors suggest' is that 'the relationship which determines all the others is that between God and everything else'.[28] Well, perhaps; but in this sentence is the word 'relationship' not just another metaphor, and if not, how is it functioning?

I have dwelt at some length on these two books partly because the features I have highlighted are going to become important in describing how Gunton's Trinitarian theology developed, and partly to indicate that direct reflection on, or deployment of, the doctrine of the Trinity was actually remarkably lacking in Gunton's major theological writing in the 1980s. Two less-noted works came out during this period, however, that did both focus on the Trinity. Gunton's third book, *Enlightenment and Alienation*, has not widely been judged his most successful or influential.[29] Its subtitle was *An Essay towards a Trinitarian Theology*, and, although published in 1985, it was written by 1982.[30]

The content of this book makes more sense when one recalls that Gunton was initially employed to teach philosophy at King's College, London. The opening chapter traces an account of the Enlightenment through Descartes, Locke, Hume and Kant; the second an alternative tradition via Berkeley, Coleridge and Polanyi; the critics of the Enlightenment cited throughout are Murdoch and Adorno, not Barth or Frei. The three sections focus on perception, freedom and interpretation as problems for contemporary Western culture. The repeated hint – and it is often little more than a hint – is that a Trinitarian doctrine of God offers ways through these problems. More specifically, understanding God as triune, and the world as the creation of this triune God, offers ways to reunite alienated concepts. In perception, objective and subjective can be brought together; freedom and obligation are no longer opposed; in interpretation, critical and canonical views of the Bible come together. Let me quote a longish section that reveals both the operative doctrine of the Trinity and the use to which it is being put here:

> A form of words, a way of allowing God to come to speech, is being employed in an attempt to allow an otherwise various set of data to be understood in a unified way.
>
> But is it an appropriate unification? One widespread modern view of the Trinity is that, far from allowing the variety of our experience to come to expression, it is a foreign imposition, restricting what we want to say about God to a narrow and ancient formula. The traditional 'three persons in one substance' tends now actively to mislead, and in two ways. 'Three persons' suggests three separate Gods, not the one God in the threefold richness of his being, while the word 'substance' suggests a static, immovable deity. On the contrary, the conception of God as triune is meant to express a view of one God who is various in his being and is, therefore, able to be seen as relating himself to the world in a variety of ways. The open and personal reality of . . . God . . . can come to speech if we conceive God in his Fatherhood, Sonship and Spiritness.[31]

Note, first, that the doctrine of the Trinity advanced follows Barth: God's personhood is single, and the use of 'person' to name the three hypostases is misleading; equally, God's life is dynamic, not static. Second, the point of the doctrine of the Trinity is still, to use Gunton's own word from *Becoming and Being*, 'hermeneutic': it is a conception of God that, once held, allows us to make sense of our experience of reality.

*Enlightenment and Alienation* draws from many sources, but the presiding genius of the book is Samuel Taylor Coleridge. I do not know the source of Gunton's interest in Coleridge, who, as an Anglican zealot who poured out scornful works in support of church establishment, was surely the most unlikely of all Gunton's inspirations, but the doctrine of the Trinity here found in Barth is echoed in Coleridge. What Coleridge gave to Gunton was a hint – and in the dense and serpentine threads of logic that make up Coleridge's prose one never finds more than a hint – that ontologies, or, even better, protologies or archologies,[32] define all that follows. In an astonishingly dense lecture, unpromisingly entitled 'On the Prometheus of Aeschylus; An Essay, Preparatory to a Series of Disquisitions Respecting the Egyptian in Connection with the Sacerdotal Theology, and in Contrast with the Mysteries of Ancient Greece',[33] Coleridge offered a tabular contrast between worldviews. One may be monist, collapsing all distinctions into one, and so identifying God and the world; this, in Coleridge's language, is the Phoenician way: 'their cosmogony was their theogony, and *vice versâ*.'[34] One may be a dualist, finding the answer to all problems in a primal opposition between two co-eternal polarities, such as spirit and matter. Or one may be Trinitarian, finding within the eternal self-existent godhead the possibility of otherness that is not opposed, for which Coleridge coined the term 'alterity'. Triunity, that is, becomes the solution to the age-old problem of Parmenides and Heraclitus, correlating the one and the many.

These ideas are present in embryo at least in *Enlightenment and Alienation*, but come to full fruition in two works with the same title. In 1985, the same year that *Enlightenment and Alienation* was published, Gunton gave his inaugural lecture in the chair of Christian Doctrine at King's College, under the title 'The One, the Three and the Many'. In it we read that 'we learn from Coleridge . . . that the question of the three in one is also the question of what kind of world we live in . . . Modern culture . . . cannot find room both for the unity of mankind and the free, particular plurality of the many'.[35] The theme is much more fully worked out seven years later, in the first Bampton Lectures to be given by a non-Anglican,[36] entitled *The One, the Three and the Many: God, Creation and the Culture of Modernity*.[37] Here, Coleridge's trinitarian mediation between the one and the many forms the basis for a theory of 'open transcendentals' which leads to a theological account of culture and createdness. The hermeneutical use of the doctrine of the Trinity first found in Barth in *Becoming and Being* was here deployed with deft handling across a stunning range of concerns.

After Gunton's death, many appreciations of his work, oral and published, pointed to this book as perhaps his greatest achievement; this includes my own obituary for Colin published in the *Guardian* newspaper.[38] At the time I made the point hesitantly because I was aware that this was not Gunton's own estimation of the work. When I put the point to him once, he dismissed it with the comment that 'there was not much theology in it [*sic. The One, the Three and the Many*]'. At the time I did not understand the comment, but now I think it reflects an awareness on Gunton's part that this work was almost the end of one trajectory of his thought – one, if truth be told, that he knew he had left behind some years before he gave the Bampton Lectures on which it is based. The hermeneutical deployment of the doctrine of the Trinity – the search, we might put it, for *vestigia trinitatis* – would soon cease to feature prominently in his work.

Gunton's inaugural lecture at King's College in 1985, however, introduces a new theme into his theology, and a new vocabulary. Alongside the concern for relationship and human community that had always been there in the criticisms of alienation and suchlike, two new words come to prominence: 'person' and 'particularity'. These terms are almost wholly absent from the first decade of Gunton's published theology, except the Barthian ambivalence about the use of the former word in trinitarian discourse. And yet Gunton's inaugural lecture takes as one of its themes 'the importance of the person'.[39] (The other theme more nearly relates to the ideas I have been discussing to this point: 'our views of what it is to be human are projected from what we believe about God.'[40])

The range of reference in the lecture is characteristically wide, but in the main text John Macmurray stands out as the key witness for the claims being argued, that 'person' is a logically basic concept, and that 'persons' exist only in 'relations'.[41] My suspicion, however, is that the real root of this new note is hidden away in a pair of footnotes, referencing two unpublished papers circulated amongst the members of the British Council of Churches (BCC) Study Commission on Trinitarian Doctrine, written by Andrew Walker and John Zizioulas.

Barth's doctrine of the Trinity is now wholly absent; indeed, the key points are repudiated. The first half of the lecture is devoted to arguing that Western theology has presented a monistic concept of God, which has resulted in an individualistic concept of what it is to be human. In the second half, it becomes central to the doctrine of the Trinity that the three hypostases are, simply and precisely, 'persons'. I suspect that Gunton saw this as development rather than reversal; that what Zizioulas's account of Cappadocian theology gave him was a way of reversing the direction of analogy, and defining human personhood in the light of divine personhood, a procedure that fits very well with the Anselmian method he had learnt from Barth in that first book. But the fact remains that he is now embracing with energy and passion positions that he had himself criticized as verging on the tritheistic not many years earlier.[42]

In 1990 Gunton published a paper in the *Scottish Journal of Theology* (*SJT*) that is something of a prospectus for the next decade of his theological writing. It was entitled 'Augustine, the Trinity and the Theological Crisis of the West'.[43] It is noteworthy that, apart from disparaging comments concerning his exegesis of the text 'compel them to come in',[44] Augustine featured fairly regularly and largely positively in Gunton's published thoughts, at least, until 1985. He is not mentioned except as an inspirer of Anselm in *Becoming and Being*;[45] in *Enlightenment and Alienation*, his epistemology is repeatedly praised, twice for the Anselmian *credo ut intelligam*, and also for the recognition of all knowledge as a gift of grace.[46] In *Yesterday and Today*, Augustine is taken to task, largely in passing, for opposing time to eternity;[47] in *Actuality of Atonement* he appears only incidentally, and generally positively. The inaugural lecture once again marks the decisive break: Augustine's lack of adequate conception of the divine persons lies behind Descartes and modern individualism, and the failure of Western theology.[48]

When we look at the themes that drive the essay on Augustine, we find almost a catalogue of the next decade of Gunton's work: not just persons, particularity and relationship, but the failure of an adequate doctrine of the incarnation, in contrast now to Edward Irving;[49] the lack of an adequate account of the mediation of creation; the failure of pneumatology; and the problem of the knowability of God. At the root of all these theological errors is Augustine's alleged failure to grasp the core achievement of the Cappadocian doctrine of the Trinity. Gunton's published theological work began with the assertion and assumption that the 'classical' doctrine of God had failed; in *Becoming and Being*, this doctrine was identified with the teaching of Aquinas, with no speculation offered on why Aquinas thought like this; by the time of this essay, Gunton had become convinced that the fault lay with the failure of Latin theologians to grasp the core insight of Trinitarian doctrine, a failure that could be laid squarely at Augustine's door.

Through the 1990s Gunton offered constructive proposals on several of these issues: *A Brief Theology of Revelation*, on the knowability of God; *The Triune Creator*, on the mediation of creation; and *Christ and Creation*, revisiting Christology and addressing pneumatology.[50] Several collections of essays revisiting the themes also appeared: *The Promise of Trinitarian Theology* in 1991; *Theology Through the Theologians* in 1996; *Intellect and Action* in 2000;[51] and a series of volumes of essays from the conferences of the Research Institute in Systematic Theology at King's College.

I discern two basic directions in the articulation and deployment of the doctrine of the Trinity over this period. On the one hand, there is a focus on the Irenaean 'two hands of God' image and a Trinitarian account of mediation; on the other hand, an increasing interest in the concept of the 'person' and how divine and human personhood might be aligned. The first focuses on the economy; the second on theology proper.

The first trajectory, on trinitarian mediation, can be seen in embryo in *A Brief Theology of Revelation* and *The Triune Creator*. Right at the start of *Becoming and Being*, Gunton had argued, or at least asserted, that a part of the failure of the 'classical' doctrine had been its inability to give an adequate account of the God–world relation. On the one hand, through the *via negativa*, God was defined primarily as whatever the world was not; this led to a vicious form of transcendence whereby God was unable to be close to the creation. On the other hand, the 'great gulf fixed' between God and the world was bridged by means of an ontological hierarchy of intermediate beings, or causes, as illustrated by the five ways in the *Summa Theologica*.[52] Up to the mid-1980s, the solution to this problem had been to find in Christology a more adequate account of mediation; in this, Gunton's discovery of the thinking of John Owen and, particularly, Edward Irving, seems to have been significant, but there is no space here to trace that story. Perhaps the most surprising datum I discovered in preparing for this chapter was the complete lack of the Irenaean 'two hands of God' theme in Gunton's published work, at least, prior to 1990. Irenaeus has been mentioned, but always for Christological and eschatological reasons. The image of Son and Spirit as the Father's two hands, through which the Father interacts with the creation, appears in print, I am fairly confident, for the first time in Gunton's 1990 Didsbury Lectures, published as *Christ and Creation*. It appears here almost fully formed: '[t]he next and fairly rapid step', Gunton writes, 'is what may appear to be an outrageous generalisation: that the only satisfactory account of the relation between creator and creation is a trinitarian one . . . because God the Father creates through the Son and Spirit, his two hands (Irenaeus), . . . we can conceive a world that is both real in itself, and yet only itself in relation to its creator'.[53] The theme appears in explicit connection with a belief that mediation must be fundamentally an account of persons in relation;[54] there is no discussion at all in these lectures concerning the analogical (or otherwise) status of this language; the logic rather suggests that human and divine persons and relations are to be understood fairly univocally, in that 'person' and 'relation' become the middle terms in the arguments linking divine and human. Of course, this recognition becomes absolutely central to *The Triune Creator*; the more interesting text, however, in this connection is *A Brief Theology of Revelation*. Here, as I have indicated, the main thrust of trinitarian deployment remains the attempt to find analogies. The Irenaean account of mediation is there,[55] but it is a very muted theme.

The second trajectory deriving from the inaugural lecture is more obvious in the essays. In a paper entitled 'Trinity, Ontology and Anthropology: Towards a Renewal of the Doctrine of the *Imago Dei*',[56] Gunton returns again to his dissatisfaction with Cartesian anthropology and proposes a solution based on comparing human personhood with divine personhood and human sociality with the triune relations. The doctrine of human creation in the image of God becomes an account of how 'person' or perhaps 'persons in relation' is the key analogue that unites divine and human. The precise status of this analogy is deliberately left unclear: on the one hand, Barth's insistence that *'person* means primarily what it means when it is used of God'[57] remains; but by the end of the paper we read that 'the question of our difference from and likeness to God becomes less pressing' under the account presented.[58] As happened with 'relation' in *Actuality of Atonement*, it seems that a particular subset of theological language is being privileged. In place of Aquinas' *analogia entis* or Barth's *analogia fide*, Gunton seems to be reaching towards an *analogia personae et relationis*.

A brief recapitulation: I am suggesting that two consistent questions drove Gunton's Trinitarian interest from *Becoming and Being* on. One was the obvious question concerning the content of the doctrine: how do we adequately speak of God? The second concerned the use of the doctrine: if the doctrine of the Trinity is the right way to speak of God, how does that make any difference to the way we understand and live in the world this God has created? I have suggested that, on the first question, Gunton rather straightforwardly assumed Barth's account of the content of Trinitarian doctrine, later supplemented and reinforced by a reading of Coleridge, until a fairly fundamental revolution in his thought, which, on published evidence, can be pinned down to between 1982 and 1985, and which I propose resulted from his working with John Zizioulas on the BCC Study Commission on the Trinity. After this point, he adopted what has become known, rightly or wrongly, as an 'Eastern' account of the Trinity, stressing the true personhood of the three hypostases and finding an account of the divine unity in their relations. In terms of the use of the doctrine, until *A Brief Theology of Revelation*, Gunton put Trinitarian doctrine to hermeneutical use, finding in it a way of narrating the world. From that point on, Gunton used his new doctrine of the Trinity to answer various questions concerning mediation.

Notice that there are two changes of mind here: the first occurring by 1985 concerning the content of Trinitarian doctrine, and very obvious from the way the word 'person' ceases to be an embarrassment, as it was for Barth (and Gunton did think this; listen again to his own words: '"Three persons" suggests three separate Gods, not the one God in the threefold richness of his being . . .'[59]), and becomes the central interpretative key to the doctrine. The second change occurs more gradually, around 1993, and concerns the use of the doctrine: trinitarian analogies are replaced by trinitarian mediation. Because of the time-lag, we might assume that these two changes are independent, but the textual evidence suggests to me that they are not. It seems that, in the eight or so years between the two changes, Gunton either deployed the doctrine of the Trinity to find analogies, with little or no mention of his new vision of the Trinity as 'persons in communion' (in *A Brief Theology of Revelation*, it is 'unity in diversity' that is the focus of the analogies, as the quotation above illustrated; even in the Bampton Lectures, 'community' appears very late in the day, with the analogy to the triune life being drawn with a great deal of hesitation[60]), or he gloried in a new doctrine of the Trinity without looking for uses for it. I suspect, therefore, that in Gunton's mind there was some connection between the shift in content and the shift in use, and that he found a certain uneasiness in the middle period when the former shift had happened and the latter was awaited.

What might this be? I have indicated at several points in the exposition that the question of the grammatical status of the words 'person' and 'relation' remained unclear for some time in Gunton's theology. This seems to me to be significant: the language of 'analogy' had received much employment in describing the earlier attempt to find implications from Trinitarian doctrine. Gunton resisted, I think, the too-simple move from a 'social doctrine of the Trinity' to human sociality. (I suspect the reason is again John Zizioulas, who claimed in *Being as Communion*[61] and elsewhere that doing this would lead inevitably to a strongly episcopalian ecclesiology, which Gunton would have found difficult . . .). The Irenaean account of triune mediation offered an alternative use for the doctrine of the Trinity that did not bring such unhappy consequences, as can be seen in the book of essays Gunton left in press when he died, *Father, Son and Holy Spirit: Toward a Fully Trinitarian Theology*,[62] where the longer section is entitled 'Triune Divine Action'. It leaves the question as to the analogical or otherwise status of 'persons in relation' language still unanswered, however.

Clarity on this point is only finally achieved, as far as I can see, with the publication of *Act and Being* in 2002.[63] Here, Gunton drew on John Duns Scotus's critique of Aquinas' account of analogy to suggest that there must be some element of shared meaning if words are to refer at all.[64] As ever in Gunton's theology, the hint from the tradition is taken up and made his own, but the hint is vital in setting the train of thought running. In this case I happen to know exactly where Gunton came across the relevant passage in Scotus: between January and Easter 2001, he, Murray Rae and I were working hard at putting together a textbook, *The Practice of Theology*,[65] as very much the junior partner, I was sourcing most of the texts, largely following up suggestions Murray and Colin made. Scotus was in the chapter on theological language, and I recall Colin's excitement after he read those few paragraphs . . .

The development in *Act and Being* finally systematizes what Gunton had been pressing towards for a decade or more. From *A Brief Theology of Revelation*, we have the idea that all language is enabled to refer by the Holy Spirit; from several other works, we have the claim that it is in God's economic action, the Father working through Son and Spirit, that we come to know God. And this action is irreducibly personal. The defining case becomes incarnation: the love of Jesus is at one and the same time human and divine love; the person of Jesus is at one and the same time a human person and a divine person; thus '[w]hat it is to be a human person is in this case identical with what it is to be a divine person, and therefore the word means the same at the levels of creator and creation'.[66]

Now, the Christological qualification in this must not be missed: the identity is only 'in this case'. The next section of the book treats the 2 Peter text that forms the basis for the doctrine of *theosis*, and so perhaps recalls the observation, borrowed from Zizioulas once more, that human personhood is an eschatological concept.[67] But the underlying ontological commonality between divine and human which Scotus believed was necessary to ground accounts of analogy is found, not in the concept of being *per se*, as in Scotus, but in an account of persons and relationships as the fundamental concepts in both divine and human ontology. What does this mean for ecclesiology? I don't know where Gunton would have gone, but I wonder whether Miroslav Volf's attempt to rewrite Zizioulas in congregational terms was helpful – although it was not a book I ever heard Gunton speak particularly highly of.

A few words of conclusion. *Becoming and Being* began with a desire to replace a doctrine of God that was discredited, indefensible and useless. From Barth, no doubt mediated quite strongly by the guidance of Robert Jenson, came the suggestion that the Trinity was the answer; from Zizioulas came an account of the Trinity that was significantly different to that which Barth had proposed, defined by a celebration of the univocal usage of such words as 'person', 'relation' and love of both God and human creatures.

I presently think the suggestion that there is any language, including language of person and relation, that is not fundamentally analogical when applied to God and the creatures is a very difficult and dangerous one. I also believe that the Cappadocians thought the same, with Basil and Gregory Nyssa's dispute with Eunomius turning almost entirely on the status of *epinoia*, of the imaginative stretching of human language to hint towards the ineffable divine reality. So I think that Guntun's solution to his problem was unhappy. More, I think that the problem itself may have been misidentified: the classical doctrine of God found in Thomas has not been shown to be useless and illogical since Schleiermacher's day; it has been so fundamentally misunderstood in both philosophy and theology that it has been effectively undiscovered. I argued some of these points, which I was beginning to grope towards four and five years ago, with Gunton in private and once or twice in public. Unfortunately, our discussions were cut short.

So what do I take from this story concerning the development of Gunton's Trinitarian theology? Several things: an immense respect for the intellectual power and clarity of positions, even when I happen to disagree with some of them; helpful ideas about the usefulness of Trinitarian doctrine, which I think can apply even without (what I take to be) Gunton's revisionist theology; some happy memories, and some pangs of regret, of course; but most of all, I want to repeat a comment I wrote at the end of an introduction to Paul Brazier's transcription of Gunton's lectures on Barth. Gunton said in the course of those lectures that more and more he disagreed with Barth about the content of theology, but it was the vision of the scope of theology, the excitement in the possibilities of theology, the confidence in the usefulness of theology, the orientation of theology only and ever towards the gospel, that he found endless inspiration in still. That's what Colin gave me – as much or more when we disagreed as when we agreed. And, remembering many conversations in seminar rooms and restaurants and conference bars, how he positively encouraged me and other apprentice theologians to question and object to his ideas, I dare to hope that he would have liked to have been remembered in such terms – not necessarily as someone whose theology we should agree with, but as someone who taught us why it was worth thinking hard enough about theology to disagree.

## Notes

1  This chapter is a version of a paper presented at a day conference hosted by Spurgeon's College, London, September 2007: 'The Triune God in the Theology of Colin Gunton'.

2  Colin E. Gunton, *Becoming and Being: The Doctrine of God in Charles Hartshorne and Karl Barth* (London: SCM Press, 2001). The original edition was published in 1978. References will be taken from the 2001 edition.

3  An essay entitled 'Karl Barth and the Development of Christian Doctrine' *Scottish Journal of Theology* (hereafter *SJT*) 25 (1972), pp. 171–80.

4  The main exceptions are a brief first glance at science, 'The Theologian and the Biologist' *Theology* 77 (1974), pp. 526–28, and a couple of broader pieces for church audiences: 'Christian Belief Today: God, Creation and the Future' *New Fire* III (1975), pp. 434–41; and 'The Biblical Understanding of Reconciliation: Paul and Jacob before God' *Free Church Chronicle* XXXII (1977), pp. 17–22.

5  Gunton, *Becoming and Being*, pp. 1–5.

6  Gunton, *Becoming and Being*, p. 114 of the edition cited.

7  Gunton, *Becoming and Being*, pp. 117–27.

8  Gunton, *Becoming and Being*, pp. 127–66 and pp. 186–212; the pages between these sections are a transitional chapter on themes of analogy and futurity, setting Barth's account of the perfections in context.

9  Gunton, *Becoming and Being*, p. 186.

10  Gunton, *Becoming and Being*, the 'Epilogue' is on pp. 225–45; pp. 227–40 concern Barth on the Trinity.

11  Gunton, *Becoming and Being*, p. 232.

12  Williams and Lossky appear on p. 233 of Gunton, *Becoming and Being*, and the discussion of the *filioque* follows.

13  See Gunton, *Becoming and Being*, pp. 229, 230, 233–34, 238 and 239. The penultimate is the most revealing: 'The Achilles' heel of all Western theology is Augustine's failure to make the Spirit *a* person' (emphasis original, although I suspect it should have read '. . . *a person*'). Interestingly, Augustine is not mentioned at all in the original text.

14  Colin E. Gunton, *The Barth Lectures* (ed. Paul H. Brazier) (London: T&T Clark International, 2007).

15  Colin E. Gunton, *Yesterday and Today: A Study in Continuities in Christology* (London: DLT, 1983). Also on Christology in this period we find: 'The Political Christ: Some Reflections on Mr Cupitt's Thesis' *SJT* 32 (1979), pp. 521–40; 'The Truth of Christology' in T.F. Torrance (ed.) *Belief in Science and in Christian Life: The Relevance of Michael Polanyi's Thought for Christian Faith and Life* (Edinburgh: Handsel Press, 1980), pp. 91–107; and 'Time Eternity and the Doctrine of the Incarnation' *Dialog* 21 (1982), pp. 263–68. The theme is picked up once more in *Christ and Creation (The Didsbury Lectures 1990)* (Carlisle: Paternoster Press, 1992).

16  Colin E. Gunton, *The Actuality of Atonement: A Study of Metaphor, Rationality and the Christian Tradition* (Edinburgh: T&T Clark, 1988). Leading up to this see: 'Transcendence, Metaphor, and the Knowability of God' *Journal of Theological Studies (JTS)* 31 (1980), pp. 501–16; 'Christus Victor Revisited: A Study in Metaphor and the Transformation of Meaning' *JTS* 36 (1985), pp. 129–45; 'The Justice of God' *Free Church Chronicle* XL (1985), pp. 13–19; 'Christ the Sacrifice: Aspects of the Language and Imagery of the Bible' in L.D. Hurst and N.T. Wright (eds) *The Glory of Christ in the New Testament: Essays in Memory of George Bradford Caird* (Oxford: Clarendon Press, 1987), pp. 229–38; and 'The Sacrifice and the Sacrifices: From Metaphor to Transcendental?' in R.J. Feenstra and C. Plantinga (eds) *Trinity, Incarnation and Atonement: Philosophical and Theological Essays* (Notre Dame: University of Notre Dame Press, 1989), pp. 488–96. On the same theme see 'Proteus and Procrustes: A Study of the Dialectic of Language in Disagreement with Sallie McFague' in A.F. Kimel Jr. (ed.) *Speaking the Christian God: The Holy Trinity and the Challenge of Feminism* (Grand Rapids: Eerdmans, 1992), pp. 84–102; and 'Universal and Particular in Atonement Theology' *Religious Studies* 28 (1992), pp. 453–66.

17  Colin E. Gunton, *Yesterday and Today: A Study in Continuities in Christology* (London: SPCK, 1997) (original edition 1983).

18  Gunton, *Yesterday and Today*, p. 221; see also Gunton, *Christ and Creation*, p. 11.

19  Gunton, *Yesterday and Today*, p. 19.

20  Gunton, *Yesterday and Today*, p. 44.

21  Gunton, *Yesterday and Today*, p. 192 (Hegel); pp. 134–36.

22  Gunton, *Yesterday and Today*, p. 134; note the echoes of the criticism of the classical doctrine of God for defining God against the world in *Becoming and Being*.

23 Gunton, *Yesterday and Today*, p. 136.

24 Gunton, *Yesterday and Today*, p. 136.

25 Gunton, *Actuality of Atonement*, pp. 143–71.

26 Gunton, *Actuality of Atonement*, p. 47.

27 Gunton, *Actuality of Atonement*, p. 169.

28 Gunton, *Actuality of Atonement*, p. 144.

29 Colin E. Gunton, *Enlightenment and Alienation: An Essay Towards a Trinitarian Theology* (Basingstoke: Marshall Morgan & Scott, 1985).

30 Gunton, *Enlightenment and Alienation*, p. ix.

31 Gunton, *Enlightenment and Alienation*, p. 141.

32 A nice Coleridgean coinage.

33 See H.J. Jackson and J.R. de J. Jackson (eds) *Shorter Works and Fragments* (2 vols) (*The Collected Works of Samuel Taylor Coleridge* vol. 11) (Princeton: Princeton University Press, 1995) II.1251–86.

34 Jackson and Jackson (eds), *Shorter Works*, p. 1270.

35 Colin E. Gunton, 'The One, the Three and the Many: An Inaugural Lecture in the Chair of Christian Doctrine' (London: King's College London, 1985).

36 Coleridge would not have been impressed . . .

37 Colin E. Gunton, *The One, the Three and the Many: God, Creation and the Culture of Modernity* (Cambridge: Cambridge University Press, 1992).

38 Steven R. Holmes, 'Obituary: Rev. Professor Colin E. Gunton', *Guardian*, 3 June, 2003.

39 Gunton, 'The One, the Three . . .', p. 3.

40 Gunton, 'The One, the Three . . .', p. 3.

41 See, *e.g.*, Gunton, 'The One, the Three . . .', pp. 6–7.

42 Zizioulas is mentioned only four times in the published Bampton Lectures; the Cappadocians not many more. 'Person' and (especially) 'particularity' are major themes, however, driving much of the social comment.

43 Colin E. Gunton, 'Augustine, the Trinity and the Theological Crisis of the West', *SJT* 43 (1990), pp. 33–58. It later appeared as ch. 3 in Colin E. Gunton *The Promise of Trinitarian Theology* (Edinburgh: T&T Clark, 1991), pp. 31–57. References are to this version.

44 Gunton, *Enlightenment and Alienation*, p. 106; see also Gunton, *Yesterday and Today*, p. 185.

45 Gunton, *Becoming and Being*, p. 183.

46 Gunton, *Enlightenment and Alienation*, pp. 3–4; 131; 51.

47 The point appears several times, but see Gunton, *Yesterday and Today*, pp. 120–22 for the most extended discussion.

48 Gunton, 'The One, the Three . . .', pp. 9–11.

49 Irving appears semi-regularly in Gunton's work of the latter half of the 1980s. I am sure this is Andrew Walker's influence.

50 Colin E. Gunton, *A Brief Theology of Revelation: The 1993 Warfield Lectures* (Edinburgh: T&T Clark, 1995); *The Triune Creator: A Historical and Systematic Study* (Edinburgh: Edinburgh University Press, 1997).

51 Colin E. Gunton, *Theology Through the Theologians: Selected Essays 1972–1995* (Edinburgh: T&T Clark, 1996); *Intellect and Action: Elucidations on Christian Theology and the Life of Faith* (Edinburgh: T&T Clark, 2000).

52 Gunton, *Becoming and Being*, pp. 2–4.

53 Gunton, *Christ and Creation*, p. 75.

54 Gunton, *Christ and Creation*, p. 73–74.

55 Gunton, *A Brief Theology of Revelation*, see, *e.g.*, on p. 63: '. . . the free personal relation of God to the world through his Son and Spirit . . .'

56 Colin E. Gunton, 'Trinity, Ontology and Anthropology: Towards a Renewal of the Doctrine of the *Imago Dei*' in Christoph Schwöbel and Colin E. Gunton (eds) *Persons Divine and Human* (Edinburgh: T&T Clark, 1991), pp. 47–61.

57 Gunton, 'Trinity, Ontology . . .', p. 55.

58 Gunton, 'Trinity, Ontology . . .', p. 61.

59 Gunton, *Enlightenment and Alienation*, p. 141.

60 Gunton, *The One, the Three and the Many*, pp. 214–15.

61 John Zizioulas, *Being as Communion. Studies in Personhood and the Church* (Crestwood, New York: St Vladimir's Seminary Press, 1985).

62 Colin E. Gunton, *Father, Son and Holy Spirit: Toward a Fully Trinitarian Theology* (London: T&T Clark International, 2003).

63 Colin E. Gunton, *Act and Being: Towards a Theology of the Divine Attributes* (London: SCM, 2002).

64 Gunton, *Act and Being*, pp. 67–71.

65 Colin E. Gunton, Stephen R. Holmes and Murray A. Rae (eds) *The Practice of Theology: A Reader* (London: SCM Press, 2001).

66 Gunton, *Act and Being*, p. 147.

67 So *e.g.* Gunton, 'Trinity, Ontology . . .', p. 60.

# Chapter 4

## THE PERSON AS WILLING AGENT: CLASSIFYING GUNTON'S CHRISTOLOGY

### Alan Spence

### *Examining the bones*

A number of natural scientists are collaborating in order to give a scholarly account of an unclassified species of animal. Their various interests are reflected in the distinct contributions they make to the discussion. Some detail the creature's diet, others its ways of reproduction and some its patterns of social behaviour. Among the scientists is a student of anatomy whose attention is directed to the animal's skeleton and, in particular, to the unusual arrangement of a small set of its bones. She believes that notwithstanding the creature's habitat, external shape or social mannerisms, the configuration of these apparently insignificant bones is determinative for its classification and contributes to our understanding of its behaviour. In this chapter I will engage in a somewhat similar task to that of the anatomy student. To help classify the theology of Colin E. Gunton I will focus my attention on an apparently innocuous observation that he made in a book published shortly before he died. I believe that it provides us with a valuable insight into the skeletal framework of Gunton's overall theology, and is therefore significant for any classification that might be made of his work.

The notion I refer to appears in Gunton's engaging and provocative study on the attributes of God, *Act and Being*.[1] It is the outcome of a somewhat technical discussion concerning the number of wills operating in God and in the person of Christ, which I believe is significant enough to be quoted at length.

> If will is an attribute, it is clear that God can have only one: the idea of three divine wills is problematic for all kinds of reasons. And yet the gospel account appears to require at least two wills somewhere, as crucially in Gethsemane . . . To avoid the problem of their being two wills in God, two were attributed

to Christ . . . a divine will and a human will, and what we see in Gethsemane is the human nature's will accepting that of the divine.

But that simply will not do. There are two reasons. First, the decision which was taken to the effect that will is an attribute of nature and not of hypostasis or person leads to saying that natures have wills, with an inevitably Nestorian outcome. A human nature and a divine nature cannot will anything. Only persons have wills, especially if by 'will' we mean that which initiates or brings about action directed to an object or end. But . . . it is a mistake to make will into a kind of entity or object. It means, rather, a person willing something rather than some hypostatized entity within the person of such a kind that one person can have two of them. It can be argued, second, that this position is supported by scripture. What we read in the gospel accounts of Gethsemane is an interaction between the will of the incarnate Christ – the eternal Son became man – and the will of the Father.[2]

In the face of the conceptual complexities put forward by the ancient Church, Gunton upholds the common sense view that a person has only one will. Taking the word 'person' when it is used Christologically or when it is applied to the members of the Trinity to mean something similar to its modern use, shaped as it is by our interest in psychology, Gunton argues that willing is that which is done by a 'person'. Consequently, there can be in Christ but one will, while in God there must be three for the simple reason that Christ is one person and God is known to be three.

Any reader who is acquainted with Gunton's theological perspective will find nothing surprising in this claim. His consistent emphasis on the unity of the person of Jesus in the face of 'Nestorian' or dualistic ways of interpreting Christ, along with his clear recognition of the distinctive roles of the trinitarian persons in the economy of creation and salvation, have long prepared his reader for the considered conclusion above. However, when it is stated as boldly as this it does strike one as a little odd that a theologian with so high a regard for the formulations of the early Church should break so clearly with the teaching of the tradition in these two areas. Monothelitism, the view that Christ has only one will, was officially condemned as heresy at the Third Council of Constantinople (680–681). Furthermore, it was generally accepted by the Church Fathers that the persons of the Trinity share one being or essence and differ from one another only by their relationships or modes of coming to being, rather than by some aspect of that being such as the will. This being so, why does Gunton depart from the dogmatic tradition in these matters and how are we to classify him within the structure of classical Christian thought in light of such a decision?

## Responding to Chalcedon

I begin by offering a brief account of the development of a central feature of that structure. The Definition of Chalcedon (451) was the Church's explication of the relation between the divine and human in Christ, framed within the parameters set by the Nicene Creed and using the conceptual tools it provided. The Definition was also shaped by three contemporary documents, each of them being formally received at the Council. These were: the second letter of Cyril to Nestorius, which defended the practice of referring to Mary as *Theotokos*, the Bearer of God; the letter of Cyril to the Antiochene bishops incorporating the Symbol of Union, which served as the basis for the reconciliation of Cyril and John of Antioch; and the Tome of Leo, written to counter the Monophysite teaching of Eutyches.

Once the Definition was formally promulgated many of the monasteries and churches in Egypt and Palestine opposed it vigorously, finding it impossible to subscribe to the 'two natures' doctrine on which it was based. The teaching of these non-Chalcedonian churches generally came to be known as Monophysite – 'one nature'. Within that broad designation were included theologians like Severus, Patriarch of Antioch, whose Christology was remarkably close to that put forward at Chalcedon, and others who were to all intents and purposes practising Docetists. The uniting feature of almost all those who were opposed to Chalcedon was the belief that there was just *one* operation, one new divine–human energy or *theandric* action, in Christ's incarnate life. By this they meant not two harmonious actions working in concert, but rather one indivisible principle of activity. Pseudo-Dionysius the Areopagite first formulated the theory of this united action as follows:

> . . . not having done things Divine as God, nor things human as man, but exercising for us a certain new God-incarnate energy of God having become man.[3]

Developing this idea of Pseudo-Dionysius, the Monophysites changed the word 'new' to 'single' and the expression 'one theandric energy' encapsulated the essence of their difference with the Chalcedonians and constituted the battleground for the ensuing debate. To their minds the Chalcedonian Definition rightly affirmed that the being of Christ was only one hypostasis, one person, one Son, but was wrong in indicating that his activity was twofold – that there were in him two distinct, albeit harmonious, principles of operation, divine and human, each acting according to its own particular characteristics. And non-Chalcedonians were implacably opposed to the apparently dualistic implications of this view of Christ.

The compromise formulation that Christ had only one will was introduced by the emperor Heraclius to side-step what had become the mired discussion of whether there were in Christ one or two principles of operation. By means of this qualification he sought to encourage the Monophysites to rejoin the imperial Church and subscribe to the Chalcedonian Definition. He was in some measure successful. The formulation was sanctioned by both Church and state and was considered orthodox for some forty years until a penetrating theological response was offered by Maximus the Confessor. Maximus argued persuasively that the inner logic of the *homoousion* formulations of Nicaea and Chalcedon required *two* wills in Christ. From 681, Monothelitism was officially proscribed and Duothelitism affirmed.

Are we able to locate Gunton's Christology within this development of Christological thought? His commitment to Monothelitism in the passage quoted earlier suggests that his position might be of the same genus as that of Sergius, Patriarch of Constantinople, the man who drew up the formal documentation for the doctrine that Christ has but one will. If so, the study of Sergius could help us to understand more about Gunton. But before making this assumption we need to consider a little more closely Gunton's relation to the Definition of Chalcedon.

Gunton certainly felt a measure of discomfort with the 'two natures theory' of Christ person, believing it tended naturally towards some form of Nestorian dualism:

> Another cause for offence in the modern world is the doctrine of 'two natures':
> that Christ was, according to the language of the tradition 'one person in two
> natures'. This has sometimes led to the appearance of a kind of hybrid being,
> two contrary realities stitched together, like a centaur, suggesting two persons
> rather than one person in two natures. That this teaching has since early
> times been labelled 'Nestorianism' and officially rejected has not prevented
> some from speaking and writing as if it were true. When, for example, it is
> suggested that when Jesus was tired and wept he did so as a man, whereas
> when he performed miracles or forgave sins he acts as God, we may be near
> to such a transgression.[4]

Apparent here is Gunton's unease with the allocation of certain of Christ's actions to his human nature and others to his divine nature, a practice he has long argued was incipiently if not actually Nestorian. Now it might of course be wrong to allocate certain operations to particular natures in this way, but it is important historically to recognize that such a practice is, in fact, orthodox Chalcedonianism. Leo's 'Tome' was one of the documents approved at Chalcedon. Leo held that: 'Each form, in communion with the other, performs the function that is proper to it; that is, the Word performing what belongs to the Word, and the flesh carrying out what belongs to the flesh.'[5] Likewise, Cyril's letter to John of Antioch was also recognized as orthodox by the Fathers at Chalcedon. In it, Cyril quotes the text of the Symbol of Union:

> And as to the expressions concerning the Lord in the Gospels and Epistles, we are aware that theologians understand some as common, as relating to one Person, and others they distinguish, as relating to two natures, explaining that those that befit the divine nature according to the Godhead of Christ, and those of a humble sort according to his Manhood.[6]

This way of distinguishing between the natures is also apparent in the actual words of the Definition itself: '. . . as regards his Godhead, begotten of the Father before the ages, but yet as regards his manhood begotten, for us men and for our salvation, of Mary the Virgin.' In short, the practice of referring certain actions or attributes of the person of Christ to either his divine or human nature is thoroughly Chalcedonian. I emphasize this point because it is important for us to have a measure of clarity about the teaching of the tradition if we are to use it as a map on which to locate and so understand Gunton's theology.

We continue to consider Gunton's disquiet with the 'two nature' theory of Chalcedon. His concern with nature language was not simply with the dualism that he believed followed from it, but also with the widespread tendency it encouraged to treat natures as if they were existent realities of some sort. Speaking of nature he argues that:

> The word is best understood to work in this context more as verbal adjective than a noun. Natures are not separate entities, but ways in which Jesus of Nazareth is fully divine and fully human, in a relationship we shall have to explore.[7]

The idea of nature in this context being a verbal adjective greatly puzzled me when I first heard Gunton use it in a discussion many years ago. I now understand him to be suggesting that the natures of Christ are to be viewed as actions or operations rather than substantial entities. As he puts it: '. . . natures . . . are not things but refer to ways which Jesus is and acts'.[8] It is an interpretation that lies at the heart of P.T. Forsyth's Christology and Gunton refers to his work with a measure of approval.

> To see Jesus as the coming together of two acts or movements assists greatly, though it is better, I believe, to say that we have a single personal action – that

of Jesus Christ, the Son of God in the flesh – which is at once God's action and that of one who is fully human.[9]

Where Gunton differs from Forsyth is that while Forsyth speaks of two operations in Christ – one of divine humbling and the other of human exaltation – coming together in his incarnate life, Gunton recognizes only one operation in Christ – there is in him a single personal action. Now this emphasis on the unity of energy or operation in Christ reinforces the perception that Gunton's Christology might belong to the pattern of thought of those non-Chalcedonians like Pseudo-Dionysius the Areopagite who contended for a single *theandric* action or energy in the life of Jesus.

There is, however, one feature of Gunton's Christology that indicates that this classification would be quite wrong. It is as though our student of anatomy came to recognize from the bone structure of the creature's flipper that the animal under investigation was a bird and not a mammal. Though penguins and seals might behave in a somewhat similar way in the sea, they are nevertheless to be classified as members of quite different animal groups.

## *An* autokinetic *humanity*

What then is the salient feature of Gunton's understanding of Christ that prevents us from counting him among the post-Chalcedonian Monophysites? It has to do with the nature of the single action of Christ. For Gunton this action is not some *theandric* operation, an amalgam of divine and human activity such as the Monophysites held. Neither is it simply a divine working or willing as had been indicated by Apollinarius or even the Docetists. According to Gunton, the single principle of operation or action in the life of the incarnate Christ was always *a fully human one*.

It was from his study of the British theologians Edward Irving and John Owen that Gunton learnt to emphasize the dynamic reality of Jesus' human life as depicted in the New Testament. Nothing Jesus did in his incarnate life lay outside the bounds of human possibilities. This is because his empowerment was not from within himself but came from the Holy Spirit. As Gunton put it in *The Christian Faith*, 'The Spirit is the one who makes Jesus of Nazareth to be who he is'.[10] He lived as a man before God, exercising faith in the Father, seeking divine help through prayer, battling with demonic temptation and striving to live a life of personal obedience so as to fulfil the Father's will. Jesus' life among us was a paradigm for our own human existence. So it is that while the post-Chalcedonian Monophysites uniformly struggled with the Gospel testimony that Jesus prayed for himself, Gunton saw such prayer as a central feature of Christ's spiritual life.

Gunton argued that any distinction that we might make between divine and human action in Jesus' life is a distinction between the external agency of God and the personal agency of Jesus rather than between two principles operating within Jesus himself.

> As we have seen, there are not in Jesus two natures in the sense of rival principles. His action is God's *action* only as the action of one who was fully human, and nothing must be said which might undermine that humanity.[11]

This insistence that all the actions of Jesus are fully human, even as he fulfils God's saving purposes in the world, places Gunton at a considerable distance from the perspectives of both the Chalcedonians who upheld that the two natures each operate according to their own principles and their Monophysite opponents who affirmed one *theandric* action in Christ. It makes the study of Gunton's thought particularly interesting. Let us consider how he sought to affirm the divinity of Christ within the parameters he set.

### Agency as a conceptual tool

By interpreting the divinity and humanity of Christ in terms of action rather than substance, Gunton has chosen a quite different path from that which was followed by the Fathers of the fourth and fifth centuries. In the critical debate between Athanasius and the Arians, the crux of the argument was whether Jesus was divine because of his obedience and conformity to the Father's will *or* whether his divinity lay in his ontological identity with God. The Church eventually ruled at Nicaea that Jesus' true divinity could only be safeguarded if he was held to be substantially one with God, that is, that Jesus was in his being *homoousios* with the Father. The Arians maintained that by conforming to the divine will Jesus showed himself to be the Son of God, but this was recognized by the orthodox to be inadequate. They contended that Jesus' divine action was a consequence of his being, not the basis of it. The *homoousion* consequently became the most significant interpretative tool for the Church in both its Christological and Trinitarian discussion. Chalcedon did no more than develop the logic of Nicaea, arguing that as Jesus was of one substance with God so he was also of one substance with humankind.

However, in choosing to eschew any dependence on the language of 'being' in his interpretation of the God–man duality of Christ, Gunton has to make use of a rather different intellectual structure to give an account of the divinity of Christ. His key conceptual tool is that of agency. Applying this notion to the Christological task, Gunton suggests that the career of

Jesus can be considered from two quite different perspectives:

> There are therefore two levels at which his action must be understood.
> The first is that of one mediating the actions – the merciful, providential,
> redemptive, forgiving, renewing, healing actions – of God the Father himself
> . . . In that regard, everything that he does is the work of God, because he
> is the eternal Son of God made man . . . all this is also, at its second level,
> authentically human achievement.[12]

In addition, the close relation between will and personal action in Gunton's
work means that this double perspective can also be recognized when he
considers Christ's volition:

> There are, to be sure, dangers in speaking of two wills in Jesus, just as there are
> in speaking of two natures . . . But there are not two wills within Jesus, only
> two at work in his career, his will and the will of his Father. The incarnate
> Lord, through the Spirit and assisted by the ministering angels, accepts the
> will of his Father and goes to the cross. The Father's will is fulfilled by the free
> human willing of the incarnate Son in the power of the Spirit.[13]

How can a single action be ascribed both to the human will of Jesus and also
to the divine will of the Father? Gunton answers this question in three rather
different ways. First, as indicated above, it is through the empowerment of
the Holy Spirit that Jesus chooses the path of obedience and so conforms
to the divine will. This is undoubtedly true, but if this is all we have to
say about Jesus' person then what we have here is no more than a form
of Arianism or Adoptionism. Secondly, a high view of divine providential
action, common in the Reformed tradition, recognizes that both a divine
and a human agency can be ascribed to the same event: '. . . it is . . . better
to understand God's relation to the world rather as that of an author or
playwright, whose pen does indeed write the story, but in such a way as to
allow the characters to develop according to its and their intrinsic logic.'[14]
But such an argument, if true, could apply to anything we do and, if so, it
is not clear why Jesus in particular should be afforded divine status. When,
however, Gunton maintains that the career of Jesus can be viewed as 'the
merciful, providential, redemptive, forgiving, renewing, healing actions –
of God the Father himself',[15] he is saying far more than 'Jesus is obedient'
or 'this is how divine providence works'. He is arguing that these human
actions of Jesus are the actions of the Father, because Jesus is the incarnation
of his eternal Son: 'The theological heart of the Christian faith, therefore,
is to be found in the affirmation that this historical human being . . . is
identical with – the same person as – the eternal Son of God through whom

God created the world'.[16] This notion is, it seems to me, the linchpin that carries the weight of Gunton's Christological model. Just what he means by this identification of Jesus and the eternal Son we will need to look at a little more closely.

## Creation and incarnation

One of Gunton's major theological concerns was to show that there is a close relation between God's redemptive and creative ministry. He was deeply dissatisfied with any suggestion that the act of incarnation was unrelated to the act of creation or that so central a theological event as the coming of Christ into the world had human sin as its primary cause. 'That is why we just reject, for all its appeal, the famous Latin saying which, in translation, reads "O happy fault, that merited such and so great a redeemer."'[17] And so it was that he sought to explain the person of Christ in ways that highlighted the continuity between God's creation of the world and his personal presence in Jesus.

Gunton's doctrine of creation is a rich and complex body of constructive theology. The principal idea, as I understand it, is that God's activity in and towards the world is mediated by his two hands – the Son and the Holy Spirit. He argues with great care that because God's action is mediated in this manner, the integrity of the world in its otherness from God is maintained. Therein, Gunton navigates a carefully chartered course between the dangers of Deism on the one hand, where God stands back from his creation, unwilling to interfere in its natural processes and of Pantheism on the other, where creation and its outworking are viewed as no more than an aspect of God's being, his thinking or his speaking.

> In the theology of creation, therefore, language of mediation by God's Word enables us to speak both of God's free involvement with his creation and, ultimately, in Christ of his equally free and sovereign identification with a part of it.[18]

The pattern in which God relates to the world in the incarnation has its foundation in the way he relates to the world in creation: both are mediated by his Son.

> . . . a theology of Trinitarian mediation is indispensable for a grasp of the shape of God's manifold action in the world. Of the first 'hand of God' – often referred to as the second person of the Trinity – we must reiterate that he is the focus of God's involvement *within* the world's structures. That

involvement, as we have seen, comes to a climax in the begetting and birth of Jesus . . .[19]

Gunton's argument suggests that the incarnation is not as conceptually problematic as we sometimes make it. God has always worked his providential will within the structures of the world through the mediation of his Son. Such action, as a particular form of mediated action, never threatens the creaturely nature of this world. Although the world is the field of God's governing and gracious activity, it remains open to scientific exploration and explication within its own categories. When God comes among us to redeem us, it is again through the world's structures, in this case, through the human career of his Son. 'The human career is as such the saving action of God.'[20] Through the mediation of the Spirit, God the Father acts redemptively through the life of Jesus without threatening the integrity of his human actions or will.

But, if this is so, why should Jesus be considered to be divine? How does this man differ from the prophets? According to Gunton, Jesus is divine because he is the incarnation of the Son of God, the one who has always mediated God's action in the world. And the Son of God's divinity flows from what he does:

> . . . because the Son and the Spirit are God in action; because they do the work of God in the world, then they are truly and fully God, as truly so as is God the Father.[21]

This is important. The divinity of the Son is related to his action. But, if that is so, how does Gunton understand the act of incarnation? He offers this formal account: 'And so the eternal Son of God empties himself by adding humanity to his being in obedience to the Father and by the enabling of his Spirit, to bear his own human body, to become human as the God-man who is the agent of our salvation.'[22] This, we should note, is a classical, orthodox expression of the incarnation. However, Gunton's use of the language of 'being' here and the dualism it suggests appears to be a concession to the terminology of the tradition. He generally seems to be far more at ease using the concepts of action and agency as a way of interpreting the incarnation. For these, he argues, can be used in a way that avoids the dualism that lies at the heart of all the ancient Christological heresies:

> All of them in some way derived from dualism, the refusal to accept that the Son of God was able, because he was the right hand of the creator of heaven and earth, to involve himself personally in the creation without loss of or threat to his eternal divinity.[23]

Here, according to Gunton, the Son is able to enter the creaturely world and be fully human without loss of his divinity because of who he is. 'Jesus is the eternal Son of God *emptied* to the conditions of humanity . . ..'[24] '. . . God *submits himself* to the logic of our human condition, to save, indeed, but also to reveal, in such a way that we may both encounter and know him.'[25] 'It cannot, however, be understood because this is the Son *become* fully human . . .'[26] We must not assume from such expressions, however, that Gunton is an incipient kenoticist, or that he believes that the divine being is in some way changeable. Rather, by considering divinity and humanity in terms of action rather than being, Gunton feels able to treat these two notions not as strict alternatives or as opposing principles, but rather as ways of behaving that can both apply to a single person. So it is that in Jesus' human actions Gunton recognizes aspects of divine behaviour:

> When Jesus does the work of his Father and when he performs the apparently menial task of washing his disciples' feet he is not only setting a model for human action, but showing what kind of divine being he is: one who is divine in not grasping at divinity.[27]

Here, Gunton seems to be arguing that in the human actions of Jesus we are able to recognize his divinity and learn just what it means for him to be divine in his own particular way: 'It is in his very difference from God the Father that the Son is divine; God in a distinct way of being God.'[28]

What are we to make of this creative way of understanding the relation of the divine and human in the person of Christ, an interpretation which is dependent on the concept of God's mediated work of creation and which uses the notions of agency and action as its principal interpretative tools? We begin our evaluation of Gunton's Christology by considering again how we might map its basic structure onto the genealogical chart, so to speak, of classical theology.

### *Irenaeus*

It will come as no surprise to his readers that Gunton's interests and perspectives are remarkably similar to those of Irenaeus, the second century bishop of Lyons. Irenaeus affirmed a strong relation between God's creative and redemptive action; he recognized that the manhood of Jesus was dependent on the empowering of the Holy Spirit; he contended against the Gnostics for the absolute identity of Jesus with the Christ; and he argued that God's work in and towards the world was mediated by his two hands, the Son and the Holy Spirit. Further, Irenaeus held that Jesus Christ was both true man and true God and was able to speak without qualification of God becoming fully human:

> But in every respect, too, he is man, the formation of God; and thus He took up man into Himself, the invisible becoming visible, the incomprehensible being made comprehensible, the impassible become capable of suffering, and the Word being made man, thus summing up all things in Himself.[29]

To classify the structure of Gunton's theology as belonging to the same species as that of Irenaeus is not controversial. Gunton made no secret of his immense respect for and dependence upon this the first great theologian of the post-apostolic Church. The value of making explicit such a categorization, however, is that there are features of Irenaeus' relation to the tradition that can help us in our assessment of Gunton's own Christological project.

It is of particular significance for our discussion that Irenaeus inhabited a theological world that had yet to face the challenge of Arianism and in which the *homoousion* was yet to become the dominant conceptual tool of Christological and Trinitarian formulation. It meant that although Irenaeus was a great biblical scholar and constructive theologian who offered a comprehensive response to Gnosticism and the issues it raised, he was, as might be expected, unschooled in the concepts and technical skills that were to develop as the Christological debate progressed. Of course, no criticism can be levelled against Irenaeus for a certain naivety in some of his theological expressions with respect to issues that had yet to be raised. But what do we say about Gunton? Can he as a modern man enter Irenaeus' world, a worldview unshaped by the formulations of Nicaea and Chalcedon, and practice his theology with integrity within an intellectual framework that is not yet determined by the *homoousion* or the challenge of the Arians?

Let me illustrate my concern. Gunton makes the following ontological differentiation between God and created reality: 'This means in turn that the only meaningful distinction between different kinds of being – in technical terms, ontological distinction – is between creator and creation.'[30] Now, in the light of that perception, the Arian debate forces upon us the following question: on which side of such a distinction are we to place Jesus Christ? Is he creator or is he creature? If we answer, as I am sure Gunton would, that Jesus Christ is both creator and creature then we are clearly faced with some form of ontological dualism when explaining the person of Christ. Arianism *avoids* this dualism by perceiving Christ as the first born or most exalted of all creatures, the one through whom God made the world. Whatever status is given to him, the Son is not truly God as the Father is God. Apollinarianism seeks to get around the problem by having the Logos replace the human mind of Christ, so that there is only one principle of mental activity in his person. Orthodoxy, however, acknowledges the ontological duality of Christ's being in its 'two natures' language, but affirms the unity of his person in the narrative of the incarnation and by emphasising his single Sonship, his particular existence (*hypostasis*), and his one mode of presentation or persona (*prosopon*).

Now, in the light of the challenge of Arianism – and there are many semi-Arians or Adoptionists in theology today – can a modern Christology, which avoids the language of being and a recognition of Christ's ontological duality, adequately protect the faith of the worshipping Church that Jesus is, in the words of Irenaeus, 'true man and true God'? Is it enough simply to affirm that Jesus Christ is the incarnation of God's agent of creation? I am not sure that it is, for the Arians were more than willing to concede this. Furthermore, does not a reluctance to be disciplined by the language of the Nicene *homoousion* result in the making of unguarded statements such as Gunton's comment above: 'It is in his very difference from God the Father that the Son is divine; God in a distinct way of being God' – an expression which would surely gladden the heart of every true Arian?[31] This is not to suggest that Gunton is Arian. It is simply to question whether he has built theological walls sturdy enough to protect the faith from their persuasive arguments in the fourth century or in modern times. Such a defence is important because Arianism surely ranks as the greatest threat the Church has faced to its understanding of Christ.

### The Son or the Father

A second concern I have with the structure of Gunton's imaginative Christology is his identification of the two agents to which he ascribes the actions of Jesus. In the human career of Jesus, Gunton recognizes both the agency of God the Father and that of Jesus.

> There are therefore two levels at which his action must be understood. The first is that of one mediating the actions – the merciful, providential, redemptive, forgiving, renewing, healing actions – of God the Father himself . . . [but] all this is also, at its second level, authentically human achievement.[32]

In the same manner, Gunton understands there to be two wills operating in Jesus: 'But there are not two wills within Jesus, only two at work in his career, his will and the will of his Father.'[33] But, when considering the career of Jesus, the allocation of agency to the Father in this way seems to me to be somewhat problematic. The divine agent of the human career of Jesus is surely not God the Father, but rather God the Son. It was not the

Father who took human form and lived a life of obedience to God. It was not the Father who cried out in prayer in Gethsemane or who suffered on the cross – these were the actions of the eternal Son of God as incarnate. Significant changes to Gunton's Christological structure occur when God *the Son* is recognized as the divine agent of the human career of Jesus and as the one willing his actions. It means that the duality of agency or volition of which Gunton speaks is a duality *within* the incarnate Christ. His careful explanation of how one action can have both a divine and human agent can now be helpfully employed to understand in what sense there are within the one Christ two wills behind each act. The eternal Son is as it were the playwright of Jesus' human career, writing the story but allowing the human character to develop its own intrinsic logic. Through the mediation of the Spirit the human actions and volition of Jesus are always enabled to be authentically human events but can nevertheless also be ascribed to the divine Son. Why is this? Because the incarnation means that Jesus' humanity is the humanity of the eternal Son of God. The second person of the Trinity has taken a human nature, both body and mind, to himself, to be his own. And the events of that one incarnate life are all willed by the eternal Son without, in any way, undermining the full and authentic humanity of his human mind and volitional action. Whatever is done through his human and divine natures or agencies, however, is always to be referred to the one person, the incarnate Christ, the proper subject of all that he is and does.

## Conclusion

An animal is far more than the sum of its bones, yet its skeletal structure fulfils a vital function by providing protection and structural support for its body. For the botanist the skeleton can also be a particularly helpful indicator of its place within the animal kingdom. In this chapter, we have examined what appear to be fairly significant bones, as it were, of Colin Gunton's theology – those of person, agency and will – and of their relation to one another. Our analysis is intended to help us classify his theology and to assess whether or not it is able to bear the weight of the gospel witness to Jesus and to safeguard Christian faith in him. Our study has been almost entirely limited to the argument made by Gunton in a systematic treatise, published soon before he died, *The Christian Faith: An Introduction to Christian Doctrine*. This book is a careful exposition of the Apostles' Creed in which Gunton details the relation between the central themes of theology. This chapter makes no attempt to chart the development of Gunton's thought over the course of his career or to balance expressions that he uses in this book with others from his wide-ranging corpus. To use a recurring metaphor, this is a study of one particular specimen of Gunton's thought. But, in seeking to outline the structure of the theology expressed in the most self-consciously systematic of all Gunton's published works, it has been illuminating to try and locate his thinking within classical Christian thought. Given a number of its features, we have argued that his work should be recognized as belonging to the same genus as that of Ireneaus. Such a classification, we have suggested, sheds light on Gunton's ambiguous relation to the language, concepts and implications of the Definition of Chalcedon and explains why he was not as careful as he might have been in protecting his ideas from the danger of an Arian interpretation. Nevertheless, I believe that Gunton's theory concerning dual agency in the events of Jesus' human career and his use of the idea of mediation can be applied with minor modification to help interpret Christ's person in line with the biblical witness and the Christian tradition. To this end I have suggested that the divine agent to which Jesus' human acts are ascribed is the eternal Son rather than God the Father. With this small adjustment Gunton's theology would be able to affirm that in Jesus Christ, who is both true man and true God, there is, without confusion, both a human and a divine willing. In my opinion, such a modification would allow Gunton to build more firmly on the ancient tradition that he so highly valued.

## Notes

1 C. Gunton, *Act and Being. Towards a Theology of the Divine Attributes* (London: SCM Press, 2002).
2 *Act and Being*, p. 29.
3 Dionysuis the Areopagite, *The Works of Dionysius the Areopagite*, translated by John Parker (London and Oxford: 1897), fourth letter, p. 143.
4 C. Gunton, *The Christian Faith. An Introduction to Christian Doctrine* (Oxford: Blackwell, 2002), pp. 78–79.
5 The 'Tome' of Leo, in *Creeds, Councils and Controversies: Documents Illustrative of the History of the Church* A.D. *337–461*, edited by J. Stevenson (London: SPCK, 1966), sec. 4, pp. 318–19.
6 Cyril's letter to John of Antioch, in *Creeds, Councils and Controversies*, sec. 106c, p. 291.
7 *The Christian Faith*, p. 91.
8 *The Christian Faith*, p. 95.
9 *The Christian Faith*, p. 95.
10 *The Christian Faith*, p. 102.
11 *The Christian Faith*, p. 105.
12 *The Christian Faith*, p. 106.
13 *The Christian Faith*, pp. 109–10.
14 *The Christian Faith*, p. 64.
15 *The Christian Faith*, p. 106.

16 *The Christian Faith*, p. 79.
17 *The Christian Faith*, p. 65.
18 *The Christian Faith*, p. 10.
19 *The Christian Faith*, p. 101.
20 *The Christian Faith*, p. 85.
21 *The Christian Faith*, p. 181.
22 *The Christian Faith*, p. 96.
23 *The Christian Faith*, pp. 88–89.
24 *The Christian Faith*, p. 114.
25 *The Christian Faith*, p. 99.
26 *The Christian Faith*, p. 114 (my italics).
27 *The Christian Faith*, p.182.
28 *The Christian Faith*, p. 182.
29 Irenaeus, *Against Heresies* III 15.6.
30 *The Christian Faith*, p. 11.
31 *The Christian Faith*, p. 182.
32 *The Christian Faith*, p. 106.
33 *The Christian Faith*, pp. 109–10.

Chapter 5

# The Taste of Cake: Relation and Otherness with Colin Gunton and the Strong Second Hand of God

Paul Cumin[1]

That God remains distinctly himself while at the same time sustaining everything else as distinctly itself was for Colin Gunton the most basic item of the gospel. Simply put, 'Only that which is other than something else can be related to it'.[2] Yet Gunton also recognized that '. . . if God and world are ontologically other, some account of their relation – some theology of *mediation* – is indispensable'.[3] He therefore set out to construct a theology of mediation and soon found that such required a particular doctrine of God. For Gunton, to ask for one is to find the other: theology about a God who mediates himself to his creation is theology about the triunity of God.

As Gunton understood it, 'the doctrine of the Trinity enables us to think both the otherness, and so relative autonomy of the world, from God, and the relatedness of the world to God'.[4] At a time when many theologians were choosing between otherness and relation as if they were alternatives, Gunton wanted to 'think both'. Such was his self-imposed mandate, even if it did, in his own confession, seem to 'want to have one's cake and eat it too'.[5]

Anyone familiar with his work will know how important Irenaeus of Lyons was for Gunton in this respect, especially his use of the 'two hands' metaphor for understanding the co-existence of God and world.[6] Unless the Father 'holds' himself, so to speak, both to and apart from creation via his 'two hands' he is bound to 'overwhelm and depersonalize' this creation. Much hangs on this. And, as we shall come to see in this chapter, the placement of the *Father,* and not God *simpliciter,* at the top of this metaphor will require especial attention.

A further Irenaean influence will get us started: '. . . because it is through the economy that scripture's God makes himself known, an account of the economy is essential to any doctrine of God's being.'[7] For Gunton, the divine economy is the only place to begin Christian theology:

We must place ourselves theologically where the action is, because if we turn away from God's actual historical self-identification in Jesus, we simply manufacture an idol, or a series of idols. One central value of the doctrine of the Trinity, therefore, is that it ties our speech of God to Jesus, and thus helps to prevent the creation of idols or of any God projected conveniently to confirm our wishes or prejudices.[8]

We listen to Gunton today for many reasons and it is a comment on our times that perhaps chief among them is our need to be reminded of a redundancy: specifically Christian theology is such only when it starts with Jesus. Yet there is a complex problem with such simplicity, and it is at least as old as Chalcedon. If Jesus is somehow one with us and with God, starting from him could slip easily back round to speculation about the latter. And such indeed would be the circle were we swimming with only *one* hand. For Gunton, starting with the economy of Jesus means starting 'paradigmatically' from the Spirit:

In sum: all divine action whether creation, salvation or final redemption is the action of God the Father; but it is all equally brought about by his two hands, the Son and the Spirit. And these hands do not act separately, like someone holding a baby in one hand and trying to bang in a nail with the other – though I fear that our talk of the Spirit might sometimes suggest that. The Spirit works through the Son, paradigmatically as Jesus' ministry was empowered by the Spirit.[9]

To begin with Jesus for Gunton is to begin from the Spirit, and only as such to truly begin with Jesus. 'Christology which is abstracted from a discussion of the relation to it of pneumatology is not Christology rooted in the actual human career of the incarnate Lord.'[10] Thus, in a version of his incomplete and unpublished *A Christian Dogmatic Theology*, Gunton proposed a specific plan, and we will follow it here too.

We shall accordingly approach the doctrine of the Trinity according to the way of knowing, beginning with the economy of the Spirit and moving from there to the economy of the Son, the economy of the Father, and thence to the doctrine of the triunity of God.[11]

And so we begin with the economy of the Spirit.

There are two kinds of action Gunton most commonly attributed to the Spirit. Both centre on Christ and both deserve our attention. The first is the way in which the Spirit is iconic, always pointing away from himself to Jesus:

'The Spirit's characteristic action is self-effacing, because the Spirit is the one who enables people and things to be themselves through Jesus Christ.'[12] At issue here is getting people and things to *be* themselves. Gunton has taken a traditionally epistemological form – we know the Son by way of the Spirit – and applied it to his specifically ontological concern. This is then set to serve his theology of mediation; in the traditional grammar, a way of having both the immanence and the transcendence of God:

> . . . while in the economy, the Son realizes God's immanence in history – he becomes flesh, history – the Spirit, contrary to what is often assumed, *is God's transcendence*. The restriction of the Spirit to forms of immanence . . . is a symptom of what is wrong with the whole tradition . . . The Spirit may be active *within* the world, but he does not become identical with any part of the world . . . That is the function of the Son, who becomes flesh; and if without more ado we think of the Spirit also as a form of God's immanence, we may be in danger of being unable effectively to distinguish between Son and Spirit.[13]

There are two distinctions at work in this: the Spirit is neither the Son, nor is he identical with any part of the world like the Son. The first distinction – the ontological two-handedness of the Fathers, so to speak – is the possibility of both immanence *and* transcendence. The second distinction – that the Father keeps, as it were, both hands on the world – is God's economic actuality. And the point here is the Spirit's 'place'. For Gunton, the Spirit's self-effacing is a mode of his transcendence. The transcendent Spirit directs creation not to himself, but to the immanent Son. Put differently: 'If the Son is the *content* of God's redemptive movement into the world, the Spirit is its *form*, and that form is its freedom.'[14] In this respect, the Son may be the content of God's immanence in the world but this is only true as he is – and this is a concept to which we will need to return – *enabled* to be such by the Spirit. Similarly, the Spirit may be the 'form' of God's transcendence but he is only such as he is forever directing creation to the Father *through* its immanent content, the incarnate Son. The Spirit as the transcendent form of God's activity effaces himself by always directing creation to the immanent content of God's mediating activity, the Son.

Yet such a picture – God holding creation to and apart from himself through the immanent content and transcendent form of his two hands – is an image too static and spatial to be left alone. And so we come to the second kind of action Gunton typically attributes to the Spirit: 'Where the Spirit is, there do creatures *become* that which God created them to be.'[15] Thus:

> The Spirit is God's eschatological transcendence, his futurity, as it is sometimes expressed. He is God present to the world as its liberating other, bringing it to the destiny determined by the Father, made actual, realized, in the Son.[16]

Now we can see that the Spirit is God creating according to a particular intention; he is God's *eschatological* transcendence. Following Basil, and perhaps Barth and Jenson, Gunton understood the Spirit to be what the former called the 'perfecting cause' of creation, 'the one who directs the creatures to where the creator wishes them to go, to their destiny as creatures'.[17] It would be difficult to overstate the significance of this claim for Gunton's work. Everything about his doctrine of creation hinges on the way in which everything that God has made is intended to 'go somewhere'; creation is not simply the finished work of an absent watchmaker but is somehow a *project in progress*.

> . . . our being in time is not a defect of being, but part of its goodness . . . Human life is eschatological *in its structuring:* it is created with a view to an end that is more than replicating its beginning, because it is given *to be perfected.* That is to say, it reaches its perfection only at its end and so needs time to become what it truly is.[18]

This need for time is not a problem: 'Creation's temporality is its glory'.[19] Much of the argument in *The One, the Three and the Many* arises from this idea.[20] Where God and creation were held by Greek and Enlightenment theology at static odds with one another, there followed an unavoidable pinch on human freedom, an ontological opposition between the 'one' and the 'many'. Gunton's reply to such a situation relied on a recovery of the dynamism available from within the doctrine of the Trinity, and in particular on the way this kind of dynamism opens the possibility of conceiving God's creative participation in time. As Gunton sees it, hesitation here – or any outright belief in a timeless God or instantaneous view of creation – would introduce 'a divorce between God's creating action, which is timeless and his saving action which takes time'.[21] Gunton's tone in the debate about God's relation to time was similar to that in one of his favourite quotes from Bruce McCormack: 'if God does something in Christ then it is obvious that he can do it'.[22] For him, the matter was simple: in Christ we see that God 'takes time' to save his creatures and since this saving is what our creating has in fact entailed, in Christ we also see that God 'takes time' to create us.

In Gunton's theology, 'taking time' is therefore understood to be God creating and saving by opening and reopening his eschatological intentions for creation through the Spirit. The position of the Spirit is specifically *transcendent* here insofar as these eschatological intentions are not yet fully realized in time. And yet a transcendent and atemporal divine 'position' is far too deistic an image since it is talk of just one hand. God is also immanent and temporal by the Spirit's self-effacing focus, Christ.

With both hands now firmly in place, Gunton could affirm a divine immanence within history in a way that avoided identifying God *with* history, in effect constituting an alternative to the modern idolatry of progress. By the Spirit, God is bringing the creation into a future that is more than simply an immanent unfolding of itself. We might say – with respect to the Apostle – *when the Spirit of the Lord is, there is future.* Thus, the two characteristic actions of the Spirit come conceptually together at this point. The eschatologically transcendent Spirit brings creation to its intended end, and, like everything else about creation, the 'end' to which the self-effacing Spirit directs us is the same Christ to whom he has brought us all along. Thus we enter the second movement of Gunton's dogmatic composition, Christology.

For Gunton, if you want to explain the humanity of the Son the best thing to do is talk about the Spirit. According to him, humanity is a particular form of relation to God:

> . . . we must conceive the Spirit as the one who indeed maintains the Son in truth as his being the only one who, after the Fall, is enabled to be in true relation to God the Father and so truly human.[23]

To be human – 'truly human' – is to be enabled by the Spirit to obey the Father. And so to suggest the Son is really human is to make a pneumatological claim: 'the whole of Jesus' authentically human life is made what it uniquely is through the action of the Spirit.'[24] Having made this clear enough, Gunton goes on to introduce another big idea: '. . . at the incarnation the eternal Son took to himself the fallen flesh that all human beings share.' Gunton continues,

> [. . . this] is not, of course, to teach the sinfulness of Christ, but to give an adequate account of the representative nature of his humanity. If salvation is really to be communicated to us, then our flesh must be healed . . . Our sinfulness, then, is not conceived *mathematically* as the accumulation of wrong acts, but *relationally* as that which universally qualifies human existence in the flesh. If so, then, as the anti-Apollinarian theologians had argued, precisely *that* fallen flesh must be assumed by the saviour.[25]

For Gunton the dictum that 'the unassumed is the unhealed' applies even to peccability. The 'representative nature' of Jesus' humanity is due neither to the fact that Jesus is also divine – his especial humanness needs to be due to something about his humanity[26] – nor can Christ's headship be contingent on an unfallen calibre of his flesh, since this too would not just distinguish Jesus from other humans but categorically separate him from us. Gunton's start in this theological direction came in a hybrid of insights borrowed from John Owen, Edward Irving and Thomas Smail: if Jesus is the Spirit enabling the Son to live a fully human relation to the Father then, 'He was sinless because he was enabled not to sin by the Spirit who maintained him in truth before the Father'.[27] Gunton explains with a dig at his favourite foil, Augustine:

> [Jesus'] human persona must be, like ours, liable to sin. That it was so without falling was due to the action of the Holy Spirit . . . The Spirit, therefore, is not conceived, as tends to be the case with Augustine, as the immanent possession of Jesus, but as God's free and life-giving activity towards the world as he maintains and empowers the human activity of the incarnate Son.[28]

This critique of Augustine is indeed critical.[29] The Spirit can no more be an 'immanent possession' of Jesus than he could be immanent within the creation at all. As God's eschatological transcendence, the Spirit is the one who opens to Jesus the particular future his obedience to the Father makes possible. In this way, God's hands are, so to speak, no longer tied. The Spirit is here 'free and lifegiving', and this mobility finds its 'paradigmatic' expression in the resurrection: 'The Lord, [the Spirit] the giver of life, transforms the body of Jesus so that it may partake of the life of the age to come, the first-born of the new creation.'[30] For Gunton, therefore, the Spirit enables Jesus to transcend both the constraints of his fallen flesh and the constraints of his death, and so partake of eschatological life. Thus we could say that the resurrection of Christ, as with any of his acts, is neither accomplished by the Son alone nor by a somehow immanent Spirit behind him. Instead, the resurrection is an event in the human life of the incarnate Son that Gunton insists we understand *humanly*, as a straightforward result of this human's particular relation to the Father as it is mediated by the Spirit.[31]

Gunton's Christology will not appeal to Jesus' special case ontology to account for the remarkable in his life. The fact that this human is also divine is just that, a matter of fact; it is not a kind of hermeneutical ace up the sleeve to explain certain episodes in his historical career.

> . . . none of Jesus' acts is, on its own, unparalleled . . . In a certain sense even miracles belong among the 'ordinary' . . . What is unique is that through this particular combination of finite historical particulars God achieved the salvation of his world.[32]

For Gunton, Jesus is an (indeed *the*) ordinary human being. And if that way of putting it whiffs of Schleiermacher, the irony signals the revolutionary nature of Gunton's thought. Simply put, Jesus must be ordinary because it is ordinary people that need saving. If Apollinarius represents one of the tradition's failures to grasp mediation, Gunton is saying that the 'unparalleled' is the unhealed. As for the converse truth – the matter-of-fact divinity of this ordinary human – this too is commandeered to serve Gunton's doctrine of creation:

> ... not the human race as a whole but Jesus Christ 'is the image of the invisible God ...' ... As Pannenberg has pointed out, when it is used of Jesus, it implies that he is not only the one of whom we are copies – the prototype – but also the one who actualizes the true human destiny by what he achieves.[33]

Now we see that Christ is not just ordinary like Adam but also extraordinary as the one who is already what Adam was intended to become. Put in Gunton's terms: the incarnate Son is immanent within history as the human 'content' according to which the eschatologically transcendent Spirit 'forms' us. He is humanity's type as the first one – and so far, the only one – to have been enabled by the Spirit to realize our 'true human destiny'. Such is the fullness of the Christological intersection of soteriology and the doctrine of creation in Gunton's thought. And, once again, the Spirit is the one who keeps things moving:

> ... once the Son is incarnate, it is the Spirit and not the Word – for he is become fully human while remaining the eternal Son – who provides the so to speak motive power behind Jesus' actions.[34]

This is a remarkable claim. There is 'space' enough for Jesus to be truly human since it is neither 'the Word' – a *Logos asarkos* behind Jesus – that is responsible for the extraordinary in the life of Christ nor even a pneumatic power possessed by him; everything is done by the incarnate Son *as human*. That the theological traffic here is about both Christ and creation signals the fact that Gunton is indeed offering some new direction. And if Apollinarius was a wrong turn then the tradition's response to him was a bottleneck: Gunton also rejected the *communicatio idiomatum*. He explains why citing John Owen:

> One implication of this [account of the human Christ] is an assertion of the hypostatic union which does not entail 'a transfusion of the properties of one nature into the other, nor real physical communication of divine essential

excellencies unto the humanity.' The humanity remains authentically human
and is not subverted by the immanently operating Word, because he *is*, to
repeat, that Word become human. Wherein, then, consists Jesus' capacity to
do the word of God? 'The Holy Ghost . . . the *immediate, peculiar, efficient*
cause of all external divine operations . . .'[35]

Gunton clearly saw the pneumatology he received from Owen and others as
an *alternative* to various *communicatio*-Christologies.[36] Abstractions about
ontological transfusions only ever appeal when the Spirit is an afterthought.
But with both hands firmly in place, we have a plausible lucidity: 'he is, to
repeat, that Word become human.'

The result is what we might tentatively call a post-metaphysical
Christology. The incarnate Son is human in the same way as, more or less,
everyone else. In this respect Gunton may indeed have much to offer whatever is beyond the current anti-metaphysical critique. But that assessment is
not entirely accurate. To explain why, we need to proceed further.

Although according to Gunton's own scheme we ought to move now to his
patrology, we are not yet – for reasons that will soon become clear – ready
for that. This is because Gunton's concern for the authentic humanity of
Christ is an instance of his wider concern for the ontological integrity of
creation as a whole, with the movement from the economy of the Son to
the Trinity having as its correlative a movement from Christ to creation. The
latter move does not give us different questions, however. Instead it gives us
different ways of asking the same ones. And when we recall the centrality of
the concept of mediation for Gunton we have the key for understanding the
connection between the two: just as we heard worry about an 'overwhelming'
or 'subversion' of the humanity of Christ without a mediating Spirit, so now
we hear Gunton similarly work to establish sufficient 'space' for creation.
And, as we saw at the outset, it is this need for creation's ontological space
that leads into Gunton's theology proper: 'Because God lives in a dynamic
order of trinitarian space, he is able to create a world that has space to be
the world.'[37]

There are two sides to this claim. The first concerns God's 'space', and
the second is about the effects of this on that of creation. In the former, we
see that as Trinity God has personal space to be the Father, Son and Spirit.

What flows from the conception of God as three persons in communion,
related but distinct? First, there is something of the space we have been
seeking. We have a conception of *personal space*: the space in which three
persons are for and from each other in their otherness. They thus confer
particularity upon and receive it from one another. That giving of particularity

is very important: it is a matter of space to be. Father, Son and Spirit through the shape – the *taxis* – of their inseparable relatedness confer particularity and freedom on each other. That is their personal being.[38]

Here, the centrality of the concept of particularity identifies Gunton's thought like a theological moniker.[39] It is his way of affirming personal space in God. Unless the Father, Son and Spirit are particularly themselves, unless they are other than one another, there is no way to understand their relation to one another and so no way to affirm the unity of God. The particularity of the three is the 'personal being' of the one. And this begins to explain why Gunton could not accept vogue attempts to reify relation:

> For Basil the persons are not relations; rather, persons are constituted by their relations to one another . . . Without a distinction between persons – as the ones who are each particularly what they are by virtue of their relations (*scheseis*) to one another – and the relations between them, the danger is that their particularity will be lost, as has been the case notoriously in the West with its excessive stress on the principle that the acts of God *ad extra* are undivided.[40]

Without a distinction between the concepts of relation and person the theologian has no way to distinguish between the persons themselves. Gunton's caution about the supposed indivisibility of God's acts *ad extra* gets us to the point: 'If all divine actions are actions of the one God, so that the actions of the Trinity towards the world are undivided in an absolute sense, the persons are irrelevant for thought, and a kind of monism results.'[41] Although he accepted the principle's value as a barrier against Tritheism,[42] he saw in its overuse a more subtle and prevalent tendency toward the opposite extreme. Simply put, when theology reserves any 'undivided-in-an-absolute-sense' notion of God it thereby loses the possibility for particularity in *any* sense 'and a kind of monism results'. Here is Gunton's nemesis: it is a single-continuum metaphysic in which God and not-God are ultimately ontological alternatives. And this gets us to his second sense of theological 'space': there is space between the divine persons and thereby there is some too for the relation and otherness of God and creation.

Gunton's thinking on this matter began to flourish when he came to grips with S. T. Coleridge:

> . . . the only real alternative to Christianity is pantheism, [this is] Coleridge's view . . . . Atheism and deistic mechanism are, in effect, identical with pantheism, for all of them swallow up the many into the one, and so turn the many into mere functions of the one. There is, that is to say, no basis in any

such unitary conception of God for freedom because there is in it no space between God and the world.[43]

Coleridge is notoriously arcane,[44] but Gunton found in his thought exactly the scheme he needed to think clearly about 'space between'.[45] He continues, 'the doctrine of the Trinity allows for such space because it enables us to conceive the world as other than God while yet in relation to God'.[46] And it is this 'other than . . . yet in relation to' that signals the parallel between his doctrine of God and his doctrine of creation.

Let us clarify the point. Gunton's concern for space between the divine persons and between God and the world is for the possibility of both relation (->) and otherness (<-). From here the grammar deteriorates somewhat since without space enough for these two dynamics to occur together (<=>), 'relation' is not possible. The language is awkward because 'relation' is used to describe both the whole dynamic (<=>) and one of the two within it (->). But there is another word for the whole-dynamic-relation (<=>), and although Gunton does not himself use it for describing the triune communion, it is what we have heard him call *mediation* in his doctrine of creation.[47] I suggest that communion and mediation are functionally the same concept for Gunton. Communion is about the otherness-in-relation of the three divine persons and mediation is about the otherness-in-relation of God and creation. Both therefore describe the way God confers particularity, freedom and space to be, either within the triune life of Father, Son and Holy Spirit or through the mediatorial economy of Jesus and the Spirit in creation. In this sense, mediation is not just something that God does as the need arises when he creates something, it is a way of describing the event that he *is*.

Such a close call between the being and act of God would not sit well with Gunton, however, and it signals a shift in his thought that brings us now to his patrology. If communion and mediation are theologically synonymous, it is only because both are attempts to secure their respective forms of particularity.

In Gunton's doctrine of God the concept of particularity functions explicitly: it is what keeps the Christian theologian from talk of an absolute monotheos. In his doctrine of creation, however, it is less explicit – appearing as 'relative independence' or *Selbständigkeit*.[48] Nevertheless, its function is the same, here keeping us from the correlative collapse into pantheism.

Before particularity was paramount for Gunton, the idea of communion held pride of place in his thinking. What we need to see now is the way these two key concepts appear to have slipped, at the mature end of his career, into a kind of loose opposition. Whereas his earlier and perhaps less metaphysically ambitious thought seemed to allow him to hold particularity and communion in a sort of sustainable mutuality, this was a mutuality with tensions that it would seem he later chose to resolve. This produced a crucial shift in his thought.

Before the 'shift', Gunton would commonly say things like,

> God *is* no more than what Father, Son and Spirit give to and receive from each other in the inseparable communion that is the outcome of their love. Communion is the *meaning* of the word: there is no 'being' of God other than this dynamic of persons in relation.[49]

And then, seven years later,[50] after this 'shift', we hear something very different: 'the personal should be primordial, and it follows that any concept like "being" or "communion" which is secondary to the persons should not usurp their pride of place.'[51] This, we should note, was not a minor change for Gunton. His most influential work, for example, hinges on the finality of communion in God:

> The theology of God conceived to exist in the interrelationship of persons in which neither the one nor the many has priority over the other provides an alternative to the two poles of modern political thought, individualism, which elevates the many over the one, and collectivism, which does the reverse.[52]

There came a time when the implied apophasis in this 'neither the one nor the many' would not suffice for Gunton.[53] And although we will find pressures in his own thinking that brought him to this change of course, it did not arise without external influence. Gunton found himself between two of his most respected theological interlocutors, T.F. Torrance and John Zizioulas:

> Now, I do not wish to adjudicate here on the dispute between, on the one hand, John Zizioulas' view that the only way of maintaining a truly personal basis for reality is by making the Father the source of all things, especially the source or *aitia* of the triune communion; and, on the other, Torrance's view that in some way or other we must understand the triune communion as a whole to be the metaphysical source of unity.[54]

Here Gunton is declining the opportunity to adjudicate a dispute, the central concern of which had to do with *source*. For Zizioulas, the Father must be this or else a 'dead ousianic tautology' smothers freedom from the top down.[55] For T.F. Torrance – and more recently and pointedly Alan Torrance – if one of the Trinity is somehow prior to the other two then the identification of being and communion unravels from the inside out.[56] There was a time in Gunton's career when he quite literally sat as a mediator between these two positions and we could say that his own thought on this point follows a movement from Torrance's side of the table to Zizioulas'. It is clear that he once sat firmly *across* from Zizioulas:

> Whence does this communion derive? According to Zizioulas, it derives from the Father, who is to be conceived as the cause of the communion in the Trinity. While such a claim preserves the due priority of the Father in the Godhead, I do not believe that it allows for an adequate theology of the mutual constitution of Father, Son and Spirit.[57]

This is Gunton in polite disagreement. He continues by offering his own view:

> Should it not rather be said that communion is a function of – a way of characterizing – the relations of all three, just as freedom is to be conceived as a relation between things, rather than as some contentless absolute?[58]

This reference to 'all three' is classic Gunton. Crucial here is his implicit critique of Zizioulas' view of freedom as a 'contentless absolute'. At this point, he not only refused to look for a single cause of divine unity, but also found in the plurality of the triune communion a constructive rubric for his theology of mediation. Gunton continues in this important passage by going on to locate the 'cause' of the divine communion:

> Whatever the priority of the Father, it must not be conceived in such a way as to detract from the fact that *all three persons are together the cause of the communion in which they exist* in relations of mutual and reciprocal constitution . . .. Beyond this, it would be better to preserve an element of reserve, and to say that God's unknowableness prevents us from further enquiry into the *cause* of his being who and what he is.[59]

Here, Gunton does not accept the pursuit of a divine 'cause' behind the three persons and is instead content with 'an element of reserve'. Then, several years after this reserve, in a manuscript to his unpublished Dogmatics, he asks a question that, on its face at least, would appear to overstep it: '. . . if the unity of God is not located in a single substance in which the persons inhere, but in three persons perichoretically united, what is the principle of their oneness?'[60]

That Gunton would even ask for such a thing – a 'principle' of God's oneness – is evidence of his high regard for Zizioulas' theology. And as with anything theological, more is decided in the framing of the question than in its answering. Gunton is searching for something and he is now looking East. And though the turn may have been charted by Zizioulas, it was Gunton's own pursuit of particularity that fueled it:

> Being may indeed be understood in terms of communion, but there is for Zizioulas no communion that is not grounded in the particular. If it is not, it will be based in some general theory of being, and that is the beginning of the end, for where the particular person is not central, the person is in danger of being submerged into the abstract and impersonal.[61]

Here we can see that communion is no longer a 'way of characterizing the relations of all three' but is now something that needs to be 'grounded in the particular'. Thus, he made a choice between Torrance and Zizioulas, and particularity was the deciding feature:

> ... T.F. Torrance's conception of the unity of God ... seems so to stress the utter equality of the persons that their particularity is submerged in a dangerously telescoped conception of their unity. To place the concept of being in the centre ... is to endanger the particularity of the persons.[62]

And, having made his choice, Gunton does follow through with his new orientation:

> Whatever we do we must not suggest that 'being' unifies. The Father unifies the Godhead by virtue of the fact that he is Father of the Son and breather of the Spirit, and is therefore eternally the 'cause' of the being of the Son and the Spirit.[63]

With the idea that the Father is somehow the 'cause' of the other two persons of the Trinity we have Gunton's shift in full relief. Originally, it was 'The priority of the Father is not ontological but economic',[64] but later, in one of his last works, 'Ontologically speaking ... the Father is prior ...'.[65] We need to recognize that the idea that the Father should be understood as ontologically causative would not have been accepted lightly by Gunton, if for no other reason than it seems, on first impression at least, to leave him liable to the very indictment he so often laid at the feet of Augustine: 'The charge against Augustine and many of his Western successors is that ... he allowed the insidious return of Hellenism in which being is not communion, but something underlying it.'[66] And so a question presents itself: what else is the Father as cause of the Son and the Spirit but 'something' – indeed some*one* – 'underlying' the triune communion? Augustine aside, such is indeed the dilemma for Zizioulas.[67] Is it Gunton's too?

There was a time in Gunton's thought when we heard much more of Coleridge than Zizioulas, more about triune 'space to be' than the causative particularity of the Father. And, if Gunton had simply traded space for particularity, we would need to ask whether the identification of the Father as cause did not put *too much* space between him and the Son and the Spirit. Such a move would only secure the Father's particularity at the expense of the Son and Spirit's. But such a question would miss the significance of other concurrent developments in Gunton's thought.

We recall his knack for pneumatology. Unlike Zizioulas, Gunton has a pneumatological route back, so to speak, from the primordiality of the Father.

> Augustine called the Spirit the bond of love between the Father and the Son, but this is in danger of leading us to think of God as a kind of self-enclosed circle. The medieval, Richard of St Victor, provided the basis of a correction by making it possible to suggest that the Spirit is the focus of a love beyond the duality of Father and Son, of a love outwards to the other. The Spirit's distinctive inner-Trinitarian being is oriented not on inwardness, but on otherness: as perfecter both of the eternal divine communion – in which there is real distinction, *otherness* – and of God's love for the *other* in creation and redemption.[68]

This is the inner-triune corollary of the Spirit's economic action as God's 'eschatological transcendence'. Not only does the Spirit enable creation to live freely into its intended future, so also does he 'free' the Father and the Son for a love that would without him be a static duality. Gunton is saying that the Spirit opens the triune life within God *and* outwards to creation. And, we might say, so too does the Spirit open new possibilities for Gunton's theology. Where Zizioulas' ontology tends to move unilaterally upward into the Father,[69] Gunton's does not because for him it is the Spirit who 'completes' the divine being:

> . . . the Spirit is the perfecting cause not only of the creation, but also of the being of God . . .. the Spirit perfects the divine and holy Trinity. As the one who 'completes', the Spirit does indeed establish God's aseity, his utter self-sufficiency.[70]

This is a crucial move. Were the Father simply the 'cause' of the Son and the Spirit in a kind of Hellenic-absolute sense, we would be hard-pressed to distinguish belief in this God from the fount-of-being theisms of Irenaeus' opponents. But by suggesting that it is the Spirit (and not the Father) who is finally responsible for God's aseity – for 'completing' the divine life – Gunton has developed a doctrine of God that looks less like the top portion of a vertical continuum and more like an open dynamic of personal love. What we have here is a revised – or perhaps, 'completed' – version of his use of the concept of perichoresis. Whereas the idea of divine interpenetration was formerly for him a kind of general description for the constitutive function of triune communion, it is here given a specific shape.[71] Now we see that the Father 'causes' and the Spirit 'completes' the divine life.

And here we must note the likely influence of Robert Jenson on his protégé. Yet Gunton's view of the Spirit's 'futurity' is unlike similar theology from Jenson in at least one important respect: Gunton's version of this kind of speculation about the Trinity is bound especially close to the divine economy:

> We should be careful of mere projection, but we can at least ask whether it is right to suggest that because the Spirit is the agent of the begetting of Jesus in the womb of Mary, he is also the agent of his eternal begottenness. The Son is the kind of eternal Son that he is by virtue of the way . . . in which he is related to the Father in the Spirit, in the eternal triune love.[72]

As the agent of the Son's begottenness – both economic and eternal – the Spirit is the divine person who mediates the triune love of Father and Son. Without such an agent in the Trinity, God would be an immediate duad of Father and Son, and – with a nod to Coleridge – we can suggest that for Gunton such a thing would be ontologically nothing more than a homogeneous monotheos. And herein lies the crucial contrast between Jenson and Gunton. Where the Spirit for Jenson tends to function like an end in himself,[73] for Gunton the Spirit's role is always about relation *and* otherness. In this respect Gunton's understanding of the triunity of God is more like the early Pannenberg, although there is also an important difference here too. The likeness is in the importance of the Son's real distinction from the Father, the difference is in the identity of the one responsible for this distinction.[74] For Gunton it is the *Spirit* and not the Son who is the 'agent of the Son's eternal begotteness', completing the causal initiative of the Father and thereby making God an *a se* communion of love. This achieves what Pannenberg sought – it finds in the triune being the Christological possibility of creation's otherness – but, unlike Pannenberg, Gunton manages to avoid placing the initiative for such a crucial distinction on the one being distinguished. Where Pannenberg may be leaning on voluntaristic or neo-Hegelian categories, Gunton names the Spirit as the one responsible for the Son's eternal begottenness and so draws plainly from the divine economy.[75]

Having dabbled in the heights we can now return to Jesus, noting that the proximity of Christology and the theology of creation is precisely the point of all this. For Gunton what the theologian does in her Christology she will do in her doctrine of creation: '. . . differences between Christologies generate differences in the conception of the mediation of creation'.[76] And so we might say – with respect again to the Apostle – there is indeed 'one mediator between God and humanity', *the one enabled to be fully human by the Spirit* 'the man Christ Jesus'. With anything less than such a deliberately two-handed Christology, the mediation between God and world collapses.

> The danger here is that without a strong pneumatology the outcome will be the excessive separation of God and the world, corresponding to Nestorianism, that in fact became deism.[77]

A line between Antioch and the Enlightenment is a classic Gunton broad-stroke and its historical validity need not occupy us. We note instead the theological symmetry between an unmediated *Logos:sarx* 'conjunction' in Nestorianism and an unmediated Creator:creation duality in deism.[78] Both establish an otherness by juxtaposing the divine and the contingent but neither can truly relate them. And we have already seen Gunton reject both the opposite extreme in Cyrilian notions of the *communicatio* and the Apollinarian backdoor to pointlessness. Now we can say that functionally Spiritless theologies of Jesus are bound to oscillate *ad infinitum* between the two poles outside Chalcedon. Thus the new possibilities with Gunton's strong pneumatology: When we dine with only one hand we must choose between having and eating our cake. But here is a theologian who did all he could to have his Christ and the creation too.

## Notes

1  For her friendship and support, especially after her husband's death, and for access to his library, I thank Mrs Jenny Gunton. A constitutive relation when this student almost got lost in too much space.

2  Colin Gunton, *The Promise of Trinitarian Theology*, 2nd edn. (Edinburgh: T&T Clark, 1997), p. 202.

3  Colin Gunton, 'Creation and Mediation in the Theology of Robert W. Jenson: An Encounter and a Convergence', in *Trinity, Time and Church. A Response to the Theology of Robert W. Jenson*, ed. Colin Gunton (Grand Rapids: Eerdmans, 2000), p. 80.

4  Gunton, *The Promise of Trinitarian Theology*, p.14. Cf., 'Are the two claims incompatible [the sovereignty of God and the relative independence of the world]? One reason for the modern world's rejection of the gospel is that it has come to the conclusion that this is indeed the case. To affirm the world,

and especially to establish the freedom of the human agent within that world it has been thought that it is necessary to deny God.' Gunton, 'Creation and Mediation', p. 82.

5  Gunton, 'Creation and Mediation', p. 82.

6  'I do not think we can do better than to hold to Irenaeus' straightforward characterization of God's action in the world: the Father works . . . by means of his two hands, the Son and the Spirit. That is not as inappropriate to the 'spiritual' nature of God as may appear: When you use your hands . . . it is you who are doing it. That is not mere metaphor, but a metaphor that conveys a great and important Christian truth. Our God's action is not immediate but mediated action. Immediate action would overwhelm and depersonalize, if not worse . . .' Colin E. Gunton, *Father, Son and Holy Spirit: Toward a Fully Trinitarian Theology* (London: T&T Clark International, 2003), p. 80 and cf. Colin Gunton, 'God, Grace and Freedom', in *God and Freedom. Essays in Historical and Systematic Theology*, ed. Colin Gunton (Edinburgh: T&T Clark, 1995), p. 127. According to such a conception, God acts mediately but directly.

7  Colin Gunton, 'A Christian Dogmatic Theology. Volume One: The Triune God. A Doctrine of the Trinity as Though Jesus Makes a Difference, 2003', Unpublished typescript given to the author by Colin Gunton, 2.7.33.2. Hereafter cited as *CDT* with part, chapter, paragraph and manuscript page number referring to the version in my possession.

8  Gunton, *Father, Son and Holy Spirit*, pp. 26–27.

9  Ibid, p. 80.

10  Gunton, *The Promise of Trinitarian Theology*, p. xxx.

11  *CDT* 2.7.33.1.

12  *CDT* 2.7.34.14; this continues: '. . . The Spirit is the one who enables the church to represent Jesus Christ in her teaching and to live in his way, so that there is a sense in which it is truer to say that she speaks *from* than *about* the Spirit.'

13  *CDT* 2.7.34.15.

14  Colin Gunton, 'The Spirit in the Trinity', in *The Forgotten Trinity. A Selection of Papers Presented to the BCC Study Commission on Trinitarian Doctrine Today*, ed. Alasdair Heron (London: British Council of Churches / CCBI, 1991), p. 130.

15  Ibid. emphasis added.

16  Ibid.

17  Gunton, *Father, Son and Holy Spirit*, p. 81.

18  Ibid., p. 136.

19  'There is nothing intrinsically fallen about time in itself . . . Creation's temporality is its glory . . . It is not time that is the problem, but the fact that those who live in it find themselves beset by sin, suffering and evil . . .. The problem with time is what happens in it.' Ibid., p. 140.

20  Colin E. Gunton, *The One, the Three, and the Many. God, Creation and the Culture of Modernity* (Cambridge: Cambridge University Press, 1993). See also: Gunton, 'God, Grace and Freedom', pp.119–33.

21  Gunton, *Father, Son and Holy Spirit*, p. 137.

22  Bruce L. McCormack, 'For Us and for Our Salvation: Incarnation and Atonement in the Reformed Tradition', *Studies in Reformed Theology and History* 1:2 (1993), p. 33.

23  Gunton, 'And in One Lord . . . Begotten, Not Made', in Christopher R. Seitz (ed.), *Nicene Christianity: The Future for a New Ecumenism* (Grand Rapids:

Brazos Press, 2001), p. 47, citing Karl Rahner, *The Trinity* (New York: Herder & Herder, 1970), thus, '. . . he is not only the one of whom we are copies – the prototype – but also the one who actualizes the true human destiny by what he achieves'. Gunton, *The Promise of Trinitarian Theology*, p. 186, citing Wolfhart Pannenberg, *Systematic Theology*, trans. G.W. Bromiley, vol. 2 (Edinburgh: T&T Clark, 1994), pp. 215–17.

24  Gunton, *Father, Son and Holy Spirit*, p. 157.
25  Ibid., p. 192, citing Edward Irving. Cf. Colin Gunton, 'Two Dogmas Revisited: Edward Irving's Christology', *Scottish Journal of Theology* 41 (1988), with citations to John Owen at p. 375 n. 20.
26  On this point see Gunton, 'And in One Lord', pp. 40 ff.
27  *CDT* 1.1.7.8., citing Smail. See Thomas Smail, 'The Holy Trinity and the Resurrection of Jesus', in *Different Gospels*, ed. Andrew Walker (London: Hodder and Stoughton, 1988), pp. 63–96.
28  Gunton, 'The Spirit in the Trinity', p. 127.
29  'It is in the incarnation and particularly in relation to the humanity of Christ in general that we discern a unique particularizing of the activity of the Spirit as the life-giving power of God in and towards his creation . . . [following Augustine's contention that Jesus could not have received the Spirit at his baptism *because he already had it*, in the West] there has always been a tendency to minimize the particularities, in contrast to assertions of a general presence, of the Spirit's action in relation to Jesus. The outcome has been a corresponding stress on the divinity at the expense of the humanity of Christ, along with developments emphasizing the virginal – and eventually immaculate – conception of Jesus as the real source of his sinless humanity.' Ibid., p. 126.
30  Ibid., p. 127.
31  Gunton, *Father, Son and Holy Spirit*, p. 153.
32  Ibid., pp. 158, 159.
33  Gunton, *The Promise of Trinitarian Theology*, p. 186, citing Pannenberg, pp. 215–17.
34  *CDT* 1.1.7.6.
35  *CDT* 1.1.7.6.
36  '. . . the communion of attributes is more of a problem than a solution, for it inevitably tends towards the truncation of the human story.' *CDT* 2.7.32.12.
37  Gunton, 'Creation and Mediation', p. 88. After quoting Barth: 'God is spatial as the One who loves in freedom, and therefore as Himself . . . God possesses His space. He is in Himself as in a space. He creates space.' Karl Barth, *Church Dogmatics*, ed. G.W. Bromiley and T.F. Torrance, vol. 2/1 (Edinburgh: T&T Clark, 1957–75), p. 470.
38  Gunton, *The Promise of Trinitarian Theology*, p. 110.
39  Thus Christoph Schwöbel's eulogy: 'If God is not simply "a sea of essence, infinite and unseen" but first of all this particular God, the Father, the Son and the Spirit . . . the particular must have paramount significance in theology . . . If we still followed the ancient custom of venerating the great doctors of the church by a particular title, Colin Gunton would have to be the *doctor particularis*, the teacher of the significance of the particular . . .' *King's College Chapel*, September 2003. Typescript p. 2.
40  Gunton, *Father, Son and Holy Spirit*, p. 46.
41  Ibid., p. 57.

42 Gunton, *The Promise of Trinitarian Theology*, p. 198.

43 Colin Gunton, 'Immanence and Otherness: Divine Sovereignty and Human Freedom in the Theology of Robert W. Jenson', *Dialog* 30:1 (1991), p. 23.

44 For the best available theological introduction to this, and the likely source of Gunton's own interest in Coleridge as a theologian, see Daniel Hardy, 'Coleridge on the Trinity', *Anglican Theological Review* LXIX, no. 1 (1987), and see too: Thomas McFarland, *Coleridge and the Pantheist Tradition* (Oxford: Clarendon Press, 1969), esp. pp. 268 ff.

45 Summarizing Coleridge on the way to his own thought, Gunton explains, 'According to the Phoenician scheme, there is no space between God and the world, and so no human freedom. According to the kind of Hellenism we have viewed, the space is placed in the wrong place: between mind and matter, so that there is too little space between the human mind and God, too much between one person and another: space is here at the expense of relation. In the third, Hebrew, scheme, there is space, because of the freedom of the immutable God to create *ex nihilo* but, we need more than space. Indeed, from one point of view, space is the problem: individualism is the view of the human person which holds that there is so much space between people that they can in no sense participate in each other's being. There is clearly space and space, and our requirement now is to find a conception which is correlative with that of relation.' Gunton, *The Promise of Trinitarian Theology*, p. 109.

46 Colin Gunton, 'Immanence and Otherness, p. 23.

47 He does, however, come close: 'To be a person is to be constituted in particularity and freedom – to be given space to be – by others in community. *Otherness* and *relation* continue to be the two central and polar concepts here. Only where they are given due stress is personhood fully enabled.' Gunton, *The Promise of Trinitarian Theology*, p. 114.

48 On this see Colin Gunton, 'Creation and Mediation' p. 90.

49 Ibid., p. 10.

50 As with any dynamic thinker, the 'shift' in Gunton's thought is not clean-cut. Even in 1988 we had a foretaste of his later position: '. . . if something other than the Father is the ontological foundation of the being of God, the world and everything in it derives from what is fundamentally impersonal. What under (or over) lies is some*thing* other than the God made known in the economy . . .. But if the Father is not the substratum of the Godhead, what is?' Ibid., p. 54.

51 Colin Gunton, 'Persons and Particularity', in Douglas Knight (ed), *The Theology of John Zizioulas: Personhood and the Church* (Aldershot: Ashgate, 2007), pp. 97–124, p. 100.

52 Gunton, *The Promise of Trinitarian Theology*, p. 171. Thus, '. . . modernity cannot do justice to the being of the human person because it has an impoverished theology. Oscillating between collectivism and individualism – which represent ultimately one and the same failure – it calls desperately for an understanding of the person not as *a relation*, but at one who has his or her being *in relation* to others. This Trinitarian and *ethical* insight flows from a theology of the Trinity in which both the one and the many are given due and equal weight'. Gunton, *Father, Son and Holy Spirit*, p. 53. At both points citing his thesis in *The One, the Three and the Many*.

53 Apophatic theology was always suspect for Gunton but, as we shall see, this was

not the rationale for his change of mind on this point.

54 Gunton, *Father, Son and Holy Spirit*, p. 55. A problem already on his mind when he wrote the second introduction to his re-published *The Promise of Trinitarian Theology*, '. . . the chief [problem] for our purposes concerns whether Zizioulas' description of the Father as the cause of the Trinity endangers his own identification of being and communion'. p. xxiii.

55 Ibid., p. 25.

56 'An *a posteriori* ontology of intra-divine communion risks being subsumed by a cosmological category of causality.' Alan J. Torrance, *Persons in Communion. Trinitarian Description and Human Participation* (Edinburgh: T&T Clark, 1996), p. 291.

57 Gunton, *The Promise of Trinitarian Theology*, p. 196.

58 Ibid., p. 196.

59 Ibid., p. 196. Emphasis added.

60 *CDT* 2.7.31.1.

61 Gunton, 'Persons and Particularity', p. 1.

62 *CDT* 2.7.31.1.

63 *CDT* 2.7.31.3.

64 Gunton, *The Promise of Trinitarian Theology*, p. 197.

65 *CDT* 1.Preface.5.1.

66 Gunton, *The Promise of Trinitarian Theology*, p. 10.

67 Or so I suggest in 'Looking for Personal Space in the Theology of John Zizioulas', *International Journal of Systematic Theology* 8:4 (October 2006), pp. 356–70.

68 Gunton, *Father, Son and Holy Spirit*, p. 86. Thus, prior to the shift we are observing, 'Similarly, because the Holy Spirit is the agent of the Father's perfecting and transforming work as it is realized by relating the creation to God through Jesus Christ, it follows that we can cautiously draw conclusions from the Spirit's perfecting work to a speculation that he may, similarly, perfect the being of God, in a way parallel to, but distinctly different from, Augustine's teaching that the Spirit is the bond of love between Father and Son.' Gunton, *The Promise of Trinitarian Theology*, p. xxvii. Similarly, citing his paper in the same collection at pp. 105 ff.: '[this] might be rather near to Augustine's doctrine of the Spirit as the bond of love, but I hope that it says more than that, particularly about the Spirit's being the focus of God's movement outwards. The Trinity locked up in itself, to use Rahner's characterization of much post-Augustinian trinitarianism, by conceiving the Spirit as the closure of an inwards-turning circle, militates against a link between the Spirit's being in eternity and his action in the world.' Gunton, 'And in One Lord', p. 46.

69 Although Gunton does indeed find occasion to critique the Western *use* of the *filioque*, his affinity for Zizioulas's theology did not extend to abandoning this classic bone of contention altogether. The remaining differences between the two at this point are crucial to the possibilities we are tracking here; there are ones available for Gunton and unavailable – or unlikely – for Zizioulas.

70 *CDT* 2.7.31.3.

71 Gunton's different answers to the question of what perichoresis means for the divine life is another way of representing the 'shift' in his thought. Whereas he once (in *The One the Three and the Many*, p. 152) said things like: 'the concept [perichoresis] is a way of showing the ontological interdependence

and reciprocity of the three persons of the Trinity: . . . so that for God to be did not involve an absolute simplicity but *a unity deriving from a dynamic of plurality* of persons' (emphasis added), he later argued that 'perichoresis cannot do anything as an abstraction, because it is the *outcome* of the relations of the persons, not their cause.' *CDT* 2.7.31.2, (emphasis is Gunton's) and: 'It [*sic, In*] its place it [the concept of perichoresis] serves to demonstrate the character of personal being, not to constitute it.' *CDT* 2.7.31.3.

72 Gunton, 'And in One Lord', p. 46.

73 I am somewhat less dismissive in 'Robert Jenson and the Spirit of it All. Or: You (Sometimes) Wonder Where Everything Else Went', *The Scottish Journal of Theology* 60:2 (April 2007), pp. 161–79.

74 For Pannenberg's concept of the 'self-distinction of the Son from the Father' see Wolfhart Pannenberg, *Systematic Theology*, trans. Geoffrey W. Bromiley, 3 vols., vol. 1 (Grand Rapids: Eerdmans, 1991), pp. 319 ff.

75 Gunton makes the point best himself: 'Pannenberg's emphasis upon the Son's self-distinction . . . does not in itself guarantee the ontological distinctness of creation, and might indeed endanger it. If the Father is not to be too much all in all, an adequate doctrine of creation requires to stress not only the Son as the focus of the creation's coherence but also the Spirit as the mediator of particularity and difference.' From a review by Gunton of the second volume of Pannenberg's *Systematic Theology*. A review shared with and unhappily received by the work's author and so, to my knowledge, left unpublished. From p. 2 of a typescript given to me in 1999.

76 Ibid., p. 85.

77 Gunton, 'Creation and Mediation', p. 91.

78 The theology is Gunton's point too. He continues by typifying the division between Alexandria and Antioch in terms of their modern equivalents in, respectively, Lutheran and Reformed Christologies: 'One can be overschematic, but perhaps it is not too much of a simplification to say that each tendency seeks to conceive the relation-in-otherness of God and the world, the first stressing the relation, the second the otherness – again, in parallel with their corresponding Christological emphases.' Ibid., p. 91.

Chapter 6

## THE DOUBLE *HOMOOUSION*: FORMING THE CONTENT OF GUNTON'S THEOLOGY

Lincoln Harvey

Christians proclaim that God created the world out of nothing. This means that the world is not made from any God-stuff, so to speak. Instead, God is God and the creation is creation and the two should never be confused. Colin Gunton never tired of championing this point. Through the course of his constructive theology, Gunton sought to guard the essential difference between Creator and creation, arguing against their conceptual collapse within a meta-ontology. God is God and the rest of us are not.[1]

Gunton's opposition to a meta-ontology was positive in purpose, however. Because the world is glorious in its own right and status as creature, human beings are freed from the weighty delusion that they are somehow divine or that God needs them in any way to complete himself. The truth of the gospel is much less burdensome than that. We are not necessary; we are not that serious; our existence is fundamentally gratuitous.[2]

According to Gunton, Christian theologians should therefore ensure that the ontological distinction between God and creation is properly respected. However, they must not push the point too far. Contingency is not independence, and the creator is not absent. If Gunton is correct, Christian theologians will need to celebrate God's glorious *presence* as much as his fundamental otherness. This twofold imperative creates an apparent paradox between some form of ontological identity (as *presence*) and ontological difference. It also means that Christian theologians owe their readers an epistemology. How can God be known positively as different?

If theologians do not settle for unqualified apophaticism – which, in hazarding statements about what God isn't, says little about who he is – Christian speech about God will employ creaturely language and categories and thereby run the risk of confusing God with the reality he has made. With this onto-epistemic problem in mind, we intend to examine the way

Gunton handles the issue. In doing so, we will see how he justifies the positive nature of Christian theology by allowing the orthodox claim that Jesus alone is simultaneously of one being with the Father *and* of one being with humanity – the double *homoousion* – to determine his thinking. To discover the epistemological impact of the double *homoousion*, we shall first examine Gunton's justification for reading the doctrine of God out of the Christological economy. Having seen how this establishes the legitimacy of the doctrine of the Trinity, we shall investigate the way in which Gunton switches the direction of thought, thereby linking the revelation of who God is in himself to knowledge of the world as well. In tracing this second movement, we will argue that Gunton's two-way train of thought manages to maintain the necessary interval between God and the world through his concept of 'open transcendentals' because he anchors creaturely knowledge precisely and exclusively in the person of Jesus Christ. We shall conclude that the methodological structuring of Gunton's theology is therefore a proper response to the most basic claims of the Christian gospel: the Word became flesh and dwelt among us.

The problem is fairly straightforward: a Christian theologian cannot justify their knowledge of God by pointing to some form of generic identity between the divine being and the created order. Whatever was promoted for this purpose – be it mind, reason, spirit, feeling or whatever – would be fundamentally inadequate for the task. This is because a universal point of contact can never provide grounds for identifying a God who is holy, sovereign, free and ontologically *other*. Instead, a generalized identity can only encourage the creature to self-project onto a confused infinite, essentially domesticating God by replacing him with a constructed idol. Simply put, general identity does not establish any 'space' in which to establish genuine otherness; God is rendered too close to be different.

According to Gunton, a properly Christian account of God and the world therefore requires a theological conceptuality which allows sufficient space for there to be difference between God and creation while also affirming God's genuine presence. Broadly speaking, Gunton constructs a theology of 'mediation' in response to this need, one in which the doctrine of the Trinity explains the way in which the God of the gospel – the eternal communion of Father, Son and Spirit – is able to relate himself to the creation simultaneously at a 'distance' and from 'within'.[3] For Gunton, therefore, the term 'mediation' denotes the way in which the triune God acts generously in relation to creation by respecting creation's integrity in relation to himself. God – through the *taxis* of his own being – has space for difference-in-relation *ad extra* because he is who he is in himself.[4]

That said, however, the purpose of this chapter is not to examine

Gunton's overarching account of ontological mediation. What interests us here is the way in which Gunton systematically links the *epistemic form* of his constructive proposal to the content of his theology. As Gunton sees it, creaturely knowledge of God needs to be structured in line with the way in which God is enjoying fellowship with the creature, thereby ensuring both unity *and* distinction at this point also. As this suggests, God's revelation of himself is therefore mediated, a point Gunton is prepared to affirm explicitly.[5] By extension, Scripture, sacraments and the Church's proclamation – to take three hefty examples – are understood as the means through which the Son and Spirit ensure the genuine-but-not-overwhelming presence of God in relation to the creature. And, in line with this, the concept of mediation is also allowed to shape Gunton's understanding of theological language. Analogy – in its twofold claim of likeness and unlikeness – is a form of speech entirely appropriate for the theological task in its affirmation of both unity and distinction. Theological speech is analogical in character.[6]

Though analogical form neatly fits the theological reality it seeks to describe (and therefore creates a pleasing systematic cohesion between form and content), Gunton knows that unqualified recourse to the structure of analogy cannot resolve the general issue. This is because analogical language may well introduce a bit of (apophatic) slack in denoting unlikeness, but it makes a positive claim nonetheless. With analogy, difference has to be transcended just as much as protected, and this means that Gunton has to develop a fuller account of the nature of his positive claims. He does so by developing a 'trinitarian analogy of being' in which the concept of an 'open transcendental' underwrites his constructive proposal.[7]

Generally considered, transcendentals are those universal features of the world, the description of which is an attempt to capture conceptually the true nature of reality. Gunton, however, knows that he is working with *two* 'realities', God and everything he has made. Given this radical complication, Gunton – as already noted – rules out any unqualified universal that brackets both God and the world within a meta-ontology. Instead, he sets out to modify the established understanding of a transcendental in a way in which the God–world duality is respected while enabling a genuine search for concepts that carry across the ontological divide.

The way in which Gunton distinguishes between an open transcendental and the unqualified universals emerges in his Bampton Lectures, *The One, the Three and the Many*.[8] Classically, transcendentals identify the clear and distinct marks of being as it is *always* known. However, an *open* transcendental is subtly different. It is a 'fallible foundation', one which remains most basically continuous with the reality it opens up, but by which it can be changed.[9] Gunton unpacks what such heuristic provisionality might mean in conversation with Samuel Taylor Coleridge, for whom the concept of an 'idea' – itself pretty much synonymous with Gunton's 'open transcendental' – denotes the most basic imaginative features of human engagement with the world.[10] Inspired by Coleridge's work, Gunton argues that human ideas arise out of the mind's dynamic interaction with reality, an interaction that provides the means for a 'deeper involvement in the truth of things'.[11] This ongoing encounter means that ideas constitute 'an inner dynamic and direction within human thought', powering and shaping the mind as it carries on exploring the world with which it is continuous.[12]

Following Coleridge, Gunton proposes that the various ideas are related to each other through the doctrine of the Trinity. In other words, the Trinity is the foundational idea – functioning as the 'Idea of ideas' – that provides an inexhaustible, suggestive category of thought.[13] Gunton explains:

> [A]lthough it [the Trinity] is not transcendental, not a mark of all being, it yet generates transcendentals, ways of looking at universal features of the world of which we are a part and in which we live. The expectation is that if the triune God is the source of all being, meaning and truth we must suppose that all being will in some way reflect the being of the one who made it and holds it in being.[14]

Here Gunton wants to place God and the world in close epistemic relation, but it is, so to speak, an 'open' identity. Knowledge of the nature of God only 'generates' our understanding of the nature of the world. Gunton does suggest that the Trinity is, as such, a mark of all being; it is not a transcendental. If it was, Gunton would fail to maintain the distinction between God and the world.[15] Instead, for Gunton, creaturely knowledge of God is more limited in function: it enables a 'new way of looking', a way of 'seeing', which is shaped by the supposition that God produces a 'reflection' of himself – a 'finite echo' – in the creaturely reality he has made.[16] The key question to be asked, however, is whether God can be linked to the world in this 'open' way. Could Gunton's use of 're-visioning' language – despite his best efforts – mask an underlying identity between God and creation? To answer this question, we will examine how Gunton's concept of 'open transcendentals' works itself out in practice. We can do so by looking at the way he handles the trinitarian doctrine of perichoresis.[17]

In Christian theology, perichoresis denotes the way in which the persons of the Trinity give and receive existence from each other in a dynamic event of interdependent reciprocity. Father, Son and Spirit do not live in isolation, so to speak. Instead they exist *into* each other, thereby dynamically constituting the shared life that is God.[18] This means, in part, that God slips the creaturely categories of thought, essentially escaping simplistic notions of oneness and manyness, refusing to be trapped by monotheism (as if we understand his oneness!) or by tritheism (as if we understand his manyness!).[19] The doctrine claims that this unique and dynamic 'singularity–plurality' *is* the eternal interrelation of three persons distinguished in their relations, giving and receiving distinct identity in concert with each other.

However, if perichoresis means that the Father, Son and Spirit permeate each other without becoming confused with each other, two – by now expected – questions can be asked. First, if God is God and the creature is not, how can we know anything about God's inner life? Second, even if we do know something about God's being, what difference could it make to creatures in a world that is *not* God? To answer these questions, Gunton brings into view the methodological function of the concept of *economy*.[20]

According to Gunton, the theological concept of the economy emerges early in the Christian tradition as a financial metaphor through which to describe the generosity of God in both the gift of Christ ('yet for your sake he became poor') and the 'down payment' of the Spirit.[21] Through the course of time, the term was extended, soon being employed more generally as a means of holding together conceptually the variable divine activity in the world within a unified whole. It was, according to Gunton, simply a short step from such use towards more radical theological claims. Gunton spells out the logic:

> Because the one God is economically involved in the world in those various ways, it cannot be supposed other than that the action of Father, Son and Spirit is a mutually involved personal dynamic. *It would appear to follow* that in eternity Father, Son and Spirit share a dynamic mutual reciprocity, interpenetration and interanimation.[22]

As the emphasized section suggests, the doctrine of perichoresis emerges as theologians think through the good news that the one God is working with created reality as Father, Son and Spirit. Gunton is claiming that there is a straightforward 'movement in thought' (as he goes on to describe it) from conceptualizing the dynamic of Godly action in creation to conceiving of the nature of the divine being.[23] The underlying judgement is clear: If we meet God in the economy, it is reasonable to suppose that the structure of this encounter *is* the being of the one who acts in this way.

Gunton's attempt to open up some kind of 'space' within the equation by talking in terms of 'movements in thought', 'implications', 'suppositions' and the like, is again worth noting.[24] Gunton's hesitance-in-inference (as it might be termed) – he never claims, to my knowledge, that we *must* think like this – reveals his continuing unease with any suggestion that there is an identity between God and the world. However, as we have already seen, positive theology will be silenced – or produce only fanciful speculation – unless our theological claims have genuine purchase *somewhere*. The question remains, where? In reply to this question, Gunton maintains that the point of contact must be found in God's movement to the creature in *Jesus Christ*: 'we need not be too anxious about finding a ladder' up to God because 'God has let that down already in the incarnation of his eternal Son within the structures of worldly being'.[25]

In and of itself, the Christological claim cannot settle the issue in hand, however. Instead, it first complicates things by pushing the problem back a notch. This is because the incarnation seems to suggest some sort of natural correlation between the general shape of the world and the specific shape of the one who fits within it. Hans Urs von Balthasar has outlined what is at stake here:

> [I]f revelation is centred in Jesus Christ, there must be by definition a periphery to this center. Thus, as we say, the order of the Incarnation presupposes the order of creation, which is not identical with it. And, because the order of creation is orientated to the order of Incarnation, it is structured in view of the Incarnation; it contains images, analogies, as it were, dispositions, which in a true sense are the presuppositions for the Incarnation.[26]

Here von Balthasar is arguing that a general identity in shape exists between the world and God that *pre-dates* Jesus, and therefore, by extension, the created order can offer an advanced and quasi-independent preview of the God who eventually turns up in Jesus Christ. That is to say, God can be known in his prior act of creating.

Aware that natural theology can enter through the back door, Gunton decides to radicalize the doctrine of the incarnation. He does so by 'beginning' the incarnation in the decision of God to elect Jesus Christ *before* creation. Gunton therefore sides with Scotus, pushing together creation and redemption, claiming that there would have been an incarnation without a Fall. This means that creation is a project that was always moving towards the coming of God to live in mediated communion with the creature; when God created, he said 'Jesus'.[27]

This move allows Gunton to follow Barth in arguing that the creation is 'fitted' for God's predetermined covenant activity in Christ (simply put, for Barth, creation is the external basis of the covenant), but, epistemologically, the order of knowing is counter-intuitive.[28] It is the actuality of the revelation of God in Jesus Christ that enables the theologian to re-imagine the creaturely realm in light of that vision. Knowledge of nature is mediated by the coming of Jesus Christ.[29]

Here we see that the incarnation, for Gunton, encourages human thought to travel in *two* directions. First, it allows Christians to understand both divine being and divine action in general.[30] And, second, Christians can read away from Jesus Christ to general *creaturely* being and action as well.[31] In effect, by refusing to divorce creation from redemption, Gunton presents a Christological *theology of nature*. By coming to us in Jesus Christ, 'Revelation – God's personal interaction with the world through his Son and Spirit – suggests ways of seeing parallels between uncreated and created rationality . . .'[32]

Formally, the dogmatic linking of Jesus to creaturely ontology simply mirrors the shift from the economic to the immanent Trinity, but this time through a 'horizontal' axis. On the basis of this belief, and with specific regard to the doctrine of perichoresis, Gunton can state that,

> To speak theologically of the economy is to speak of the way in which God constitutes reality: makes it what it is through the activities we call creation and redemption. To speak of divine perichoresis is to essay a conceptual mapping, on the basis of that economy, of the being of God: God is what he is by virtue of the dynamic relatedness of Father, Son and Spirit. The question now is whether we can make significant moves in the reverse direction. Can we use the concept of perichoresis not only analogically but transcendentally, to lay to view something of the necessary notes of being?[33]

Answering his own question positively, Gunton argues that perichoresis is 'a concept which, because it derives from reflection on the involvement of God in time and space, is not conceptually foreign to createdness'.[34] Thus, on the basis of the single Christological economy, perichoresis becomes an open transcendental, which means that the pattern of being found in God can also be found *alongside* God in the creaturely realm.[35] Gunton is therefore able to offer a theological anthropology of creaturely personhood, essentially, as Trevor Hart puts it, developing a notion of the '*perichoresis* of time and space in which we, as the particular persons that we are, and without ceasing to be particular, are nonetheless constituted as such by our relatedness to all that has been and all that will be, as well as all that is'.[36] In sum, human persons are constituted in relation through 'perichoretic reciprocity'.[37]

So what are we to make of this? It is clear that Gunton is fully committed to thinking through the question of how God and the world are related. Broadly speaking, his neo-Irenaean theology of mediation is his proposed settlement. The Son and the Spirit, as the 'two hands' of the Father, hold the world close-yet-at-a-distance, the generosity of God thereby affording the creature relative self-standing but never at the cost of God's genuine presence. For Gunton, this overarching framework is underwritten by God's very own nature. Because of the eternal priority of Father, Son and Spirit, God is able to mediate himself in relation to the world.

As we have seen, however, Gunton's account of communion-based, trinitarian mediation is also being used to inform a subsidiary account of relations within the created order. This approach could be termed 'trinitarian philosophizing',[38] a tactic, as Ted Peters explains, that affirms the way in which knowledge of God is received in faith, God thereby revealing himself as ultimate reality, and, as ultimate reality, revealing something about the structure of creaturely being as well.[39] Gunton, however, knows that great caution is needed here. The doctrine of God and the doctrine of creation are not to be confused: God is God and the creation is not. And so, given the ontological disparity between the two, a general ontology cannot serve epistemology because God would be rendered too close to be different.

In consequence, Gunton believes that any identity between God and the world needs to be particular, precise and miraculous, and so, for Gunton, the answer is *exactly* Christological: the ontological structuring of identity and space pivots on the hypostatic union. It is only because the one Lord Jesus Christ is of one being with the Father *and* of one being with humanity (the double *homoousion*) that genuine identity exists between God and creation – but it exists precisely *as* this particular person, in him alone. In other words, the person of Jesus Christ is the non-analogical point of identity which finances all subsequent theological speech. At this point alone, language is univocal.[40]

For Gunton, therefore, a theology of nature can be read from Jesus Christ: 'Our knowledge of general revelation is the fruit of the gospel, christologically centred as that is'.[41] One thing for us to recognize, however – and it can be all too easily overlooked – is that Gunton's method is radically counter-cultural. The truth of the incarnation now carries little weight in public discourse. The doctrine is often held to be an unsophisticated myth, irredeemably scandalous because it excludes harmonious, pan-religious knowledge of God. The God of the gospel is thereby rendered redundant, the particularity of Jesus of Nazareth an embarrassment, and specific God-talk illegitimate. Under these prevailing conditions, contemporary theologians face a tough choice: either leave the doctrine of the incarnation behind or instead apologetically transform it into an anodyne justification for intellectual engagement with the cultural fashions of the day; either way, it is difficult to maintain that knowledge of the living God is definitively shaped by one man alone, Jesus of Nazareth, the Christ.

With Gunton, however, theologians are presented with another option. Here we find a Christian academic who is prepared to take the creedal confession of incarnation with full seriousness. God, without ceasing to be God, has come to his creation at a particular time and particular place as a particular human being – the Word became flesh and dwelt among us. Good theology can only ever proceed within the jurisdiction of this event, with everything that we say about God – not just in soteriological form[42] – needing to be shaped by this fundamental confession. And, on this point, Gunton is in good company. This is because the systematic relation between incarnation and theological speech was clarified for the Church during the Arian controversy. In designating the Son a creature, Arius was understood to be cutting *God* out of the economy of salvation.[43] God was therefore rendered 'alien' and 'foreign' to the world, the ontological dichotomy between God and creation necessarily establishing an epistemological division as well.[44] In consequence, Christian theologians knew that they would be rendered mute (or, at best, blindly speculative) unless they affirmed *divine* incarnation. The Nicene Creed – in claiming that the incarnate Son is of one being with the Father – thus established the bedrock of theological speech: it is only because *God* is truly present as Jesus Christ that God can be spoken of at all. Gunton most definitely honours the tradition on this point, and we would do well to follow suit.[45]

Yet, for Gunton, Jesus Christ is not simply the point where the unknown God can be known; he is also the point from which Christians are to re-imagine the world, and it is here that he finds himself at some distance from the mainstream tradition.[46] This is because, as Gunton reads it, the anti-Arian sensitivities of post-Nicene theology created an intellectual climate in which Christ's humanity was downplayed too readily in favour of promoting his divinity.[47] By overplaying the communication of attributes to the detriment of Jesus' distinct and functioning humanity (and thereby also downplaying the distinct role of the Spirit in the economy),[48] the early theologians created a Jesus who was of little earthly use. In contrast – and strongly influenced by his reading of John Owen and Edward Irving – Gunton wanted to redress this fault, outlining the way in which the functional humanity of Jesus Christ, perfected by the Spirit, is the proper basis for a genuine theology of nature. Because this one alone is fully and truly human, he tells us something about the world that God has made.[49]

Is this 'horizontal' move reasonable? On my reading, yes. If Jesus is truly divine *and* truly human then we can surely look 'sideways' to discern the nature of the world just as much as we can look 'upwards' to discern the nature of God. Of course, our theology of creation will need to cohere with our pneumatology, eschatology and ecclesiology – no easy task – but the methodological point remains: Jesus is the ground of *all* theological speech and speech about the world is most-basically theological. As a result, it would seem to me that Gunton's method is to be applauded. His work encourages us to stop using the doctrine of the incarnation simply as a means to underwrite our favourite engagement with contemporary culture and instead use it to detail the transformative impact of the gospel, which includes its ability to change the way we understand the nature of our world. For this reason alone, Gunton's contribution to the theology of creation should be widely celebrated.

## Notes

1 Gunton underlined the ontological distinction between God and the world in both protological and eschatological forms, thereby warning against crude understandings of divinization. For example, see Colin E. Gunton, 'Creation and Mediation in the Theology of Robert W. Jenson: An Encounter and a Convergence' in Colin E. Gunton (ed.), *Trinity, Time, and Church: A Response to the Theology of Robert W. Jenson* (Grand Rapids and Cambridge: Eerdmans, 2000), pp. 80–93.

2 '[A] distinction between God's reality and that of the world serves the world's interest . . . God's personal otherness from the world is needed if there is to be a true establishing of the world in its own right, as truly worldly creation.' Colin E. Gunton, *Father, Son and Holy Spirit: Essays Toward a Fully Trinitarian Theology* (London: T&T Clark, 2003), p. 24. For a complementary account on the non-serious nature of the world to which I am indebted, see Rowan Williams, *Not Being Serious: Thomas Merton and Karl Barth,* http://www.archbishopofcanterbury.org/2070, accessed 21/08/09.

3 '[B]y virtue of his triune nature, God the Father is able to enter into personal relations with the created order by the mediating activity of his two hands, the Son and the Spirit, who are as truly God as he is God. Irenaeus' God is thus ontologically transcendent of the world – he is a different kind of being, creator as distinct from creation – but by virtue of his triune being able to enter into relations with that world.' Colin E. Gunton, *The Triune Creator. A Historical and Systematic Study* (Edinburgh: Edinburgh University Press, 1998), p. 60.

4 'Mediation denotes the way we understand one form of action – God's action – to take shape in and in relation to that which is not God; the way, that is, by which the actions of one who is creator take form in a world that is of an entirely different order from God, because he made it to be so.' Colin E. Gunton, *The Christian Faith: An Introduction to Christian Doctrine* (Oxford: Blackwell, 2002), p. 5. Therefore, 'the doctrine of creation, trinitarianly conceived, enables us to understand the world as other than God, but as the product of a free act of creation and of a continuing free relatedness'. Colin E. Gunton, *The Promise of Trinitarian Theology*, 2nd edn. (London and New York: T&T Clark, 2003), p. 203.

5 For a full treatment of these themes, see Colin E. Gunton, *A Brief Theology of Revelation* (Edinburgh: T&T Clark, 1995). For an explicit statement about the mediation of revelation, see p. 18.

6 Gunton, *A Brief Theology of Revelation*. See also Gunton's celebration of

metaphor in Colin E. Gunton, *The Actuality of Atonement: A Study of Metaphor, Rationality and the Christian Tradition* (London and New York: T&T Clark, 1988), pp. 27–52.

7 Colin E. Gunton, *The One, the Three and the Many: God, Creation and the Culture of Modernity* (Cambridge: Cambridge University Press, 1993), pp. 141 ff.

8 This has been identified as 'his most ambitious book'. John Webster, 'Systematic Theology after Barth: Jüngel, Jenson and Gunton' in David Ford and Rachel Muers (eds), *The Modern Theologians* (Oxford: Blackwell, 2005), p. 261.

9 'An open transcendental is a notion, in some way basic to the human thinking process, which empowers a continuing and in principle unfinished exploration of the universal marks of being.' Gunton, *The One, the Three and the Many*, p. 142.

10 Gunton, *The One, the Three and the Many*, pp. 136 ff. As most basic, they are inherently 'vague and woolly', p. 143.

11 Gunton, *The One, the Three and the Many*, p. 144.

12 Gunton, *The One, the Three and the Many*, p. 147.

13 Gunton, *The One, the Three and the Many*, p. 144.

14 Gunton, *The One, the Three and the Many*, p. 145.

15 Gunton, *The One, the Three and the Many*, p. 145.

16 Gunton, *The Promise of Trinitarian Theology*, p. 73. In this instance, Gunton applies the notion of a 'finite echo' to the Church. However, it therefore applies to the wider creation but this time within an account of eschatological redemption. Thus, in other places, Gunton happily applies the term to the created order. For example, see Gunton, *The One, the Three and the Many*, p. 166, where we also find a clear statement of Gunton's belief that it is 'reasonable to suppose' that theologically generated transcendentals will 'throw light on' a range of phenomena (p. 167, p. 151).

17 Gunton, *The One, the Three and the Many*, pp. 152 ff.

18 'In its origins, the concept was a way of showing . . . how they [the persons of the Trinity] were only what they were by virtue of their interrelation and interanimation, so that for God to be did not involve an absolute simplicity but a unity deriving from a dynamic plurality of persons.' Gunton, *The One, the Three and the Many*, p. 152.

19 As Joseph Ratzinger (now Benedict XVI) puts it: 'People realized, if still quite unreflectively, that while God is indeed radically One, he cannot be forced into our categories of singular and plural; rather, he stands above them, so that in the last analysis, even though he is truly one God, he cannot be fitted with complete appropriateness into the category "one".' Joseph Ratzinger, *Introduction to Christianity* (San Francisco: Ignatius Press, 2004), p. 125.

20 Gunton, *The One, the Three and the Many*, pp. 157 ff.

21 Gunton, *The One, the Three and the Many*, p. 158.

22 Gunton, *The One, the Three and the Many*, p. 163. Emphasis added.

23 Gunton, *The One, the Three and the Many*, p. 163.

24 Gunton is clear: perichoresis is an '*implication*' of the economy. Gunton, *The One, the Three and the Many*, p. 163, emphasis in original.

25 Gunton, *A Brief Theology of Revelation*, p. 63. 'It is of the essence not only of our creaturehood but of its fallenness that we are unable to approach the holy God apart from his initiative.' Colin E. Gunton, *Christ and Creation: The Didsbury Lectures 1990* (Eugene, Oregon: Wipf & Stock, 2005), p. 67.

Gunton's method is evident in the title to his (as yet) unpublished dogmatics: Colin E. Gunton, *A Christian Dogmatic Theology. Volume One: The Triune God. A Doctrine of the Trinity as Though Jesus Makes a Difference*, 2003.

26 The question is asked of Barth in this case but applies equally to Gunton, see Hans Urs von Balthasar, *The Theology of Karl Barth*, trans. E.T. Oakes, S.J. (San Francisco: Ignatius Press, 1992), p. 163, cited by Bruce McCormack, 'Grace and Being' in John Webster (ed.), *The Cambridge Companion to Karl Barth* (Cambridge: Cambridge University Press, 2000), p. 108.

27 See, for example, the brief discussion in Gunton, *The Triune Creator*, p. 121, or his defence of the Christological 'thrust' of original creation in Gunton, *Christ and Creation*, pp. 94–98. See also Gunton, *The Actuality of Atonement*, pp. 151–52.

28 Karl Barth, *Church Dogmatics* (13 vols.), edited by G.W. Bromiley and T.F. Torrance (Edinburgh: T&T Clark, 1957–975), III/1, pp. 94 ff.

29 Gunton, *A Brief Theology of Revelation*, pp. 40 ff. In revealing the Christ, God also reveals something about the human creature: '[W]e are able to appropriate the revealedness of nature because we are the kind of beings we are: a part of nature, yet also such as we are able to transcend and understand that of which we are a part' (p. 34).

30 The latter is evident in the way Gunton systematically links the classic models of atonement to divine creative action in Gunton, *The Actuality of Atonement*.

31 'A teaching of God's economic openness to the world walks hand in hand with a view of the world that is open both to God and within its own structures of being . . . "Economy" embraces the being of the world in its relation to God and the action of God in relation to the world.' Gunton, *The One, the Three and the Many*, p. 160.

32 Gunton, *A Brief Theology of Revelation*, p. 63.

33 Gunton, *The One, the Three and the Many*, p. 165.

34 Gunton, *The One, the Three and the Many*, p. 167. Gunton continues to recognize the dangers of analogy, however: 'Such an enquiry is, of course, a perilous one, for it is free if guided speculation: looking at the world in the light of the concepts whose primary usage is elsewhere.' Gunton, *The One, the Three and the Many*, p. 167.

35 Gunton draws on post-relativity theories in modern physics to suggest that everything contributes to the being of everything else. Gunton, *The One, the Three and the Many*, p. 166.

36 Trevor Hart, 'Redemption and Fall' in Colin E. Gunton (ed.), *The Cambridge Companion to Christian Doctrine* (Cambridge: Cambridge University Press, 1997) p. 196.

37 Gunton, *The One, the Three and the Many*, p. 170.

38 Cited in Ted Peters, *God as Trinity: Relationality and Temporality in Divine Life* (Louisville: Westminster/John Know Press, 1993), p. 84.

39 Peters, *God as Trinity*, p. 84. Knowledge of the Trinity creates 'a quite tremendous extension of the field of vision', as Karl Barth put it. Karl Barth, *Dogmatics in Outline*, translated by G.T. Thomson (London: SCM Press, 1949), p. 26.

40 In *Act and Being*, Gunton explicitly identities the Christological 'place' where language is univocal: 'What it is to be a human is in this case [i.e. Jesus] identical with what it is to be a divine person, and therefore the word means the same at the levels of creator and creation'. On the same page, he asserts that 'love' is also

univocal precisely here. Colin E. Gunton, *Act and Being. Towards a Theology of the Divine Attributes* (London: SCM Press, 2002), p. 147. In other words, as Barth argued, Jesus Christ is the 'point on the line of intersection', the space – or, better, the only space where there is no space – where no interval exists between God and the world. Jesus is where that which is different is truly united to the glory of both. 'In this name two worlds meet and go apart, two planes intersect, the one known and the other unknown . . . The point on the line of intersection at which the relation becomes observable and observed is Jesus, Jesus of Nazareth, the historical Jesus – born of the seed of David according to the flesh. The name Jesus defines an historical occurrence and marks the point where the unknown world cuts the known world.' Karl Barth, *The Epistle to the Romans*, translated form the sixth edition by Edwyn C. Hoskyns (Oxford: Oxford University Press, 1933), p. 29.

41 Gunton, *A Brief Theology of Revelation*, p. 55.
42 As Barth argued, 'this is the presupposition everything starts with'. Barth, *Dogmatics in Outline*, p. 53.
43 Rowan Williams shows that Arius' *Thalia* is dominated by the theme of the 'absolute unknowability of the Father'. Rowan Williams, *Arius,* 2nd edn. (London: SCM Press, 2001) p. 105.
44 'Encyclical Letter of Alexander of Alexandria and his Clergy', in J Stevenson, *A New Eusebius: Documents Illustrating The History of the Church to AD 337,* (2nd edn. Revised by W.H.C. Frend) (London: SPCK, 1987), p. 323.
45 Thus, as Alan Torrance puts it in an essay to which I am very much indebted: '[T]he incarnation constitutes the hinge between God and humanity. Without it all out "God-talk" loses its grounds and can only collapse into the unwarranted projections onto the transcendent of the self-understandings of creatures who were literally without knowledge (*agnôsis*).' Alan Torrance, 'Jesus in Christian Doctrine' in Markus Bockmuehl (ed.), *Cambridge Companion to Jesus* (Cambridge: Cambridge University Press, 2001), p. 203.
46 Interestingly, Lewis Ayres argues that the early Christians actually encouraged a re-imagining of the world: 'Like almost all early Christian writers, pro-Nicene's read Scripture as a providentially ordained resource for the Christian imagination. It is an intrinsic part of Scripture's purpose to enable description of the God who acts *and* of the structure of the cosmos within which God acts: the reshaping of the cosmological imagination is a central aspect of the Incarnate Word's mission.' Lewis Ayres, *Nicaea and its Legacy: An Approach to Fourth-Century Trinitarian Theology* (Oxford and New York: Oxford University Press, 2004), p. 335.
47 Colin E. Gunton, *Theology Through the Theologians: Selected Essays 1972–1995* (Edinburgh: T&T Clark, 1996), pp. 151–68.
48 'The function of the Spirit in relation to Jesus is, accordingly, as the perfecter of his humanity. Just as the *enhypostasia* reminds us of the origin of our salvation in the eternal love and action of God, so attention to the Holy Spirit reminds us of the way in which the saving action of Jesus is accomplished humanly in time. Too much stress on either can lose essential dimensions of the gospel.' Gunton, *Christ and Creation*, p. 50.
49 So, for example, Gunton writes: 'If we ask how it is that the humanity of Jesus of Nazareth is maintained in its autonomy, the answer is in part pneumatological. If Jesus' humanity was in no way imperilled by its being that of the Word, that

is because of the action of God the Spirit. The Spirit is the one who mediates the action of God the Father in such a way that the life of the Son, while deriving from the Father and dependent upon him, is given space to remain authentically human. An account of the proper autonomy of the world *must run in parallel* with this . . .' Gunton, *Theology Through the Theologians*, p. 147. Emphasis added.

Chapter 7

PROVISIONALITY AND PROMISE:
AVOIDING ECCLESIASTICAL NESTORIANISM?[1]

John E. Colwell

In the foreword to a collection of Colin Gunton's sermons, members of the Brentwood United Reformed Church (URC) recalled a definition that Gunton suggested should be put on a banner in the entrance hall to their church building: 'The Church is a community of all ages called to praise God in worship and in life'.[2] Of course, it would be somewhat unfair to treat a headline statement as indicative of a comprehensive ecclesiology, but, nonetheless, the banner could be interpreted as focusing on that which the Church does rather than on what the Church is, and, as such, the statement could be viewed as somewhat Pelagian. Even a cursory acquaintance with Gunton's account of the Spirit would demonstrate such a suspicion to be unfounded, yet I do want to take Gunton's banner statement – or rather that which is omitted from the statement – as a means to engage more broadly (and I trust more fairly) with that which Gunton does and does not say concerning a doctrine of the Church.

No reader of Gunton's could doubt the formative and foundational place of the Church in his life and work. For Gunton, as 'a community of worship, belief and action', the Church is always the proper context for the theological task.[3] Throughout his career, Gunton was therefore fully committed to his local church in its stark particularity, together with its inevitable frustrations and parochialisms – indeed, maybe because of them rather than despite them. Both collections of his published sermons are therefore replete with personal and particular allusions to the reality of the church in Brentwood.[4] These show that there was nothing even remotely docetic in Gunton's understanding of the Church; no hint of Platonic abstraction; that which the Church is, is to be encountered in the particular and local community of faith and is to be identified there:

The Church is the concrete place where certain human beings accept a call to associate themselves with the reality of him who is the logic of the divine love. They do it not in order to exercise institutional authority over others, but on behalf of the rest of humanity. In that sense the universality is construed not Platonically but factually . . . Because Jesus Christ takes form in the here and now, in part of mankind and on behalf of others, we are able to bring to expression the universality of his significance. Underlying that universality is the Church's confession that his reality is at once human and divine, a presence whose basis is in eternity.[5]

Given the practical centrality of the Church for Gunton's thinking, the relative scarcity of any sustained treatment of ecclesiology in his work is perhaps surprising. As far as I am aware, his first sustained engagement with ecclesiology occurs in the seventh chapter of *The Actuality of Atonement*.[6] Here we find the Church defined in terms of its spatial and temporal particularity as a community called into being, not apart from the world, but on behalf of the world:

All the talk of the cosmic Christ, of his work in creation and redemption, must be realised in a community whose life takes place in time and space. The church is called to be that midpoint, the realisation in time of the universal redemption and the place where the reconciliation of all things is *from time to time* anticipated . . . The point about the Christian community is that it is in receipt of a particular call and mission: to orient itself to the place where the universal salvation of God takes place in time and to embody in community and for the world the forms of life which correspond to it.[7]

And again . . .

. . . we require an ecclesiology which seeks neither to be identical with the surrounding world nor to be isolated from it: a church which is, as a distinctive community, both *in* and *for* (and therefore sometimes *against*) the world, just as Jesus was at once in, for and against the religious culture of first century Israel. In this respect, the church as a whole can profit from insights derived from the traditions of Dissent.[8]

The emphasis upon the phrase 'from time to time' in the first of these quotations is my own, and I draw attention to it because of its strangeness – a strangeness that we will encounter again and again as this occasionalist qualification becomes more prominent in his ecclesiology. To understand its place in Gunton's thinking, however, it is important to recognize that Gunton was a Congregationalist, not merely by birth and background, but by deep conviction. This is one reason why John Owen was to become one of his key conversation partners in the development of a doctrine of the Church.[9] From Owen, Gunton gleaned not just an understanding of the local church in its particularity – developed in parallel to his own interpretation of a Cappadocian understanding of the Trinity – but a distinctive and somewhat controversial Calvinist understanding of the person of Christ which, I shall argue, is somewhat problematic for his ecclesiology.[10]

Gunton's first explicit and sustained engagement with John Owen appears under the title 'The Church on Earth: The Roots of Community' as Gunton's own contribution to *On Being the Church*, a collection of essays he edited together with Daniel Hardy.[11] The chapter appears again under the title 'The Community. The Trinity and the Being of the Church' in a collection of his own essays entitled *The Promise of Trinitarian Theology*.[12] The essay begins with the reflection that, too often, understandings of the Church appear to have been derived by analogy to earthly empires or human societies rather than to an account of the triune nature of God.[13] Noting the particular significance of pneumatology for ecclesiology, Gunton arrives at the point of deeming that '[w]hat is required . . . is a reconsideration of the relation of pneumatology and Christology, with a consequent reduction of stress on the church's institution by Christ and a greater emphasis on its constitution by the Spirit'.[14] Predictably, there follows an engagement with a Cappadocian account of the Trinity as represented in the work of John Zizioulas, but perhaps less predictably this is followed by an engagement with John Owen, focusing not just or primarily on his account of voluntarism,[15] but more specifically on a summary of his understanding of the humanity of Christ and his severe qualification of the doctrine of the *communicatio idiomatum*, a rejection of the notion that the distinctive properties of Christ's divine nature were in any sense or any manner communicated to Christ's human nature.[16] Gunton's summary serves as a response to the question concerning the shape of an ecclesiology that reflects a more radical account of Christ's humanity:[17]

> An inescapable characteristic of the church in this context is that as part of the creation it, too, is finite and contingent. That is to repeat the point that was made in the previous section as an implication of conceiving the church in the image of the humanity of Christ.[18]

From both Owen and the Cappadocians Gunton derives a notion of the Church, not as a direct analogy, but as a 'finite echo or bodying forth of the divine personal dynamics';[19] the 'being of the church consists in the relations of the persons to each other'.[20] This echo occurs in the life of the believing community through those distinctive practices of proclamation and sacramental worship that constitute its distinctive being,[21] but this echo is no mere human affair – that it is realized within the church through its proclamation and worship is wholly an outcome of the work of the Spirit:

> Too much is therefore not being claimed for the theology of the church that is being attempted in this paper. The hope is to have created the framework by which a link may be drawn between the being of God and that which is *from time to time* realised by the Spirit. It is a kind of analogy of echo: the church is what it is by virtue of being called to be a temporal echo of the eternal community that God is.[22]

Here again we encounter the occasionalist qualification, 'from time to time', and here again we note its strangeness.

Surprisingly (but perhaps typically), explicit reference to the Church occurs only at the end of Gunton's Bampton Lectures, where, in conversation with Daniel Hardy's chapter in *On Being the Church*,[23] Gunton dismisses as 'foolish romanticism' the notion that we can be human without institutions. Nevertheless, Gunton also identifies the greater danger of the Church functioning as an institution rather than as a community:[24] to be human 'is to be created in and for relationship with God and with other human beings' and, consequently, ecclesiology is 'sociality made explicit'.[25] Perhaps more interestingly, towards the end of his Didsbury Lectures, Gunton again qualifies the Church both pneumatologically and eschatologically – since the 'church is the community placed by Word and sacrament under the rule of Christ', it is itself the location in time and space of 'the beginning of the re-formation of the image of God';[26] but it is but a beginning, it is eschatologically orientated, and it is wholly dependent upon the Spirit for the realisation of its true being and identity:

> There are two features of ecclesiology, therefore, which obviate a triumphalist understanding: the free and *unpredictable* action of the Spirit and its eschatological orientation . . . And it is in the Spirit as the one through whom the end is realised that the movement in both directions can be understood to take shape.[27]

As previously, the emphasis upon the word 'unpredictable' is my own and, as with the phrase 'from time to time', it is indicative of the concern that motivates this chapter.

Gunton's essay 'God, Grace and Freedom' provided him with a further opportunity to commend an 'ecclesiology of the personal' in distinction to the polarities of the individualistic and the authoritarian;[28] a freedom granted by the Spirit rather than a mere human voluntarism; a unity that enables particularly and diversity rather than a coerced homogeneity:[29]

The point that should be stressed is that particularity is realized in community. But, and here we come to the link with the secondary features of freedom, it must be free community in the sense of being unconstrained and entered into voluntarily. It should not be suggested that freedom under grace, enabled by divine action, is not the exercise of the free human will. But it is a will whose direction is given shape by the patterns of relation in which it is set. It is not the freedom of empty space. Only in relation to God and to others can we be particularly who and what we are, and therefore only so can we be free.[30]

Gunton's distinctly pneumatological account of the Church is again developed in a collection of essays entitled *Theology Through the Theologians*. First an essay specifically on the Holy Spirit enables Gunton again to affirm the Church as 'the community of the last days', the community that, through its worship and life, anticipates 'the reconciliation of all things in Christ'.[31] But it is in the course of the essay in which he again engages explicitly with the work of Owen and Zizioulas that these characteristic themes receive further development.[32] Here Gunton's overarching concern is with the tendency to treat the promise of the Spirit's presence in the life and worship of the Church as if it were a 'claimed possession' to the point at which the actions of the Church and the action of the Spirit become confused, a confusion that manifests itself both in clericalism and in Congregationalist assumptions concerning the decisions of church meetings.[33] Again Gunton affirms that, as a 'historically given reality', the Church cannot but be an institution;[34] again he notes the danger inherent in Owen's voluntarism of a collapse into individualism – a collapse that can only be avoided if 'our concept of churchly freedom is' explicitly the 'freedom given by the Spirit who creates community';[35] again he affirms that the 'heart of the constitution of the Church by the Spirit is to be found in worship'; that '[w]hen true worship takes place, there is a sharing in the worship of heaven'; that '[i]t is then that the Church truly *is*'.[36] But here also we encounter a reiteration of the occasionalism previously encountered: the church is 'a community that must, ever and again, take place'.[37] Yet, earlier in the essay, Gunton revisits the Pauline metaphor of the Church as the body of Christ, but now with marked hesitation:

In the Pauline writings, Christ is variously the body which is the Church and the head from which the body takes its shape. In both cases, there is nearly but not quite an identification of the Church with Christ, enough to make it understandable that the Church has sometimes been claimed to be the extension of the incarnation. But that is precisely where the difficulty emerges. If that is all that we have to say, we may come very near to making claims for some kind of absoluteness of the Church as it institutionally is . . .[38]

The theme of the Church's spatial and temporal particularity, a particularity serving a universal end, is further explored in an essay entitled 'Election and Ecclesiology in the post-Constantinian Church',[39] but in this same collection we also find an essay written chiefly in response to the writings of Yoder and Hauerwas that reiterates this concern lest the Church 'make historically and morally implausible claims': the Church must be defined 'exocentrically', by 'reference to the primacy of the Word and sacraments' rather than by any 'moralistic criterion'.[40] However, it is in his attempt at an outline of Christian doctrine that we encounter Gunton's most developed sketch of ecclesiology – and here also we encounter the most developed expression of his ecclesiological hesitation: certainly the church 'is the place – the living space – where the kingship, priesthood and prophetic work of Jesus is appropriated . . .';[41] but there can be no sense in which the Spirit, who realizes 'in the life of particular human beings and groups of human beings the reality of what God in Christ achieved on the cross' ought ever to be considered as 'in some way at the disposal of the church'.[42] And, as much in response to a distinctively Reformed understanding of the Incarnation as in response to Irenaeus, this limitation is identified as an outcome of the significance of Christ's ascension, as the 'one whose presence to both church and world is essentially problematic'.[43] And, consequently, we find here Gunton's most developed hesitation regarding the significance of the phrase 'body of Christ' as a metaphor for the Church:

> The church can no more claim automatically to be the body of Christ than it can claim to possess the Spirit. The risen Lord is made present only by the Father's Spirit, and any institution claiming either in some sense automatically to mediate – let alone to be – the presence of Christ or automatically to be in possession of the Spirit is in danger of subverting its own constitution. Here, as so often in theology, we meet perils on both sides. On the one hand, we neglect the promise of God that the church is called and empowered to represent his love in the world in a particular way, one shaped by the career of Jesus; on the other, we forget that this becomes real only by the Spirit's free giving. The conception of the church as the body of Christ can in this regard cause as much harm as good . . .[44]

It certainly is not my intention to gainsay this proper emphasis on the freedom of the Spirit but, following Barth and following Gunton in other contexts, I want to re-attest that freedom as distinctively divine freedom, as determinate and not indeterminate, as bounded by *promise*. The question, therefore, is whether this note of promise is dulled in Gunton's work by a rather less than determinate freedom; whether an occasionalist account of the Spirit's presence and action displaces presumption but at the price of uncertainty and caprice.

The starkest expression of this occasionalism (of which I am aware) occurs in Gunton's Drew Lecture, delivered at Spurgeon's College on 11 November 1999 – a lecture which Gunton notes could be subtitled 'a conversation with Robert Jenson, with particular respect to the first letter to the Corinthians'.[45] The lecture begins with the observation that the key issue of eschatology is 'the right relation of beginning, middle and end',[46] and that rightly to conceive of this relation in turn raises the question 'of the limits we should place on what we might expect of the church'.[47] Gunton observes that '1 Corinthians 15 describes Jesus Christ as a particular human being rather than . . . [an] apparently social or corporate person . . .' and that, in this passage, 'Christ is patently distinguished from the church' just as his resurrection is distinguished from ours;[48] Christ here 'is one with the church only as also its transcendent Lord'.[49] Moreover, in chapter 11 of the Epistle, phrases such as 'in memory of him' and 'until he comes' presuppose that Christ 'is in fact absent'; that 'Paul is speaking of real absence, not real presence'.[50] While resisting the possibility of reducing the reference here to 'discerning the body' moralistically,[51] Gunton takes these distinctions of the passage as warrant for reiterating that

> . . . any too close identification of the church with Christ . . . risks two offences against eschatology . . . empirical self-deception or special pleading that presumes upon the judgment of God . . . an immediacy that is simply unjustifiable because it derives from an overrealised eschatology.[52]

As one would expect, it is at this point that Gunton introduces a doctrine of the Spirit as the 'key to ecclesiology as to eschatology': it is the Spirit who enables the church to be the church both in its worship and its obedience; it is the Spirit who enables Christ, as 'other than' the Church, to be 'present to and in' the Church; it is thus that the Spirit enables the Church 'to be that which it is elected to be'.[53] But all this is again qualified by the repeated phrase 'from time to time':

> While being other than the church even when that is understood as his body, he is present to and in it in so far as the Spirit enables it *from time to time* to be that which it is elected to be.[54]

> . . . in so far as the church's mode of life does *from time to time* anticipate that of the age to come, it is enabled to do so by the Spirit who both makes present the life-giving death of Christ and will complete its eschatological perfecting on the last day.[55]

Though, with Gunton, I want to affirm that 'Christ's presence in all its manifold forms is realized only through anticipation ... through the mediation of the eschatological Spirit',[56] I find myself greatly troubled by this repeated 'from time to time', by this disturbing qualification of the Spirit's presence and action within the Church, by this ecclesiological occasionalism. Anecdotally, of course, the qualification is all too understandable: one does not need to participate in any local church for any length of time to be acutely aware of aspects of its life, worship and ministry for which one would not wish to hold the Spirit accountable. But the question is whether we can so easily separate the all too human from the presence and action of the Spirit without denying the Church's essence? And here we arrive at the significance of the subtitle of this present chapter: how do we avoid ecclesiastical Nestorianism?

Nestorius, a fifth century Bishop of Constantinople who formerly had been a monk in Antioch, famously objected to the title 'bearer of God' as applied to the Virgin Mary, preferring to call her 'bearer of Christ' or 'bearer of the human' and, consequently, (justly or unjustly) was accused of separating the two natures of Christ and, implicitly, dividing Christ's single person. Nestorius initially was condemned at a council at Ephesus held in 431 and subsequently at the so-called 'robber' council at Ephesus in 449, the latter commending the teaching of a monk from Constantinople named Eutyches who argued that, subsequent to the Incarnation, Christ had but a single nature. The issue was 'resolved' – though, considering its consequences, this is hardly the most appropriate term – at the Council of Chalcedon (451) that confessed Christ . . .

> . . . in two natures without confusion, without change, without division, without separation, the distinction of these natures not being abolished through their union but rather the distinctive characteristic of each nature being preserved and concurring in one person and one essence . . .

This final phrase concerning the preservation in the one person of the distinctive characteristic of each nature, the divine and the human, came to be expressed in the Western Church through the doctrine of the *communicatio idiomatum* (the participation in distinctive properties) whereby the single person of Christ was confessed to participate fully in the distinctive characteristics of both his divine and human natures without these natures becoming confused. Occasionally, however, the doctrine is more radically (and problematically) understood with respect to each nature (as distinct to Christ's single person) participating fully in the distinctive properties of the other nature.[57] It can be argued that it was this more radical interpretation of the doctrine that was employed by Martin Luther as a means of affirming the reality of Christ's bodily presence at the Eucharist: the ascended Christ's human nature participates fully in the ubiquity of his divine nature and, consequently, Christ can be bodily present at the Father's right hand and simultaneously bodily present at any number of Eucharistic celebrations.

Contrary to Luther, Calvin regarded the radical reading of the doctrine as explicitly Eutychean and Monophysite, confusing the two natures of Christ in a manner that contravenes the Chalcedonian definition and that effectively undermines the reality of Christ's human nature.[58] Rejecting this interpretation, Calvin (following Athanasius[59]) instead spoke of that of Christ's divine nature that cannot be contained by the human nature; he is born of Mary without having to leave heaven and without ceasing to fill the universe[60] – which leads unsurprisingly to Calvin being accused by Lutherans of Nestorianism, of dividing the two natures of Christ, of effectively denying that the Word *becomes* flesh.

But what, you may well ask, has this to do with a doctrine of the Church? If the Church is *not* Christ and Christ is *not* the Church (the New Testament references to the Church as Christ's body being understood metaphorically rather than literally), then, at face value, not a lot – and it is in this sense that the subtitle of this paper is contradictory: ecclesiastical Nestorianism, if not an oxymoron, is at least an inappropriate confusion of terms. But it is in the work of John Owen, the seventeenth-century Puritan, that the Calvinist interpretation of the Incarnation comes, I think, to its fullest expression, and it is this aspect of Owen's work that is formative for Gunton's ecclesiology (his affirmation of the particularity and stark humanity of the Church and, thereby, his hesitations concerning the use of the metaphor of the Church as Christ's body and, what I have termed, his pneumatological occasionalism). Conversely, it is within Lutheran theology that we typically encounter a realistic employment of the metaphor (for the Christ who can simultaneously be bodily present at any number of Eucharistic celebrations can similarly be bodily present in – and perhaps even 'as' – his Church). As a result, the question of Christ's identity or non-identity with his Church, historically at least, appears to be consequent upon an interpretation of the two natures of Christ's single person. In short, Christology is determining the ecclesiology. If this is so, how are we to resolve the long-standing debate between Lutherans and Calvinists, both with respect to Christology and with respect to ecclesiology? How are we to avoid Eutycheanism on the one hand and Nestorianism on the other?

With respect to Christology, at least, I really don't know. At the risk of offending my friends, I cannot see how the Lutheran position avoids the charge of Eutycheanism: I cannot conceive how human nature participating fully in the characteristic properties of divine nature remains human nature in any meaningful sense (and, with Calvin, I want to retain the distinction between Christ and his Church – his presence and action here is mediated by the Spirit rather than a consequence of any property of his own nature or person). But at similar risk of offending other friends, I cannot see how Calvin avoids the charge of Nestorianism: if there is that of Christ that is effectively excluded from the Incarnation then the Incarnation is no longer truly an Incarnation and, consequently, Revelation is no longer truly Revelation; we are left with a 'God' behind and beyond the gospel story – a notion which at least one reading of Calvin's account of predestination would seem to confirm.

If there is a path through this Christological conundrum I suspect it lies, following the trajectory indicated in Gunton's own exposition of Christology (itself taking its cue from Karl Barth),[61] in not importing presumed notions of divine and human nature, together with their respective properties, to the gospel story; in allowing the gospel story itself to define both human nature and divine nature in the single person of Christ. But turning to the issue of ecclesiology I am a little more optimistic. While I think I understand and sympathize with the motivation underlying Gunton's pneumatological occasionalism, I deem it unnecessary and avoidable. This is because the more realistic appropriations of the body of Christ metaphor to which Gunton alludes in passages already cited are usually associated with Catholicism alongside Lutheranism.[62] Though there are instances in the early twentieth century of some Catholic theologians speaking of the Church as an extension or continuation of the Incarnation[63] – there may indeed be earlier instances of the trend – at the Second Vatican Council the Church is instead spoken of as being 'in the nature of a sacrament'[64] and, in Catholic tradition, sacramental presence is *distinct* and *particular*.

Luther had developed his idiosyncratic understanding of the manner of Christ's presence at the Eucharist, partly in response to Zwingli's effective denial of any real presence, and partly in rejection of Aristotelian categories of substance and accidents as an unhelpful and pernicious intrusion to Christian doctrine. In this latter respect, however, I believe Luther was seriously mistaken. The objection raised at the time to Aquinas' distinction of substance and accidents in his exposition of the Eucharist, and the nub of the objection in the immediately ensuing disputes over the next two hundred years, was precisely that this distinction offended *Aristotelian* categories and conceptions. Both in his distinction between substance and accidents, and in his employment of the distinctions of causality, Aquinas was using Aristotle's terminology creatively to the point of affirming something *entirely contrary* to that received tradition.[65] For Aquinas, therefore, as clearly as for Zwingli or Calvin, the ascended Christ remains bodily located at the Father's right hand (however that may be conceived);[66] his presence in the Eucharist is distinctive and extraordinary; his presence in the Eucharist is sacramental.[67] In the Eucharist, therefore, while the 'accidents' (perhaps we could say 'physicality') of the bread and the wine are miraculously preserved, their 'substance' (perhaps we could say 'identity') is miraculously transformed into that of the Body and Blood of Christ. Moreover, for Aquinas (as distinct from some of his contemporaries and successors) the efficient cause of this transformation, and of the grace imparted through the sacrament, remained God alone – there is no opportunity for manipulation here; no space for sacerdotalism; Christ becomes present here, in this extraordinary manner, because he said he will – for Aquinas, as for the Reformers, the sacraments are *res promissa*, 'the stuff of promise'.[68]

For Luther, however, though Christ's presence at the Eucharist is similarly an outcome of promise, that presence issues from a property of Christ's ascended human nature rather than being a distinctive and extraordinary act of God. In other words, it is Christ's own ubiquitous presence rather than a presence mediated by the Spirit – Christ can be simultaneously present here because he is ubiquitous. But – and this is the vital point – an essential presence everywhere is a particular presence nowhere. In effect, Luther's device affirms too much, and, thereby, too little.[69] For Calvin, remarkably reminiscent of Aquinas in described dynamic if not terminology,[70] Christ's real presence in and through the Eucharist, as also our anticipated eschatological presence with him, is mediated by the Spirit;[71] it is not the outcome of a supposed property of Christ's ascended human nature, rather, it is a particular and mediated presence, promised through the Word and received by faith.

My own bias towards Aquinas and Calvin over Luther on this matter should be clear, but what unites each of their accounts is the way in which Christ's sacramental presence is a matter of *promise*. Of course, promise lends itself to presumption and manipulation – once Thomas' careful qualifications are abandoned, the possibilities for presumption and manipulation abound; and once Calvin's focus on the Word and the Spirit is qualified by a focus on divine hiddenness, promise becomes submerged in radical uncertainty – but such developments are neither inherent nor inevitable: divine promise can be the basis of a humble assurance of faith without succumbing to presumption and manipulation. Positively, however, by underlining the relation between Christ and promise, Christ's mediated presence in and through the Eucharist, as also in and through Holy Baptism, does not need to be qualified by any 'from time to time'. This does not mean that Christ's mediated presence in and through the Eucharist is immediate and automatic; instead it is a being-given presence, mediated afresh by the Spirit, a mediated presence that can be anticipated and trusted – though never manipulated – since it is a *promised presence*. And this brings us back to ecclesiology.

If the Church too is 'in the nature of a sacrament' – sacramentally constituted if not itself simply a sacrament – then Christ's presence in and through the Church is similarly a matter of promise. It is not a presence to be presumed upon or manipulated – it is a presence mediated by the Spirit who is the Lord. But as a promised presence, a presence mediated by this Spirit who is this free Lord, neither is this presence subject to any uncertainty, caprice, or occasionalism. Certainly it is a being-given rather than a given, but this being-givenness is a constant of the Church's constitution, it is not a presence being given 'from time to time'. To put the matter otherwise, there should be no place for 'ecclesiastical Nestorianism' here. The Church that is constituted through (though not 'by') its proclamation of the Word and its celebration of the sacraments is through (though not 'by') these means constituted *by* the Spirit as a living sacrament of Christ's presence in and to the world; the divine and the human here, as in the proclamation of the Word or the person of Christ himself, must not be confused, but neither may they be separated or divided. Of course, the stark particularity and humanity of the Church remain – we cannot observe this sacramental dynamic anymore than we can observe Christ's presence in and through bread and wine; the Church, after all, is the one sacramental mystery explicitly named as 'mystery' within Scripture[72] – but faith trusts the promise and is content to rest in the mystery. Though it must not presume upon the promise nor manipulate the promise, through its proclamation of the Word and celebration of the sacraments the Church cannot cause the promise to be fulfilled (in an efficient sense), but, through its faithful proclamation and celebration, it does what it is called to do as the means through which the Spirit mediates this promised presence – to complete an earlier quotation from Gunton:

> . . . [t]hat is why worship, and especially what we call sacramental worship, cannot but be the focus of the church's life . . .[73]

To speak then, as Gunton did, of the Church as 'a community of all ages called to praise God in worship and in life'[74] is certainly not inherently Pelagian, nor is it the sum of that which Gunton wished to say and did say concerning the Church. It identifies the Church's calling as the means of its essence rather than its essence itself; it identifies a human dynamic through which a divine dynamic is promised to be realized – but rightly to define the Church's essence this human dynamic and this divine dynamic must never be confused or separated; we are encountered by a promised dynamic issuing in a promised identity that can be trusted as being neither capricious nor occasional. The imagery of the Church as the body of Christ, then, though never to be pressed in any literal or intrinsic sense, is truly significant of this promised mediated presence and consequent identity. Through the Spirit – and the centrality of the Spirit in the pertinent chapters of 1 Corinthians should be noted – the Church in its life and worship is the means of the presence of Christ within the world, a presence anticipating an eschatological fulfilment certainly, but certainly not a presence that is in any sense occasional or capricious. The Church is the Church 'in the nature of a sacrament' and a sacrament is a matter of promise.

## *Notes*

1  This paper was first read at a day conference, 'The Triune God in the Theology of Colin Gunton', held at Spurgeon's College on Monday 10 September 2007.

2  Tony Cheer, Sheila Maxey, Charles Steynor, 'Foreword' in Colin E. Gunton, *The Theologian as Preacher: Further Sermons from Colin E. Gunton*, eds Sarah J. Gunton and John E. Colwell (London: T&T Clark, 2007), pp. ix–x, p. x.

3  Colin E. Gunton, *Yesterday and Today: A Study of Continuities in Christology* (London: DLT, 1983), p. 205.

4  Colin E. Gunton, *Theology Through Preaching: Sermons for Brentwood* (Edinburgh: T&T Clark, 2001); cf. Gunton, *The Theologian as Preacher*.

5  Gunton, *Yesterday and Today*, pp. 176 ff.

6  Colin E. Gunton, *The Actuality of Atonement: A Study of Metaphor, Rationality and the Christian Tradition* (Edinburgh: T&T Clark, 1988).

7  Gunton, *The Actuality of Atonement*, pp.170 ff. [my emphasis].

8  Gunton, *The Actuality of Atonement*, p. 181.

9  '. . . it seems to me that the theology of the Church in terms of free congregating, which plays so large a part in Owen, is not sufficiently safeguarded from a later collapse into an individualistic and merely secular concept of freedom. Yet unless our notion of freedom is controlled pneumatologically; unless, that is to say, our concept of churchly freedom is the freedom given by the Spirit who creates community, we shall be in danger of a collapse into the kind of individualistic autonomy that encourages us to think that we do it all by ourselves, and which, as I have already suggested, sometimes marks later times.' Colin E. Gunton, 'John Owen and John Zizioulas on the Church' in Colin E. Gunton, *Theology Through the Theologians: Selected Essays 1972–1995* (Edinburgh: T&T Clark, 1996), 187–205, pp. 195 ff.

10  Gunton, *Yesterday and Today*, pp. 176 ff., referring to Dietrich Bonhoeffer, *Ethics*, ed. Eberhard Bethge, trans., Neville Horton Smith (London: SCM, 1955), p. 20.

11  'The Church on Earth: The Roots of Community' in *On Being the Church: Essays on the Christian Community*, eds Colin E. Gunton and Daniel W. Hardy (Edinburgh: T&T Clark, 1989), pp. 48–80.

12  Colin E. Gunton, *The Promise of Trinitarian Theology* (Edinburgh: T&T Clark, 1991), pp. 58–85.

13  '. . . the manifest inadequacy of the theology of the church derives from the fact that it has never seriously and consistently been rooted in a conception of the being of God as triune.' Gunton, *The Promise of Trinitarian Theology*, p. 58; cf. p. 60.

14 Gunton, *The Promise of Trinitarian Theology*, p. 58; cf. p. 69.
15 Gunton, *The Promise of Trinitarian Theology*, p. 77.
16 For this account in Owen see John Owen, *A Discourse Concerning the Holy Spirit (1674) in The Works of John Owen*, vol. 3, ed. W.H. Goold (London: Banner, 1965), pp. 159–88.
17 Gunton, *The Promise of Trinitarian Theology*, p. 67.
18 Gunton, *The Promise of Trinitarian Theology*, p. 73.
19 Gunton, *The Promise of Trinitarian Theology*, p. 74.
20 Gunton, *The Promise of Trinitarian Theology*, p. 76.
21 'The concrete means by which the church becomes an echo of the life of the Godhead are all such as to direct the church away from self-glorification to the source of its life in the creative and recreative presence of God to the world. The activity of proclamation and the celebration of the Gospel sacraments are temporal ways of orienting the community to the being of God.' Gunton, *The Promise of Trinitarian Theology*, p. 82.
22 Gunton, *The Promise of Trinitarian Theology*, p. 79 [my emphasis].
23 Daniel W. Hardy, 'Created and Redeemed Sociality' in *On Being the Church*, pp. 21–47.
24 Colin E. Gunton, *The One, the Three and the Many: God, Creation and the Culture of Modernity: The Bampton Lectures 1992* (Cambridge: Cambridge University Press, 1993), p. 217.
25 Gunton, *The One, the Three and the Many*, p. 223.
26 Colin E. Gunton, *Christ and Creation: The Didsbury Lectures 1990* (Carlisle & Grand Rapids: Paternoster Press & Eerdmans, 1992), p. 108.
27 Gunton, *Christ and Creation*, p. 110 f. [my emphasis].
28 Colin E. Gunton, 'God, Grace and Freedom' in *God and Freedom: Essays in Historical and Systematic Theology*, ed. Colin E. Gunton (Edinburgh: T&T Clark, 1995), pp. 119–33, p. 132.
29 Gunton, 'God, Grace and Freedom', p. 131.
30 Gunton, 'God, Grace and Freedom', p. 132.
31 Colin E. Gunton, 'God the Holy Spirit: Augustine and his Successors' in Gunton, *Theology Through the Theologians*, pp. 105–28, p. 121.
32 Colin E. Gunton, 'John Owen and John Zizioulas on the Church' in Gunton, *Theology Through the Theologians*, pp. 187–205.
33 Gunton, 'John Owen and John Zizioulas on the Church', p. 187.
34 Gunton, 'John Owen and John Zizioulas on the Church', p. 198.
35 Gunton, 'John Owen and John Zizioulas on the Church', pp. 195 ff.
36 Gunton, 'John Owen and John Zizioulas on the Church', p. 202.
37 Gunton, 'John Owen and John Zizioulas on the Church', p. 202.
38 Gunton, 'John Owen and John Zizioulas on the Church', p. 198.
39 'The Spirit's creating work is, before it is anything else, universal. However, the point of the story of Israel's election and Jesus' resurrection is that the universal end of creation – "to bring all things in heaven and on earth together under one head, even Christ" (Eph. 1.10) – is achieved through particularities . . . Among those particularities, and indeed, pre-eminent among them, are Israel as the people of God, and the Church as the body of Christ. The election and calling of the *particular* communities is rooted in the universal mediation of creation in Jesus Christ.' Colin E Gunton, 'Election and Ecclesiology in the post-Constantinian Church' in *Intellect and Action: Elucidations on Christian Theology*

*and the Life of Faith* (Edinburgh: T&T Clark, 2000), pp. 139–55, pp. 147 ff.

40 Colin E Gunton, 'The Church as a School of Virtue? Human Formation in Trinitarian Framework' in Gunton, *Intellect and Action*, pp. 101–20, p. 119.

41 Colin E. Gunton, *The Christian Faith: An Introduction to Christian Doctrine* (Oxford: Blackwell, 2002), p. 123; cf. 'The church is the society whose distinctive way of being in the world – distinctive polity, we might say – is oriented to God primarily in terms of thanksgiving and worship.' Gunton, *The Christian Faith*, p. 127.

42 Gunton, *The Christian Faith*, p. 121.

43 Gunton, *The Christian Faith*, p. 121.

44 Gunton, *The Christian Faith*, pp. 121 ff.

45 Colin E. Gunton, '"Until he Comes": Towards an Eschatology of Church Membership' in *Called to One Hope: Perspectives on Life to Come*, ed. John E. Colwell, (Carlisle: Paternoster Press, 2000), pp. 252–66, p. 264.

46 Gunton, 'Until he Comes', p. 252.

47 Gunton, 'Until he Comes', p. 253.

48 Gunton, 'Until he Comes', pp. 257 ff.

49 Gunton, 'Until he Comes', p. 258.

50 Gunton, 'Until he Comes', p. 258; referring to Richard B. Hays, *First Corinthians* (Louisville: John Knox, 1997), p. 199.

51 Gunton, 'Until he Comes', p. 260.

52 Gunton, 'Until he Comes', p. 261.

53 Gunton, 'Until he Comes', p. 262.

54 Gunton, 'Until he Comes', p. 262 [my emphasis].

55 Gunton, 'Until he Comes', p. 263 [my emphasis].

56 Gunton, 'Until he Comes', p. 264.

57 '. . . Turretin's account of the *communicatio idiomatum* relies on a distinction between communication between natures and person and communication between the two natures. Properties of each nature may be meaningfully and rightly applied to the person, but properties of the one nature may not be applied to the other.' Stephen R. Holmes, 'Reformed Varieties of the *Communicatio Idiomatum*' in *The Person of Christ*, eds Stephen R. Holmes and Murray Rae (London: T&T Clark, 2005), pp. 70–86, p. 77.

58 'For . . . we do not doubt that Christ's body is limited by the general characteristics common to all human bodies, and is contained in heaven . . . so we deem it utterly unlawful to draw it back under these corruptible elements or to imagine it to be present everywhere.' John Calvin, *Institutes of the Christian Religion*, ed. McNeill, J.T., trans. Battles, F.L. (Philadelphia: Westminster Press, 1960), IV xvii 12.

59 Athanasius, *On the Incarnation*, trans. A. Religious (London: Mowbray, 1953), III 17.

60 'For even if the Word in his immeasurable essence united with the nature of man into one person, we do not imagine that he was confined therein. Here is something marvelous: the Son of God descended from heaven in such a way that, without leaving heaven, he willed to be borne in the virgin's womb, to go about the earth, and to hang upon the cross; yet he continuously filled the world even as he had done from the beginning!' Calvin, *Institutes*, II xiii 4.

61 Gunton, *Yesterday and Today*, especially pp. 177–82; cf. 'Who God is and what it is to be divine is something we have to learn where God has revealed Himself

and His nature, the essence of the divine. And if He has revealed Himself in Jesus Christ as the God who does this, it is not for us to be wiser than He and to say that it is in contradiction with the divine essence.' Karl Barth, *Church Dogmatics* IV/1, trans. eds G.W. Bromiley and T.F. Torrance (Edinburgh: T&T Clark, 1956), p. 186.

62  Gunton, *Yesterday and Today*, pp. 176 f.; cf. Gunton, 'John Owen and John Zizioulas on the Church', p. 198.

63  See for instance Henri de Lubac, *Catholicism, Christ and the Common Destiny of Man* (London: Burns and Oates, 1950), p. 2.

64  '*Lumen Gentium*' or 'The Dogmatic Constitution of the Church' (Vatican II, 21 November 1964) in *Vatican Council II: The Conciliar and Post Conciliar Documents*, ed. Austin Flannery (Dublin: Dominican Publications, 1975), 350–426, I 1; cf. '. . . God has gathered together and established as the Church, that it may be for each and everyone the visible sacrament of this saving unity.' '*Lumen Gentium*', II 9.

65  For a discussion of the non-Aristotelian use of language by Aquinas, see Edward Schillebeeckx, *The Eucharist* (London: Sheed & Ward, 1968), p. 58 ff.

66  '. . . in no way is Christ's body locally in this sacrament'. Thomas Aquinas, *Summa Theologica* (*ST*), trans. Fathers of the English Dominican Province (Westminster, Maryland: Christian Classics, 1981), III 76 5; '. . . Christ's body is at rest in heaven. Therefore it is not moveably in this sacrament.' *ST* III 76 6.

67  'Christ's body is not in this sacrament in the same way as a body is in a place, which by its dimensions is commensurate with the place; but in a special manner which is proper to this sacrament. Hence we say that Christ's body is upon many altars, not as in different places, but *sacramentally*: and thereby we do not understand that Christ is there only as in a sign, although a sacrament is a kind of sign; but that Christ's body is here after a fashion proper to this sacrament . . .' *ST* III 75 1; cf. 76 3–6.

68  Robert Jenson identifies promise as '. . . the decisive maxim of all the Reformation's theology: God's gifts are *res promissa*, "the stuff of promise."' Robert W. Jenson, *Systematic Theology*, vol. 1, *The Triune God* (Oxford and New York: Oxford University Press, 1997), p. 14.

69  'What is sacrificed for the sake of this *Christus praesens*, as Calvin noticed long ago, is his specificity as a particular man. Christ everywhere really means Jesus of Nazareth nowhere.' Douglas Farrow, *Ascension and Ecclesia: On the Significance of the Doctrine of the Ascension for Ecclesiology and Christian Cosmology* (Edinburgh: T&T Clark, 1999), p. 12 ff.

70  For an excellent discussion of the similarities between the accounts of the Eucharist in Thomas and Calvin see Varujan Richard Smallwood, 'A comparison of Thomas Aquinas' and John Calvin's understanding of the Eucharist' (Spurgeon's College, University of Wales: unpublished BD dissertation, 2003).

71  '. . . he feeds his people with his own body, the communion of which he bestows upon them by the power of his Spirit. In this manner, the body and blood of Christ are shown to us in the Sacrament.' Calvin, *Institutes* IV xvii 18.

72  Ephesians 3.9-10.

73  Gunton, 'Until he Comes', p. 263.

74  Gunton, *The Theologian as Preacher*, p. x.

Chapter 8

CREATED FOR ACTION:
COLIN GUNTON'S RELATIONAL ANTHROPOLOGY

Paraskevè Tibbs

In recent years, a number of voices have decried the absence of relational categories with which to describe what is known intuitively: we humans are relational beings.[1] Colin Gunton was one such voice, and an enthusiastic one at that. He regularly highlighted the scarcity of relational concepts in Western thought, arguing that their absence elevated the 'one' over the 'many', and thereby created the numerous problems associated with rampant individualism in modern society. For Gunton, the solution to this crisis lies in part in *theology*: we need to help people understand that we are relational beings because we are made in the image of the triune God, the one whose being *is* the relation of the Three in communion, Father, Son and Holy Spirit.

Driven by this underlying vision, 'relationality' and 'communion' were to become dominant themes in Gunton's systematic thought, shaping both his doctrine of God and his doctrine of creation and their intrinsic interconnection. As he saw the matter, 'the created world . . . reflects in different ways the being of God in communion'.[2] However, despite Gunton holding that *all* creation in some way reflects the being of God, he also maintained that it is the *human* creation alone that is in some way genuinely 'like God' because it alone is made in his *image*. As he saw it, this meant that the human creature must be afforded a special place within any general ontology of relationality. The purpose of this chapter is to investigate critically how Gunton himself handled this task.

On reading Gunton's work on this subject, the reader will discover two overriding themes at the centre of his account of the *imago Dei*. First, the principal consideration for any Christian anthropology is humanity-in-relation to God (as opposed to the uniqueness of human creation vis-à-vis non-human creation). Second, the doctrine of creation is linked closely to redemption, both present *and* eschatological, and so anthropology must be closely tied to an account of Jesus Christ. Given this twofold pattern, we will need to outline the way in which Gunton develops a properly Christological anthropology in relation to God if we are to fully understand his thinking on this subject, as well as highlight his conclusion that there is a physical likeness to Jesus Christ bestowed upon humankind. In so doing, we will be able to show that Gunton prioritizes only one way of active relatedness in his anthropology. Though he wrote prolifically on the horizontal relationality of creation to other creation – specifying the kinds of activities necessary to maintain those relations – Gunton was less specific about whether the unique vertical relationship between God and human creation in the image is to be nurtured and maintained by *human action*. Given this oversight, I intend to supplement Gunton's account of the image, underlining the way in which human worship of God also needs to be considered as the ontological aspect of the *imago Dei*, with the Fall therefore being understood as a failure to give adequate worship to the Creator.

In making my case, I will also argue that Gunton's articulation of the Christological function of the image needs to be more closely aligned to his view that the project of creation begins in a garden. I will argue that worship and priesthood need to be understood as ontological attributes of the *imago Dei*, both as it applies to the High Priesthood of Christ and derivatively to the priesthood of all believers.

### *Anthropology derived from Christology*

Given the paucity of specific biblical passages relating to the 'image', Gunton attempts to do justice to the broad witness of Scripture rather than attempt a too literal and too limiting conception based on narrow readings.[3] For example, the story of humankind being created in the image and according to the likeness of God is described in Genesis 1.26-27. For Gunton, however, any proper investigation could never be limited to these two verses alone. Instead, these verses must be read in the context of the entire chapter, with the chapter itself then being understood within the wider canonical whole.[4] Given Gunton's expansive approach, he was not particularly concerned with fine details of exegesis. For example, he did not endeavour to distinguish image[5] from likeness,[6] and, in fact, took exception with this aspect of Irenaeus' thought (or at least he took exception with those commentators who believe Irenaeus made a marked separation between the two terms in order to associate the image with reason).[7] In Gunton's discussions, 'image' and 'likeness' are therefore used synonymously simply because Gunton was interested primarily in the overall shape and texture of the biblical witness.

In seeking the broad shape of scripture, Gunton often called attention to the fact that the creation narrative takes place in a garden and not a paradise, and that this setting was significant: 'In paradise, the fruits simply fall off the trees and on to our tables; in a garden, trees have to be tended'.[8] As Gunton reads it, this means that there was work needing to be done as creation began to move towards its *telos*. Thus, referring to original creation as God's project, Gunton maintained that it should only be considered perfect because it is God's doing, but that this does not mean it is complete in itself. On this point, Gunton agreed with Irenaeus' notion of the imperfection of original creation – insofar as it was *incomplete* – and the associate human task to move the project onwards towards its perfection and completion.

Significantly though, for Gunton the movement toward completion can only be accomplished by human creation *in* Christ, who, through the Spirit, achieves what the first Adam had failed to do, and – through the same Spirit – redirects the universe along the 'right direction'.[9] A key tenet of Gunton's viewpoint, therefore, is that anthropology must be derived from Christology, with the New Testament witness to Christ being essential for a proper understanding of the human creature. The image – whatever its precise content – is also therefore inextricably connected to the one who would redeem and complete it. This means that the destiny of the first Adam is bound up with the second Adam, with the eschatological and teleological being systematically linked with the soteriological aspects of the image of God.[10] In effect, to see what true human personhood should be, Gunton insists that we must look to Jesus Christ – the only human person in whom the divine image is truly and perfectly manifest – as the image (*eikon*) of the invisible God (Colossians 1.15).

For Gunton, however, Christ is not only the archetypal bearer of the image, but the one through whom the image under sin is reshaped.[11] Referring to Irenaeus' doctrine of the recapitulation of human history in Christ, Gunton argues that 'Jesus Christ recapitulates our human story in order that the project of the perfection of all things may be achieved'.[12] Notably, for Gunton, Christ is not only the end of God's project of creation as its perfection and perfecter; he is also the beginning of creation as Creator and prototype of humanity. Gunton refers, for example, to Colossians 1.17-18 to back up this claim, where Christ is described as the one 'before all things . . . the beginning, the first-born from the dead, that in everything he might be pre-eminent'.[13] Given the priority of Christ in creation, Gunton was interested in pursuing the image/likeness in decidedly (though not exclusively) physical terms – precisely as physical as Jesus, he would say.[14]

Given his interest in the physicality of Jesus, Gunton agreed with Francis Watson that Ezekiel 1.26 should be read in close correspondence with Genesis, in that God will resemble the human form if and when he makes himself visible.[15] However, without additional qualification, it is clear that this view appears to be unduly anthropocentric. For example, we might wonder how Jesus could possibly be the prototype for human creation if the Incarnation was subsequent to human origins. Such difficulties could be resolved if temporality – a strictly linear movement from beginning to end – is removed from the equation. This would mean that though Genesis 1.1 certainly describes a watershed moment in God's eternity, the 'beginning' described there was for creation, not for God. In effect, there is an eternal reality beyond created time (before and after, in a sense) in which the eternal eschaton to which time-bound creation is now heading was already a reality at its origin. Therefore, Christ, as incarnate God, who ascended bodily into his eternal kingdom, no longer limited by time and space, could indeed be spoken of as the prototypical human person in whose image and likeness Adam was created.

Gunton's conflation of beginning and *telos* in Christ is certainly not unique, especially if patristic thought is taken into account. Gunton himself directly refers to Irenaeus in this regard: 'the Word of God himself is a pattern in the creation of human beings'.[16] Others who spoke of Christ as the prototypical human include Maximus the Confessor, who proposed that only by exercising appropriate movement toward Christ may one lay hold of one's proper beginning and cause.[17] Though Maximus spoke of Christ's embodiment – through which God accomplishes all things – the material needs to become spiritually charged (i.e. deified) through the deified corporeality of the Word.[18] For Gunton, however, this runs a number of risks, and so he instead places considerable emphasis on the physical aspect of the image in Christ. I believe that Gunton's desire to preserve relationality necessarily took him in this direction. Since relationality requires particularity, Gunton wanted to preserve the proper balance between particularity and unity, and thus avoid any tendency to 'belittle' materiality. Thus, in emphasizing a physical resemblance to God in Christ, Gunton did not abolish particularity, which is the unfortunate consequence of theologies that emphasize entirely spiritual or mental elements of the image. Platonism, for example, explains that the real self is immaterial and distinct from its temporary dwelling place in a body. For Gunton, however, 'our particular embodiment – the sense that in certain respects, however much that has to be qualified, we are our bodies – is inseparable from our being in the image of God'.[19] In short, our bodiliness is essential to the *imago Dei*.

Despite the emphasis on physicality, Gunton's primary concern remained with relationality, and therefore he was unambiguous that there are both physical and non-physical ways of being related to God and others. Limiting the image to the physical or non-physical, as have so many throughout the centuries, is to fall prey to either Platonism's spiritualizing on the one hand or modernity's humanism on the other hand. As Gunton saw it, 'Relations are [instead] of the whole person, not of minds or bodies alone'.[20] Any improper imbalance towards bodies or minds simply threatens a fully relational anthropology.

## *Vertical relationality*

Gunton believed that inquiries into the *imago Dei* have tended to be far more interested in how human beings differ from non-human creation than in our relation to God. Is the image to be located in rationality since non-human creation has not been created with the faculty to reason as humans do? Is the image found in the ability to walk upright or in some other physical attribute not shared by animals? The problem Gunton found in these kinds of comparisons is that inevitably the contrast becomes limited to either a physical or a mental capacity. Instead, he noted that human beings have been given something that the rest of creation does not share in: 'a particular and unique kind of relation' with God.[21] For Gunton, the fact of our unique relationship with God as humans – and not our differences from rocks and animals – should be kept at the fore of any investigation of anthropology.

Whatever constitutes the specific image given to human creation, it is enduring: 'that something given cannot be taken away, except by God, because it is part of what it is to be a created human being.'[22] If the triune God removes his continuing subsistence in relation to the entire created order, it ceases to exist, and for this reason Gunton called all creation's relationship with the Creator 'indelible'.[23] Here we also observe Gunton's movement from a general ontological principle of creation to anthropology: 'this holds for human and non-human creature alike, even though the form of the relation is different'.[24] Furthermore, since the image given to human creation is essentially one of a God-originated relationality, and not one defined by human intellect, the image as such is maintained even in human beings with mental limitations and even in those who choose to turn away from the knowledge of God. Even human beings 'moving in the wrong direction are upheld by the Son and drawn to perfection in the Spirit'.[25]

For Gunton, this unbreakable relatedness of Creator to creation – and in particular the unique and special relationship with God bestowed upon human beings – constitutes the essential and pre-eminent vertical element of the *imago Dei*.

## *Horizontal relationality*

'To be created in the image of God places us first in relation to human beings especially to the "other" that man and woman are created to be and second to the rest of the created order.'[26] This statement outlines the core thesis of Gunton's relational view of the image. We humans have been created to be in relation to one another (like the Holy Trinity) and secondarily to the rest of creation. The horizontal inter-relationship among human beings directly affects personhood as well: 'Likeness to God consists in the fact that human beings are persons while the remainder of the created world is not.'[27] Using language identical in many cases to his trinitarian writings, Gunton described human beings as 'authentically personal', thereby imaging the divine Trinity only insofar as they subsist in 'mutually constitutive relations with one another'.[28] While, as we have already seen, the image is indelible when described as a continuing relation to God, it is not clear in Gunton's model what the eternal consequences are (if any) if one fails to subsist in the appropriate inter-human relationships, and is thus less-than-authentically personal. This point should not be overlooked. Gunton did not speculate as to what God does about individual evil, rather he focused on what the Son and the Spirit have mediated as a universal potential.[29] Though he asked all the right questions (for example: 'what are we to make of those who so violate the order of being that their likeness to the human Jesus is discernible only by their physical shape?'), he never explicitly answered them, other than to conclude that these people too, in some respects, remain in the image of their Creator.[30]

The horizontal aspect of image-as-relation is also closely aligned with the discussion of the human care of non-human creation in Gunton's writings. As noted above, rather than finding value in extended comparisons of human to non-human creation, Gunton believed that there was no ontological distinction, but rather an 'asymmetry of relation' and therefore only a relative difference between humans and other creation: 'As created beings, human persons are bound up closely with the fate of the rest of the material universe, as stewards rather than absolute lords.'[31] Again, noting that the biblical creation account describes not paradise but a garden that requires naming, tending, and subduing, Gunton believed that the obvious implication of the narrative is that there is a task for the human creature to complete. This involves a general 'ethic of createdness',[32] though not a developed theology.

His writings attest, however, to somewhat conflicting opinions about whether the garden narrative provides any ontological 'meat' adequate to describe the image. For example, in 1991, Gunton expressed the opinion that the stewardship of creation was 'too literalistic and too restricted'[33] as a theology of the image, but two years later, he expanded on the notion of stewardship and wrote that 'being in the image of God has something to do with the human responsibility to offer the creation, perfected, back to its creator as a perfect sacrifice of praise'.[34] His later view, that the garden and stewardship of creation have at least some ontological potential for a functional definition of the image, in my opinion, begs for further discussion. How are humans to offer creation to God as a perfect sacrifice of praise? I suggest that this phrase of Gunton is in essence a definition of the priesthood of believers described by the Apostle Peter as the essential mark of communion with God: 'you also, as living stones, are being built up a spiritual house, a holy priesthood, to offer up spiritual sacrifices acceptable to God through Jesus Christ' (1 Peter 2.5).

Consistent with this view, Gunton believed non-human creation requires human creation to bring all things to the *telos* where God will be all in all: 'the created world is not truly itself without us.'[35] Citing Irenaeus, Gunton wrote that it is the bread and wine of the Lord's Supper that shows that it is human creatureliness through whom all creation speaks.[36] Writing from a decidedly liturgical point of view, this second-century bishop intended to convey that the non-human elements of creation – the grain and the grape – are made by human activity into bread and wine, and are offered by human action in the penultimate divine–human communion of the Eucharist. In this way, through human action, the inanimate grape and grain 'speak' and also participate in communion with God. So while Gunton believed that worship of the Creator is the proper goal of creation (and I believe he is quite correct in this regard) he offered a very broad definition of what, in fact, constitutes proper worship. In his opinion, proper worship of the Creator would include every act of proper relationality, an example of which would be refraining from polluting creation.[37] Gunton indicated further that he did not wish to stress sacraments at the expense of the Word, though he believed there was something to say about matter representing elements of Christ's life, death and resurrection.[38] Nevertheless, it seems that the element of worship – of proper doxology offered to the Creator through the stewardship or priestly care of creation – has potential to describe the functional aspect of the image. This is the heart of liturgical theology, and, though Gunton never truly ventured into that arena,[39] concentrating more on systematic conceptions, I believe his ideas, brought together and expanded upon, could indeed provide ontological significance for describing the *imago Dei*.

## *The image and the Fall*

If Genesis speaks about creation in the image of God, one should not overlook that it also speaks of a critical and destructive change in the status quo of original creation, which is typically thought to have affected the image in some way. Gunton correctly points us to consider the indelible relationship between Creator and creation sustained by the Creator, although he has not equally systematized the ways in which the Fall contributed to the breaking or harming of that vertical relationship. It may be that the seldom-mentioned 'Fall' is logically less important in Gunton's model since he believed that creation was incomplete from the beginning. It is clear that, for Gunton, since the image is 'indelible' despite human failings, the original image was not obliterated by the Fall.

There are other related questions to be asked of Gunton's anthropological proposals, however. First, if human beings were created in order to develop mutually constitutive relations with other human beings (i.e. to seek authentic personhood according to the image of Christ), does failure to do so affect the image? It seems that the answer would be that failure to do so affects genuine personhood, but not the image. We are less Christ-like, and therefore less in the image, but the image is ultimately indelible. Secondly, does failure to be genuinely personal affect salvation in Gunton's model? The answer to this question is also unclear since Gunton's discussions in the works cited have not been framed within the perspective of salvation, but of ontology. While Gunton spoke of Christ as the redeemer of humanity, by redemption Gunton meant 'the completion of the whole project of creation, not the saving of a few souls from hell'.[40]

In general terms, Gunton described the Fall as 'a rebellion against God's gracious promise'.[41] Whatever was the failing or condition resulting from the Fall, it was not specifically articulated by Gunton.[42] The Fall led to a breach of proper relationships within creation, with murder as 'the most serious sin against the image of God'.[43] In reflecting upon this statement, I believe it is noteworthy to emphasize that murder, which in its primary dimension is a horizontal offence, is described by Gunton as the most egregious violation of the image. This is consistent with the weight given by him to horizontal relationality within creation.[44] If the image was damaged in the Fall as a result of human sin, however, this perspective is somewhat unsettling since the first biblical murder does not occur until after the expulsion from the Garden of Eden. In other words, how can murder be the worst breach against the image if 'humans in the image' had already done something in the garden that led to expulsion and death? Though Gunton is correct to state that the image of God as a special relationship with God is irrevocable, Genesis undeniably speaks of catastrophic damage to the relationship caused by human action *against God*, not by an offence against other creation. It therefore seems that consideration must first be given to the damage done to the image in the garden before redemption in Christ can be properly understood.

Additionally, in what way is this 'original' breach with God repeated in our fallen world today? Gunton had also often suggested that residual Enlightenment ideas have contributed to contemporary individualism in the West. But I wonder whether the problem of individualism in our day (improper horizontal relationality) is indeed a consequence mainly of inadequate ideas about triune relationality, as Gunton suggested, or more a consequence of sin and death entering the world as a result of a breach of human communion with God (improper vertical relationality)? Perhaps it would be more accurate to consider that the Enlightenment itself was merely a symptom of this same primal failure described above? The Genesis narrative describes a rupture of communion with God that specifically points to human action, the result of which is a subsequent rupture in horizontal relations. This fact may point at lacuna in the logical expansion of Gunton's ontology of human creation as it considers relationality in the contemporary world. I would therefore like to briefly revisit the garden to suggest an embellishment upon his foundations, and perhaps a solidifying of his less-concrete ideas in a way that connects the image and the original problem of broken communion with God with its remedy as growing in communion with God in likeness to Christ.

## Commentary: the priesthood of human creation

Gunton articulated mixed opinions on whether or not sufficient specific biblical warrant could be found to pursue the garden as anything more than an analogy. His general attitude leaned towards thinking that the concept of human stewardship of creation was too restrictive and literal, with no ontological principle of the image to be derived from it. So as far as garden-tending goes, Gunton is quite correct that the analogical limits are easily reached. However, quite a bit more could be said about humanity's intended ontological function as described in the garden if we revisit the garden through the lens of liturgical theology. It also provides the theological apparatus needed to address appropriate correctives to the problem of individualism in the present day. The point I wish to make is very much in agreement with Gunton's view of Christ as the prototypical image of God and also as the *telos* of the image, but with some terminological embellishment: the image of God is related ontologically to Christ's priesthood, and, by extension, its renewal and restoration in the royal priesthood of all believers (1 Peter 2.5).

I will attempt to connect the dots of this idea by borrowing from the late twentieth-century liturgical theologian Alexander Schmemann. What Schmemann understood from the Genesis narrative, and what he believed was confirmed throughout the whole of Scripture, was that Adam was intended to be not merely 'steward' but 'priest'. In Schmemann's view, all of biblical history presents food given by God as not only for sustenance, but also expressly as communion with God. Even in the garden, every creature must eat in order to live, and so likewise the fruits of the earth were offered to Adam in order to live, but also and more importantly, to be communion with the divine Giver. Adam's naming, tending, reaping and even consuming of creation, was to be his *priestly* response to this gift (and would encompass both the vertical and horizontal aspects in Gunton's model). Instead, wrote Schmemann, Adam sought the only thing expressly not given to him by the Creator to be communion: the fruit of that one particular tree. More than merely being disobedient, Adam sought creation as an end in itself rather than in relationship with the Creator, thus radically damaging (if not destroying) communion with God and failing to be priest.[45]

Schmemann's argument is consistent with Scripture, as well as with Gunton's belief that 'being in the image of God has something to do with the human responsibility to offer the creation, perfected, back to its creator as a perfect sacrifice of praise'.[46] Scripture indeed attests to the divine intention of human creation to assume roles much greater than garden tending – to nurture and even create from non-human creation, and to offer all things back to God in thanksgiving (literally, *eucharistically*). This priestly role is at the heart of what Irenaeus meant when he wrote that the bread and wine of the Eucharist speak through human creation. Despite Gunton's initial reluctance (though in his later writings he moved in this direction), I suggest that there may indeed be ontological anthropological implications for the meaning of the garden, food, naming, blessing, tending and creating when taken in this way, especially with regard to the royal priesthood of all believers.

According to Schmemann, Adam ceased seeing creation as the means to communion with God and sought creation itself, above the Creator.[47] Since creation has no life or meaning in itself apart from God, Adam's disobedience brought all creation into a realm of death. Gunton expressed a striking parallel idea in a later writing: 'the one meant to be like God has sought sustenance from other sources, and so has experienced a fall through worship of the creature rather than the creator'.[48] Gunton was also correct to point to Jesus Christ as the prototypical image of God, but a sacramental and specifically eucharistic meaning can be derived from Christ's cosmic priesthood and should also be considered as an element of the *imago Dei*. In Christ we see the intended role of all humankind – to be priests of creation, never forgetting the divine Giver.

Schmemann suggested that individualism in our age is the symptom of the failure to be 'priest'. It is the failure to recognize that all things – all creation and all people – are from God, and are given precisely to 'be' communion with him. Envisaging the image of God in terms of the unique relationality of priesthood works to correct the destructive division between the religious and the secular that has taken place in the West and gives the potential for all of life to be a sacramental action (thus extending Gunton's view that all of life was to simultaneously include both a vertical and horizontal functional aspect of the image).

It may also be helpful to introduce at least some distinction between image and likeness at this point, with 'image' as a static given (the indelible relation with God, as per Gunton) and 'likeness' as intentional movement towards – or away from – conformity with Christ's likeness. Retaining a distinction between the two terms, without attributing one to reason as Gunton was correct to eschew, may emphasize the necessary ontological dynamism of the image that is somewhat less well defined in Gunton's discussions. Stavropoulos, like Gunton, also uses the metaphor of a garden. The cultivation, however, is not of other creation but of the human person growing in likeness to Christ: 'Within each human being God sows all those seedlike gifts which make us his image and lead us toward his likeness, insomuch as we cultivate these gifts'.[49]

## Conclusion

There is much to commend in Colin Gunton's view of human personhood, among which is his reintroduction (or perhaps even introduction) of relationality as a primary concept in contemporary Christian systematic theology in the West. Individualism is pervasive in both the secular world as well as much of the Christian world, and Gunton's renewing of Greek patristic themes (in many cases as a direct contrast to Latin patristic themes influenced by Augustine) did much to redirect the theological mindset towards this essential concept of relationality.

Gunton was also most helpful in revisiting Irenaeus' notion of recapitulation in Christ, especially with the understanding that Christ has universally healed Adam's failure to give proper worship to God. Another key patristic theme that Gunton emphasized was the perception of Christ as both *Protos* and *Telos*: the prototypical model of human creation as well as its perfection, which included a particular kind of physicality. He was also correct to redirect attention to the primary issue in theological anthropology: that the image should not be defined by the way humans differ from non-human creation (i.e. walking upright, ability to reason), but by the unique and special relationship in and with the triune God. This relationship is the nucleus of the *imago Dei,* which is given and sustained by God out of love for his creation. Gunton believed that we humans are relational solely because we have been given the image of the triune Creator, whose being is communion.

Indeed, human beings have been created for action, which Gunton described as a specific active relationality with other human beings according to the image of the Trinity, as well as an asymmetrical active relationality with non-human creation. Especially helpful was his interpretation of the garden as depicting a work-in-progress requiring human creation to act in moving God's project towards its perfection in Jesus Christ. As expressed especially in his later writings, however, we humans were created to not only be inter-relational, but also for the unique action of offering proper worship and sacrifice to our Creator. Adding an intentionally eucharistic or liturgical layer to the discussion brings a much-needed focus on the necessity of human action to actively pursue communion with the Father, through the Spirit, in Christ. It is summed up by the biblical concept of priesthood. Because of Christ's priesthood, all humanity has been restored to the potential of its proper function in the created world: we were created to be priests who offer all things in thanksgiving and worship to our Creator.

## Notes

1  'I am because we are, and since we are, therefore I am.' John S. Mbiti, *African Religions and Philosophy,* 2nd edn. (London: Heinemann, 1989), p. 106.

2  Colin E. Gunton, *The One, the Three and the Many: God, Creation and the Culture of Modernity* (Cambridge: Cambridge University Press, 1993), p. 217. This is the idea at the core of his conception of 'open transcendentals'. See discussion at pp. 141 ff., pp. 211 ff. Also note similar discussion in 'Trinity, Ontology and Anthropology: Towards a Renewal of the Doctrine of the Imago Dei' in Colin Gunton and Christoph Schwöbel (eds), *Persons, Divine and Human. King's College Essays in Theological Anthropology* (Edinburgh: T&T Clark, 1992), pp. 47–61.

3  'We need more than an extended exegesis of Gen 1.26f, and in particular a broader treatment of the topic, if we are really to make more satisfactory use of the concept of the *imago dei.*' Gunton, 'Trinity, Ontology and Anthropology', p. 58.

4  Colin E. Gunton, *The Triune Creator. A Historical and Systematic Study* (Edinburgh: Edinburgh University Press, 1998), p. 198.

5  *tselem* in the Masoretic, or *eikon* in the LXX.

6  *demut* in the Masoretic, or *omios* in the LXX.

7  While Irenaeus did sometimes distinguish the two terms, he also uses them interchangeably as in *Against Heresies* 3.18.1 and 5.12.4. He would not be alone in the Greek Fathers in doing so. Others, including Diodochos of Photoki (5th c.),

Maximus the Confessor (7th c.), John of Damascus (8th c.) and Gregory Palamas (14th c.), spoke of salvation as a process of movement from the divine 'image' to the divine 'likeness'.

8  *The Triune Creator*, p. 197. Also see Colin E. Gunton, *Father, Son and Holy Spirit: Essays Toward a Fully Trinitarian Theology* (Edinburgh: T&T Clark, 2003), pp. 109–10.

9  *The Triune Creator*, p. 202.

10 *The Triune Creator*, pp. 193 ff.

11 'Trinity, Ontology and Anthropology', p. 58.

12 *The Triune Creator*, p. 202.

13 *The Triune Creator*, p. 210.

14 *The Triune Creator*, p. 200.

15 *The Triune Creator*, pp. 199–200, referring to Frances Watson, *Text and Truth. Redefining Biblical Theology* (Edinburgh: T. & T. Clark, 1997).

16 *The Triune Creator*, p. 200, referencing Irenaeus *Against the Heresies*, 5.1.1 and 6.1.

17 Maximus the Confessor, *Ambiguum* 7:1080C in *On the Cosmic Mystery of Jesus Christ*, trans. Paul M. Blowers and Robert Louis Wilken. (Crestwood, NY: St Vladimir's Seminary Press, 2003), p. 56.

18 For expanded discussion see Adam G. Cooper, *The Body in St. Maximus the Confessor: Holy Flesh, Wholly Deified*. (Oxford: Oxford University Press, 2005).

19 *The Triune Creator*, p. 205. Irenaeus also argues in *Against Heresies* (5.6.1) that the human body and the soul together constitute the image. It is the gift of the Holy Spirit that moves us toward the likeness.

20 'Trinity, Ontology and Anthropology', p. 59.

21 *The Triune Creator*, p. 207.

22 *The Triune Creator*, p. 204.

23 *The Triune Creator*, p. 207.

24 *The Triune Creator*, p. 207.

25 *The Triune Creator*, p. 207.

26 Colin E. Gunton, *The Christian Faith: An Introduction to Christian Doctrine* (Oxford: Blackwell Publishers, 2002), p. 41.

27 *The Triune Creator*, p. 208.

28 *The Triune Creator*, p. 208.

29 *The Triune Creator*, p. 196, for example.

30 *The Triune Creator*, p. 203.

31 'Trinity, Ontology and Anthropology', p. 61. Also see: Colin E. Gunton, *The Promise of Trinitarian Theology*, 2nd edn. (Edinburgh: T&T Clark, 2004), p. 116.

32 *The Triune Creator*, pp. 228 ff.

33 'Trinity, Ontology and Anthropology', p. 57.

34 'Trinity, Ontology and Anthropology', p. 60. Also: 'true end of all human action is praise of the creator, of rendering to him due response for his goodness, we have a common light to illuminate all the dimensions of human cultures.' *The One, the Three and the Many*, p. 227.

35 'Trinity, Ontology and Anthropology', p. 60.

36 *The Triune Creator*, p. 197. Gunton also points to the suggestion implied by certain translations of Psalm 19.3-4 that creation has its own 'voice' as well.

37 *The Promise of Trinitarian Theology*, p. 187 and *The Triune Creator*, p. 235. Also:

'we shall . . . begin to understand the nature of sacrifice when we come to see its function in the removal of uncleanness which pollutes the good creation' in Colin E. Gunton, *The Actuality of Atonement: A Study of Metaphor, Rationality and the Christian Tradition* (Grand Rapids: Eerdmans, 1989), p. 119.

38 *The Triune Creator*, pp. 234–35.

39 He did, however, write that 'liturgical worship . . . is both the matrix for and model of the more broadly construed worship that is the proper service of the creature to the creator'. *The Triune Creator*, p. 235.

40 *The Triune Creator*, p. 171.

41 *The Christian Faith*, p. 29.

42 Although in places he had spoken of the Fall as originating in human sin, he also left room for the possibility of some kind of corruption of creation by another force or agency (such as the angels) before the human fall. See Colin E. Gunton, 'The Doctrine of Creation' in Colin E. Gunton, (ed.), *The Cambridge Companion to Christian Doctrine* (Cambridge: Cambridge University Press, 1997), p. 143.

43 *The One, the Three, and the Many*, p. 216. Also see discussion in *The Triune Creator*, pp. 171 ff.

44 'To be created in the image of God places us first in relation to human beings.' *The Christian Faith*, p. 41.

45 Alexander Schmemann, *For the Life of the World: Sacraments and Orthodoxy* (Crestwood, NY: St Vladimir's Seminary Press, 1998), pp. 11–16.

46 'Trinity, Ontology and Anthropology', p. 60. Also: 'True end of all human action is praise of the creator, of rendering to him due response for his goodness, we have a common light to illuminate all the dimensions of human cultures.' *The One, the Three, and the Many*, p. 227.

47 Schmemann, *For the Life of the World*, p.16.

48 *The Christian Faith*, p. 122.

49 Christoforos Stavropoulos, *Partakers of Divine Nature*, trans. Stanley Harakas (Minneapolis: Light and Light Publishing, 1976), p. 26.

Chapter 9

COLIN GUNTON'S DOCTRINE OF ATONEMENT:
TRANSCENDING RATIONALISM BY METAPHOR

Justyn Terry

While Gunton's most significant legacy is his work on the doctrine of
the Trinity and the implications this has for all other Christian doctrines,
especially the doctrine of creation, he also made important contributions to
the doctrine of atonement. Gunton found that atonement, like the Trinity,
was suffering from something of an eclipse in British theology. Debates
about which theory of the atonement gave the best explanation of the work
of Christ had become highly polarized over the previous century and had
brought such discredit to all the apparent alternatives that the result was
what Colin Grant described as a tacit 'abandonment of atonement'.[1]

In *The Actuality of Atonement: a study of metaphor, rationality and the
Christian tradition*, published in 1988,[2] Gunton looked to rehabilitate the
doctrine of the work of Christ by reassessing the form of the revelation to
which it was a response. He argued that the biblical teaching on sacrifice,
victory and justice is best understood as speaking of God's reconciling work
in Christ, not as theories, but as metaphors. Those who had tried to develop
a full-orbed doctrine of reconciliation[3] from any one biblical image were
making the mistake of treating these illuminating metaphors as complete
theories. This insight enabled him not only to give an account of how the
doctrine of atonement had found itself languishing to such an extent, but
also allowed him to offer his own constructive insights into how the subject
should better be understood. For both of these reasons, *The Actuality of
Atonement* has now become a standard text on the saving work of Christ.

In order to see the significance of what Gunton achieved and to
appreciate his own contribution to the subject, we shall lay out the context
in which he wrote. We shall then expound and evaluate his own views on
the subject in light of that context, arguing that while Gunton helps liberate
the atonement from the confines of rationalism by his use of metaphors, he

does not go far enough in bringing the metaphors together to show how Christ reconciles sinners to a holy God.

## *The problem of the doctrine of atonement in British theology*

At the start of the twentieth century, debates about the doctrine of atonement in Britain had become sharply polarized by the rise of modernism. Those who sympathized with this movement, like Hastings Rashdall, R.S. Franks and V.F. Storr,[4] wanted to formulate Christian doctrine in ways that were sympathetic to Hegelian idealism, scientific reductionism and historical and literary criticism of the Bible. They found moral exemplarist accounts of the atonement the most satisfying, since they explained the work of Christ crucified in terms of its transformative effect on people, not the forgiveness of sin. It was the repentance and amendment of life that the cross inspired that brought reconciliation to God. This enabled these authors to give an account of the cross without speaking of God's wrath, original sin or vicarious atonement, each of which were thought to create difficulties for a modern audience.

Other theologians, however, like R.W. Dale, James Denney and J.K. Mozley,[5] felt that the tendencies of modernist rationalism had to be resisted rather than accepted, and advocated the penal substitution theory as providing the best account of the atonement. For them, the work of Christ was essentially his bearing of human sin and suffering its punishment, namely death, which was to be seen as the inevitable consequence of the wrath of God. Christ died so that sinful humans could be forgiven. Here it was the objective taking away of human sin that enabled sinners to be reconciled to God when they turned to Christ in repentance and faith.

Advocates of these two alternatives were keen to point out the flaws in each other's positions. Rashdall, for instance, carefully delineates a Pauline theology of sin leading to death, and the work of Christ as taking that punishment as our substitute.

> [I]t is clearly St. Paul's conception that Christ has paid that penalty in order that man may not have to pay it. It is impossible to get rid of this idea of substitution, or vicarious punishment, from any faithful representation of St. Paul's doctrine.[6]

Then he rejects it by saying,

> It is because for modern minds it does not meet the difficulty, that St. Paul's theory of the atonement cannot be our theory of it; and in spite of all

St. Paul's authority, it was never really accepted by a great deal of later Christian thought.[7]

Nor could Rashdall see a place in modern theology for theories of atonement based on ransom, victory or sacrifice. He dismissed the theory of a ransom paid to the devil as 'monstrous' and 'hideous',[8] and sacrificial imagery is described as 'primitive' and 'crude'.[9] The only theory deserving a place in contemporary expositions of the atonement in his estimation was that of the subjective moral response to the example of Jesus Christ because 'our Lord never taught that his death was necessary for the forgiveness of sins, or that any condition was required for forgiveness but the supreme one of repentance and that amendment which is implied in all sincere repentance'[10] – a view that relies on a very selective reading of the Gospel accounts. Peter Abelard is applauded as the main protagonist of this view, with Rashdall expressing regret that Anselm's more objective view of Christ satisfying God's honour on behalf of sinners who have failed to give God the honour due, has been more prominent in subsequent Christian thought.[11]

Yet Rashdall's project was in turn criticized by others. R.W. Dale, for example, strenuously opposed such thinking:

St Paul's doctrine of Justification is practically destructive of the 'moral theory' of the Atonement; for if we were justified through the Death of the Christ only because the Death of Christ makes us better men, the Pauline theory of Justification would have to be re-cast.[12]

Dale therefore raises pointed questions, asking, 'Does God forgive? Or does He simply change the condition of a man so that he does not need to forgive?'[13] He has little time for Abelard's subjectivist approach to the atonement, seeing it as, 'only a transient and disturbing influence on the development of the theory of the Atonement in the Middle Ages, and he did nothing to affect the fundamental principle on which all Anselm's speculations are built'.[14]

Dale instead wants to speak of Christ's work in terms of ransom and propitiation,[15] though he sees his main task as demonstrating that the death of Christ is the basis of the forgiveness of sins understood forensically:

The Death of Christ is the objective ground on which the sins of men are remitted, because in His submission to the awful penalty of Sin, in order to preserve or restore our relations to the Father through Him, there was a revelation of the righteousness of God, which must otherwise have been revealed in the infliction of the penalties of sin on the human race. He endured the penalty instead of inflicting it.[16]

Here again we see rival theories of atonement being set as radical alternatives, with advocacy of one view being combined with a sharp rebuttal of others.

Despite notable exceptions such as P.T. Forsyth – to whose theology we will return when we study Gunton's constructive proposals[17] – J.S. Whale[18] and F.W. Dillistone,[19] this trend dominates theologies of the atonement well into the twentieth century.[20] In his influential book, *Christus Victor*,[21] Gustaf Aulén said that he did not so much wish to enter the debate between the subjectivists and objectivists as to reshape it into a three-way discussion with the addition of what he called the 'dramatic' and 'classic' idea of Christ's victory over the evil tyrants. However, he was very critical of both the moral response and the objective view of atonement, which was associated with Anselm and therefore dubbed, 'Latin'. Aulén concluded that neither the subjective view, nor the Latin, has a continuing place in Christian theology:

> In the course of the long controversy, the two rival doctrines have thoroughly exposed one another's weak points; and now it is becoming clearer with every year that passes that they both belong to the past.[22]

Likewise, when Frances Young set out to restore sacrificial imagery to greater prominence in atonement theology in *Sacrifice and the Death of Christ*,[23] she too rejects other theories of the atonement, only to replace them with a set of ideas about sacrifice: expiation, propitiation and aversion, none of which are described in any detail.[24] They are only preserved from the kind of criticism Young levelled against others by reducing their claims from being 'theories' to being, in her case, 'images'. Once again, one view of the atonement is proposed in such as way as to eliminate the alternatives.

Many other important contributions on the doctrine of atonement could be mentioned, but we have seen sufficient material here to identify the three main challenges that Gunton faced. The first was the problem of how best to respond to modernist rationalism that wanted to minimize the problem of sin, the wrath of God and divine intervention in the world. Should this approach be embraced in order to win modern people to the Christian faith, as Rashdall thought? Or should it be rejected in order to clarify the nature of the Christian faith, as Dale proposed? The second problem was that of the status of New Testament images like sacrifice, victory and redemption. Should they be treated as theories, ideas, metaphors, or in some other way? The third was the question of how these images, however they are to be understood, should then be related to each other in order to set out a coherent account of the atonement. While Gunton proved highly effective in addressing the first two of these issues, the weakness of his proposal lies in the third, where he fails to provide a co-ordination of these metaphors.

## *A metaphorical approach to the problem*

In *The Actuality of Atonement*, Gunton begins his project by offering a sustained critique of the rationalisms of morality, experience and concept stemming from Kant, Schleiermacher and Hegel respectively. He does not do so in order to justify past formulations of the doctrine of atonement, but rather as a preparation for reinterpreting traditional atonement imagery in terms of metaphor, and thereby to transcend the narrow confines of rationalism. In effect, Gunton refuses to choose between an account made from within modernist assumptions, or from broad-brush rejections of rationalism. Instead, he begins by examining the ideas that led to such of a dichotomy in the first place.

Gunton's resulting discussions of Kant, Schleiermacher and Hegel show a deep appreciation for their insights as well as a sharp awareness of the problems each introduced into later theology.

> Kant, Schleiermacher and Hegel are important because they are the geniuses of our age. And genius is the word, for they have all marked our intellectual times indelibly and cannot be evaded by simply ignoring or going behind them. Rather, an attempt must be made to go beyond and to some extent against them.[25]

To this end, Kant is taken to task first for promoting a moral rationalism that either throws into question the meaning of the Christian language he uses, like satisfaction and justification, or changes its meaning at a fundamental level. As Gunton sees it, if we are saved from moral evil by our own innate capacity, even if that is assisted by a God located within us as Kant suggests, then we do not really need to be saved by Christ crucified. Schleiermacher is also accused of making Christian terms 'cease to mean what they once did', though he avoided the Pelagian tendencies of Kant.[26] His doctrine of redemption falls short of maintaining key elements of the tradition, 'failing to hold to its teaching that on the cross Jesus in some way or other underwent the judgement of God on human sin'.[27] Hegel likewise is criticized for changing the traditional meaning of Christian terms, for instance allowing 'reconciliation' to mean not so much reuniting sinful people with a holy God, as overcoming the opposition between the finite and the infinite. As a result, for Hegel, matters of cosmic and human evil, and indeed the historical cross of Jesus, are not needed for an account of reconciliation. For all the excellent questions they raise, Kant, Schleiermacher and Hegel are seen as playing leading roles in shaping the intellectual conditions in which the doctrine of atonement had come to languish.

Having identified the difficulties of these three forms of rationalism, Gunton begins to develop his case for a metaphorical reading of biblical accounts of atonement. As Gunton acknowledges, he was by no means the first to use metaphor to describe the relationship between biblical imagery and the work of Christ. We see it, for instance, in Rashdall,[28] Storr,[29] and prominently in Whale.[30] Gunton's contribution is to harness recent philosophical writing on metaphor in order to spell out more precisely how traditional atonement imagery relates to the work of Christ itself, without diminishing the claim to the objective reality of the ontological change in relationship that it has secured.[31] He set out to 'show that metaphor is both a pervasive feature of our language and that it is a way of telling things as they are'.[32]

To establish his case, Gunton draws on scholarship, largely from the philosophy of science, which almost unanimously rejects the view propounded by Hobbes and Locke that metaphor is an abuse of language and instead advances the claim that it is a major clue as to what language is and does. He considers its characteristics in comparison to those of the rationalist conception of language mirroring reality and concludes that 'simply in virtue of the greater modesty of the claims for comprehension, metaphor is a primary vehicle of human rationality and superior to the pure concept (if such exists, as must be doubtful)'.[33] Here lies the importance of metaphor: it enables us to speak of things without which we could only remain silent. As Gunton later says, '[A] metaphor or family of metaphors takes its shape from the divine and human story it seeks to narrate, and so enables aspects of the meaning of an unfathomable mystery to be expressed in language'.[34]

Gunton then examines the New Testament imagery of victory, justice and sacrifice in the light of this research. He begins with, 'The Battlefield and the Demons'[35] which is largely occupied with analyzing Aulén's *Christus Victor*. He argues that by taking the victory over Satan metaphorically rather than literally some of the historic problems with this theory, such as the attribution of rights to the devil, can be avoided.[36] It is, in Gunton's view, precisely because Aulén presses the imagery too far that the cosmic battle becomes a myth, placing it, 'in a sphere outside the course of concrete divine-human relations'.[37] This is by no means to withdraw the claim that by his death Christ gained a mighty victory. It is instead to say that we have here a metaphorical way of expressing the victory that Christ has won:

> These biblical metaphors, then, are ways of describing realistically what can be described only in the indirect manner of this kind of language. But an indirect description is still a description of what is really there.[38]

And since this is a victory in which the evil and lies of an enemy are overpowered not by force but by goodness and truth, it is an example of how a metaphor can transform our understanding of a word (such as 'victory'), our understanding of the world in which this victory has occurred and our understanding of the God whose victory it is.

> If the victory of Jesus is the victory of God, then the language in which the story is told is one of the ways in which we are enabled to speak of God. We learn, that is, that God is the kind of being who makes his presence felt in our world in the way in which the life and death of Jesus take shape. The metaphor of victory is therefore one of the means by which God is enabled to come to human speech as a *saving* God.[39]

Gunton has drawn criticism for the way that he interprets the evil that Christ has overcome.[40] He follows one of his teachers, G.B. Caird, in taking biblical references to the devil and demons as referring to political, social, economic and religious powers:

> The victory is not over forces which inhabit a transcendent world, separate from ours, and intervene from outside, as Aulén's account might appear to suggest. Paul is speaking about 'earthly realities . . . the corporate life of men and nations.' But they are not forces which can adequately be described in everyday empirical terms. The forces are 'cosmic' in the sense that they *as a matter of fact affect the way things are on earth*, not simply as aspects, but as qualifications of them.[41]

While this does helpfully draw attention to the corporate and structural sin that Christ overcame, it is not clear that this provides an adequate account of Jesus' own encounters with the devil and his demons, nor does it sufficiently affirm the victory of Christ in those encounters.[42] Gunton here deploys the kind of demythologizing that was a characteristic of some of the rationalists he was seeking to refute. The cosmic dimension of the work of Christ is in danger of being underplayed here unless there is a more explicit recognition of a victory over a demonic realm that transcends the mundane.[43]

Gunton's use of metaphor pays further dividends in his discussion of the justice of God. Anselm receives a sympathetic reappraisal, not least because he avoids being bound by a literal reading of cosmic law; Jesus after all freely offers himself to the Father, and God is not primarily a judge exacting compensation. Anselm also makes a rather limited use of the 'classic theory' of overcoming the devil, which shows an awareness that his judicial account does not stand alone. However, Anselm is criticized for making the atonement primarily an act of power rather than love, for making God appear overly concerned with getting numbers to balance and for equating salvation with remission of penalty rather than also being about reconciliation with the Father and the renewal of creation.

Gunton then discusses Luther's insight on justification by faith and examines its biblical roots. He provides a summary of the argument of the Letter to the Romans and calls into question Luther's excessive preoccupation with personal experience to the detriment of the corporate and cosmic dimensions of God's justice. This provides a fitting backdrop to a discussion of two twentieth-century theologians who make substantial use of Luther to give accounts of atonement in terms of justice: P.T. Forsyth and Karl Barth.

In *The Justification of God*, P.T. Forsyth writes about the justice of God in relation to the First World War. How can divine justice be related to such a catastrophe? Only through the cross:

> The cross is not a theological theme, nor a forensic device, but the crisis of the moral universe on a scale far greater than earthly war. It is the theodicy of the whole God dealing with the whole soul of the whole world in holy love, righteous judgement and redeeming grace.[44]

Forsyth stresses God's concern with the moral fabric of the world and uses justice not only in a narrowly legal way, but also in a metaphorical manner. War is divine judgement on human wickedness, a 'giving over' to disordered passions,[45] and this is just one of many ways in which God's justice is brought to bear in the present. But if we are to see the justice of God revealed most clearly, we must turn to the cross of Christ. 'God's justification of man . . . was by His justification of Himself in man.'[46] It is in Christ bearing the judgement of God against the sin of the world that we see God's justice revealed.

Karl Barth takes a strikingly similar approach to Forsyth in his doctrine of reconciliation in Volume IV of his *Church Dogmatics*.[47] He too uses judgement as a metaphor to expound the work of Christ under the heading, 'The judge judged in our place'.[48] Gunton draws attention to the way Barth contrasts the sinful human propensity to stand in judgement of others and the willingness of Jesus to stand under judgement:

> To understand the cross as a judgement is to hold that just as a court decides and so declares a verdict of guilt, so the cross lays bare certain aspects of our condition – for example, the pride of our standing in judgement of others.[49]

Gunton also commends Barth for how he treats the biblical witness to God's justification of sinners in Christ crucified, not as a parallel to a modern courtroom, but as a metaphor.

When he comes to discuss sacrifice, Gunton moves from an introduction of the subject to a discussion of the biblical material, as he does with victory and justice. The variety of ways in which sacrifice is used in the Scriptures is furnished as evidence that already in the Old Testament sacrifice is being used metaphorically. 'The sacrifice acceptable to God is a broken spirit' (Psalms 51.17; cf. 27.6 and 107.22) is quoted as a prime case in point.[50] Then, in the New Testament, we have Hebrews 9.26c, '[Christ] has appeared at the end of the age to put away sin by the sacrifice of himself'.

> This is clearly a metaphorical use of language: there is no altar, but a cross; he is killed by soldiers not (directly – see John 11-50) by priests; and there is no provision in the sacrificial regulations as they appear in the canon of the Old Testament for the sacrifice of a human victim. Therefore, the death is described with the help of a true metaphor, for it both is and is not a sacrifice.[51]

This point is further reinforced by the way that Christ is not only the sacrifice, he is also the priest – the high priest indeed – that makes the sacrifice. Unless this is all taken metaphorically, there is a real danger that important biblical teaching on how Christ brought about expiation for sins on the cross will be either distorted or discarded.

Gunton then engages with the nineteenth-century Calvinist Edward Irving, applauding his consistency and originality, his development of Calvin's theology of Christ's human priesthood, and the cosmic context in which Irving deploys the sacrificial metaphor. Irving is also commended for avoiding a mathematical conception of sin and salvation and for his rich doctrine of the Holy Spirit, which he also received from Calvin. Gunton concludes:

> What, then, is potentially an abused and overused metaphor can also become the most living and expressive of all, the heart of the doctrine of the atonement as an expression of the unfathomable power and grace of God.[52]

At this point, we might expect Gunton to show how sacrifice relates to justice and victory and provide an account of how they may be understood in terms of sacrifice, addressing the third of the problems we identified above. Instead, however, he moves to set these three metaphors in a wider context.[53] He asks, *what* do they say about God, his creatures and their mutual relationships? All three metaphors considered are at root about relationships, but Gunton now wants to explore 'whether a consistent pattern can be discerned in the various relationships which have come to light'.[54] He then considers these metaphors in terms of the twin themes of creation and eschatological redemption, which provide common origins and ends but no particular connection in between. The question of how the metaphors of victory, justice and sacrifice might be regarded in relation to each other, which would have made his case stronger still, is not attempted.

While this might be explained in terms of Gunton's careful avoidance of any over-schematizing of theology – something that he deplored – I think it is more likely a sign that there is no ready way to carry this project forward. While the sacrificial metaphor can speak of the incarnation, of a life lived in obedience to the Father and of the representative and substitutionary death for sin, it cannot encompass the resurrection, ascension, session or the second coming of Christ. Once the sacrifice is made, its work is done, whereas the ascended Christ continues to intercede for sinners.[55] Considering the crucial role of the resurrection for the forgiveness of sins – 'if Christ has not been raised, your faith is futile and you are still in your sins' (1 Corinthians 15.17, ESV) – this is a significant weakness. It might also help explain why the resurrection – and indeed the ascension – has so little part to play in Gunton's book. There is also the additional difficulty with making sacrificial imagery primary, in that its language about sin and guilt offerings can only be understood in terms of justice – the laws of the covenant – suggesting that, if any atonement metaphor deserves to be given priority, it is the judicial.[56]

Gunton then uses this work to address some of the perennial questions about the atonement like the relationship between the subjective and the objective in the atonement, and the issue of whether Jesus' role is best seen as a substitute or as a representative. Gunton wishes to affirm the need for a subjective response to Christ crucified, but he is not willing to let go of the objective side of Christ's work on the cross. That would be to overlook aspects of the biblical testimony, to trivialize evil and to make the atonement a legal fiction, a charge proponents of moral response theories sometimes level at those who affirm an objective atoning work.[57] He also affirms a substitutionary view of Christ's work, not in order to endorse a form of penal substitution, but because 'he does for us what we cannot do for ourselves'.[58] The victory, sacrifice and judgement were his work for sinners. They were not, however, only the work of a substitute, but also of a representative. It was by virtue of his freely chosen relationship with sinful people that Christ overcame evil, offered himself as a sacrifice for sin and faced God's judgement on sin. Substitute and representative are, then, not to be seen as alternative explanations of Christ's work, but rather as different sides of the one work.

Gunton's criticism of penal substitution theories is another issue on which he has drawn fire.[59] He says that to support such a view would be to commit the sins of treating the legal metaphor in isolation from others, to read the metaphor literally, and to create a dualism between God and

Jesus.[60] That may indeed be so in some formulations of the doctrine, but as Barth shows in the passage to which Gunton refers his readers,[61] it is possible to affirm both penalty and substitution in Christ's work by setting it in the wider context of judgement without committing any of these sins. Once we recognize that Jesus is the ruler-judge, to be compared with the Old Testament judges and kings rather than contemporary judges who only interpret the law rather than make it, the possibility arises of seeing his death in terms of both penalty and substitution. Jesus is the one entrusted by the Father with the judgement of the world, who not only implements covenant justice in his life, but also chooses to be judged as the one bearing the penalty for transgressing that covenant in his death. As a ruler-judge, Jesus is the representative of his people, and since his death is the means by which sinners are judged and find forgiveness, it is also a substitution: 'he does for us what we cannot do for ourselves',[62] to use Gunton's phrase.[63] So Barth interprets judicial accounts of the work of Christ metaphorically and in a way that can readily be related to sacrifice and victory,[64] and does so without driving a wedge between the Father and the Son, breathing new life into the concept of penal substitution.

Lastly, Gunton addresses the question of how the Church is to be a 'community of reconciliation' in its preaching, administration of the sacraments and wider life in the world. Here he suggests how victory, justice and sacrifice should shape ecclesial practice. It quickly becomes clear that the implications are so manifold that another book could be devoted to them. But it is striking how Gunton relates preaching to the metaphor of victory, baptism to justice, and the Lord's Supper to sacrifice. This is, of course, not in any exclusive sense, since all three actions are related to all three metaphors. However, it does lead to important insights into Gunton's view of the priority of preaching, and into his understanding of baptism and the Lord's Supper.

Both baptism and the Lord's Supper are seen as 'particular ways in which God the Spirit creates free human life'.[65] They are events in which the atonement is brought into connection with particular sinners so that they enjoy its benefits as they respond to the preaching of the Gospel. Both baptism and the Lord's Supper involve a realization of what Christ has done for us, and an appropriate surrender to that revelation that includes both the seriousness of sin and the graciousness of God.

Baptism symbolizes not only washing, but also, perhaps more importantly, a death by drowning. It marks the end of the life of sin. So Gunton says, 'To be baptised is to undergo judgement, by accepting the work of Christ in our stead'.[66] It is to bear the death sentence on sin in order that there may be a rebirth to new and everlasting life. That death is metaphorical, but it is also real. As Paul says, 'all have died' (2 Corinthians 5-14).

What is claimed is no more a magical transmogrification than it is literally the clinical death of the baptised. The judgement which is undergone in baptism is rather the means of entry into the living space created by the substitutionary death of Christ. Because he has undergone judgement for us and in our place, we may undergo it as a gift of life rather than as a sentence of death. But that means that it is, metaphorically but really, a sentence of death on us.[67]

While Gunton does not want to suggest that baptism brings about the fullness of new life apart from repentance and a life of discipleship of Christ in the community of the Church, he does want to stress that it brings about an ontological change. That change is relational. To enter a new set of relationships with God and with the community of faith in the life of the Church is to be a new creation.

This leads into his discussion of the Lord's Supper. At this point, Gunton's Congregationalist commitments come to the fore, with criticism of clericalization of the Lord's Supper and of individualistic reception that militate against the unity of the body that it is supposed to foster. He is also concerned that the role of the Spirit can be downplayed in eucharistic liturgies. As a remedy for these ills, Gunton proposes greater attention to the sacrificial metaphor. The biblical institution narratives draw attention to the sacrifice of Christ, but they do so in the context of other metaphors of atonement. For instance, Luke's use of Passover rather than covenant language links sacrifice with liberation (Luke 22-15). 'Thus', he also points out, 'Paul links sacrifice with judgement [1 Corinthians 11-32] and so, we might say, the eucharist with a renewal of baptism'.[68] This makes clear the need for baptism prior to participation in the Lord's Supper, but it also connects these two sacraments in a way that roots them both in Christ's atoning work, and demonstrates that both the Gospel and the responses to the Gospel are to invoke his people's praise.

## Conclusion

Colin Gunton's work on the doctrine of atonement not only helped lift it from the ruts into which it had fallen, but also served to open up new vistas of possibility, not only for understanding this central Christian doctrine, but also for doing theology in general. By attending to the roots of the problem before him and seeing strengths as well as weaknesses in his interlocutors, Gunton provides a fresh perspective that offers not only clarity but also charity. In so doing, he established a greater sense of the glory of the work of Christ and at the same time an awareness of the grandeur of Christian thought. His metaphorical reading of biblical images of atonement does need further development to show how they may be related to one another and how they address the central human crisis of sin. However, Gunton offers not only a vital contribution to the doctrine of atonement that continues to demand the attention of all who now wish to take the discussion further, but also provides a model for doing theology that is itself potentially reconciling.

## Notes

1 Grant's article, entitled 'The Abandonment of Atonement', was published in the *Kings Theological Review* IX, 1986.

2 Colin E. Gunton, *The Actuality of Atonement: a study of metaphor, rationality and the Christian tradition* (Edinburgh: T&T Clark, 1988). While this is not Gunton's only writing on the atonement, it is certainly the most significant. We shall therefore make this the main focus of our study and refer to his other contributions in relation to it. For a full list of all Gunton's works, see Colin Gunton, *The Barth Lectures*, ed. P.H. Brazier (Edinburgh: T&T Clark, 2007), pp. 262–71.

3 Gunton takes 'atonement' to mean the bringing together of two parties that have become estranged, literally at-one-ment. As such, atonement is a synonym for reconciliation, as it has been throughout its history in the English language. Gunton, *Actuality of Atonement*, p. 110, referencing R.S. Paul, *The Atonement and the Sacraments* (London: Hodder and Stoughton, 1961), p. 20 ff.

4 Hastings Rashdall, *The Idea of Atonement in Christian Theology* (London: Macmillan, 1919); R.S. Franks, *The Work of Christ* (Edinburgh: Thomas Nelson, 1918/1962); V.F. Storr, *The Problem of the Cross*, 2nd edn. (London: SCM, 1924).

5 R.W. Dale, *The Atonement* (London: Congregational Union of England and Wales, 1888); J. Denney, *The Atonement and the Modern Mind* (London: Hodder and Stoughton, 1903); J.K. Mozley, *The Doctrine of Atonement* (London: Duckworth, 1915).

6 Rashdall, *Atonement*, p. 92. The gender-specific pronoun is being retained to be faithful to the original. The reader is invited to make their own adjustments here and in later such instances.

7 Rashdall, *Atonement*, p. 108. Rashdall is referring here not only to the apostolic Fathers and apologists but also to all the non-Pauline books of the New Testament (he accepts all New Testament claims to Pauline authorship except that of the pastoral epistles [p. 84]). He claims that they 'shrank from the substitutionary theory which St. Paul attempted' (p. 206). This is a highly questionable point as Leon Morris makes clear. L. Morris, *The Apostolic Preaching of the Cross* (Grand Rapids, Michigan: Eerdmans, 1965), p. 33 ff.

8 Rashdall, *Atonement*, pp. 259 and 350.

9 Rashdall, *Atonement*, pp. 66 and 151.

10 Rashdall, *Atonement*, p. 45.

11 Rashdall, *Atonement*, p. 360 ff.

12 Dale, *The Atonement*, p. 490.

13  Dale, *The Atonement*, p. 497. James Denney also raises questions about whether those who support the moral theory of the atonement make too much of the human response and challenges the idea that our repentance could have the effect of, 'putting God under obligation by it'. J. Denney, *The Death of Christ* (Carlisle, Cumbria: Paternoster, 1902/1997), p. 190.

14  Dale, *The Atonement*, p. 285.

15  Dale, *The Atonement*, pp. 12 ff. and 356. He is, however, hardly more sympathetic than Rashdall to theories of ransom expounded in terms of a mousetrap, like those of Origen and Bernard, calling them 'rude and coarse' and 'preposterous' (p. 277).

16  Dale, *The Atonement*, p. 431 ff.

17  Forsyth was scathing of the moral response theory, but he was not a proponent of penal substitution, which he thought focused too narrowly on only one aspect of divine judgement and therefore failed to convey the grandeur of God's holy love in Christ. Forsyth instead considered there to be three great aspects of the Church's understanding of the work of Christ: the triumphant, the satisfactory and the regenerative aspects, or redemption, justification and sanctification, and he set out to relate them to one another as a 'threefold cord'. Forsyth also offered the co-ordinating principle of 'the perfect obedience of holy love which [Christ] offered amidst the conditions of sin, death and judgement'. P.T. Forsyth, *The Work of Christ* (London: Independent Press, 1910/1938), pp. 199–201. However, it is unclear if Forsyth was able to make the case that he proposed. See Justyn Terry, *The Justifying Judgement of God* (Milton Keynes: Paternoster, 2007), pp. 103 ff.

18  See J.S. Whale, *Victor and Victim* (Cambridge: Cambridge University Press, 1960). Whale used a threefold approach, with Christ as victor, victim and criminal, taking victory, sacrifice and judgement as three metaphors, not theories, of atonement. This study played an important part in Gunton's own thinking on the subject, as Gunton acknowledges in his preface. Gunton, *Actuality of Atonement*, p. xi.

19  F.W. Dillistone, *The Christian Understanding of Atonement*, 2nd edn. (London: SCM, 1980). He attempted to construct an all-embracing showcase in which to display the doctrine of atonement. It did enable him to embrace a huge breadth of material, but it remained a rather scattered exhibition without sufficient integrating themes.

20  For a fuller survey of the development of British atonement theology in the twentieth century, see Terry, *Justifying Judgement of God*, chapters 2 and 3.

21  G. Aulén, *Christus Victor* (translation by A.G. Herbert) (London: SPCK, 1931).

22  Aulén, *Christus Victor*, pp. 161 ff.

23  F.M. Young, *Sacrifice and the Death of Christ* (London: SPCK, 1975).

24  The nearest Young comes to explaining what it is that Christ has achieved in these three respects is given on pp. 121–24, but even here the brief discussions are dominated by their accessibility to modern culture and to their psychological effect.

25  Gunton, *Actuality of Atonement*, p. 23.

26  Gunton, *Actuality of Atonement*, p. 12.

27  Gunton, *Actuality of Atonement*, p. 13.

28  Rashdall, *Atonement*, pp. 159, 356, 370.

29  Storr, *The Problem of the Cross*, chapter VIII.

144      *Justyn Terry*

30  Whale, *Victor and Victim*, pp. 36 f., 46 f., 69, 78.
31  Some critics, like Vernon White and Michael Winter, question whether Gunton
    truly does make a case for ontological change here, suggesting it might be more
    a matter of revealing a change that has already come about. However, as we
    shall see, Gunton does make it clear that the metaphors of victory, sacrifice and
    justice speak of an actual, historical event through which atonement comes
    about. Vernon White, review of Colin Gunton, *The Actuality of the Atonement*
    in *The Journal of Theological Studies*, Vol. 41, 1990, pp. 318–20. Michael
    Winter, *The Atonement* (London: Geoffrey Chapman, 1995), p. 35.
32  Gunton, *The Actuality of Atonement*, p. 25.
33  Gunton, *The Actuality of Atonement*, p. 39.
34  Gunton, *The Actuality of Atonement*, p. 113.
35  Gunton, *The Actuality of Atonement*, p. 53.
36  Gunton criticizes Aulén for failing to provide the basis for a theory (p. 61),
    although Aulén did not intend to produce a theory, only an 'idea'.
37  Gunton, *The Actuality of Atonement*, pp. 63 f. A 'myth', says Gunton, is what
    results when a metaphor is allowed to dictate reality.
38  Gunton, *The Actuality of Atonement*, p. 65.
39  Gunton, *The Actuality of Atonement*, p. 80. Gunton's italics.
40  For example, Derek Tidball, *The Message of the Cross* (Leicester: IVP, 2001), p. 251.
41  Gunton, *The Actuality of Atonement*, p. 65, quoting G.B. Caird, *The Language
    and Imagery of the Bible* (London: Duckworth, 1980), p. 242. Gunton's italics.
42  Tidball replies to Gunton that in the ancient world, 'there can be little doubt
    that [Paul] had personal demonic intelligences in mind'. Tidball, *The Message
    of the Cross*, p. 251.
43  Gunton does seem to be more open to this interpretation in his chapter on 'A
    Theology of Salvation' in *The Christian Faith* (Oxford: Blackwell, 2002), p. 80.
44  P.T. Forsyth, *The Justification of God* (London: Duckworth, 1916), p. 136,
    quoted Gunton, *Actuality of Atonement*, p. 106.
45  Rom. 1.26.
46  Forsyth, *The Justification of God*, p. 174, quoted Gunton, *Actuality of Atonement*,
    p. 109.
47  Karl Barth, *Church Dogmatics* IV/1. E.T. by G.W. Bromiley, edited by G.W.
    Bromiley and T.F. Torrance (Edinburgh: T. & T. Clark, 1953/1956).
48  Barth, *Church Dogmatics* IV/1, pp. 211–83.
49  Gunton, *The Actuality of Atonement*, p. 111.
50  Gunton, *The Actuality of Atonement*, p. 121.
51  Gunton, *The Actuality of Atonement*, p. 122.
52  Gunton, *The Actuality of Atonement*, p. 141.
53  Gunton develops this metaphor more fully elsewhere, such as in a chapter
    entitled 'The Sacrifice and the Sacrifices: From Metaphor to Transcendental?'
    in *Trinity, Incarnation and Atonement*, ed. R.J. Feenstra and C. Plantinga Jr
    (Indiana: University of Notre Dame Press, 1989). But here again sacrifice is
    'one of several central metaphors' (p. 213) used to illustrate and defend his
    claims about the value of metaphor for Christian doctrine, rather than to
    draw together the other metaphors. He takes the same position in 'Christ
    the Sacrifice: Aspects of the Language and Imagery of the Bible' in *The Glory
    of Christ in the New Testament*, eds L.D. Hurst and N.T. Wright (Oxford:
    Clarendon Press, 1987).

54 Gunton, *The Actuality of Atonement*, p. 144.

55 Heb. 7.25.

56 See Terry, *The Justifying Judgement of God*, especially chapters 6 and 7. It is also significant that the metaphor of justice can span the incarnation of the ruler-judge, the death as condemnation of sin, the resurrection as the Father's vindication of the Son by the Spirit, and the coming of Christ at the last day to judge the living and the dead.

57 Gunton notes with admiration Dale's position on this issue in 'The Atonement: R.W. Dale on the centrality of the Cross' in Colin E. Gunton, *Theology Through the Theologians* (Edinburgh: T&T Clark, 1996), p. 175.

58 Gunton, *The Actuality of Atonement*, p. 165.

59 Richard Gaffin, 'Atonement in the Pauline Corpus' in *The Glory of the Atonement* (Downers Grove: IVP, 2004), p. 161; Steve Jeffery, Mike Ovey and Andrew Sach, *Pierced for Our Transgressions* (Nottingham: IVP, 2007), pp. 250 ff; Robert Letham, *The Work of Christ* (Leicester: IVP, 1993), pp. 137 ff; Kevin Vanhoozer, 'The Atonement on Post Modernity' in Charles Hill and Frank James, *The Glory of the Atonement* (Downer's Grove, Illinois: IVP, 2004), pp. 380 f.

60 Gunton, *The Actuality of Atonement*, p. 165.

61 Barth, *Church Dogmatics* IV/1, pp. 211–83; cf. Gunton, *The Actuality of Atonement*, p. 109.

62 Gunton, *The Actuality of Atonement*, p. 165.

63 Terry, *The Justifying Judgement of God*, pp. 114 ff.

64 Terry, *The Justifying Judgment of God*, p. 168 ff.

65 Gunton, *The Actuality of Atonement*, p. 184.

66 Gunton, *The Actuality of Atonement*, p. 184.

67 Gunton, *The Actuality of Atonement*, p. 185.

68 Gunton, *The Actuality of Atonement*, p. 197.

Chapter 10

## Colin Gunton on Providence:
### Critical Commentaries

Terry J. Wright

### *1. Introduction*

The Christian doctrine of providence testifies to God's ongoing provision and care for the world. However, the history of the doctrine's development indicates the difficulty of articulating an account of God's provision and care in a way that expressly and faithfully substantiates the action of God confessed as Father, Son and Holy Spirit. An increasing number of scholars now recognize the need to reverse this tendency, but there is still much work to be done before the doctrine is loosed from its quasi-unitarian shackles and given full trinitarian form.[1]

Given this situation, it is surprising that Colin Gunton wrote little that is explicitly concerned with divine providence. Nonetheless, what he did write is fertile. My aim in what follows is to identify insights in Gunton's theology that could help to develop a contemporary account of providence. In doing so, I shall not attempt to synthesize a doctrine of providence from Gunton's writings, but rather will offer critical commentaries on the relevant chapters in *The Triune Creator* and *The Christian Faith*,[2] supplementing these with references to his other works where appropriate.

### *2.1 Synopsis of* **The Triune Creator**

Early in *The Triune Creator*, Gunton outlines a number of 'essential features' that constitute the Christian doctrine of creation.[3] The cumulative effect of these features is to affirm the goodness of the created order – a goodness, Gunton later observes,[4] not of original, absolute perfection, but of a sort that allows for the world's proper development according to its status as God's creation. Even so, God continues sovereignly to act in the world, guiding it towards its eschatological perfection. Gunton is clear that divine action is not to the detriment of the creature, for God mediates this action by means of the Son and the Holy Spirit, God's two hands.[5] Such mediation means that the world is structured by Jesus Christ, while the Spirit, as the 'perfecting cause',[6] empowers the world to become that which God had desired for it. In this way, God gives creation the space to be itself.[7]

These themes permeate Gunton's extended treatment of providence, which begins with an affirmation that the universe is not a closed order, resistant to God's action. Inspired by field theory, Gunton suggests that physical reality consists of various forms of energy, all prompted, and given shape and direction, by the divine energy that is the love of the triune God.[8] This loving, divine action towards the world is the heart of the doctrine of providence. For this reason, Gunton holds that the traditional distinction between general providence and particular or special providence is untenable, for God simply *acts*;[9] and nowhere is God's action more definitively observed than in the man Jesus of Nazareth. God's action in Jesus Christ reorients the fallen world to its eschatological perfection, *and so* enables the continuation of so-called general providence.[10]

Gunton suggests that the distinction between general and particular providence is avoided by focusing on God's Spirit in relation to Christ. The Spirit sustains the world in all its ordinariness, but does so in Christ. Moreover, given the world's fallenness, the Spirit first sustains Jesus to ensure that the latter fulfils his calling to effect the world's redemption; and secondly, the Spirit is the medium by which the Father raises his Son and transforms the body of Jesus into an eschatologically perfected body. It is the notion of particularity here that Gunton deems important. 'All particular acts of providence', he comments, 'derive from and take something of the shape of that paradigmatic redemptive act. But', he continues, 'the point is: both of these forms of providence [general and particular] serve the same divine project of enabling the created order to be that which it is called to be'.[11]

Following these initial observations, Gunton moves to explain why creation and providence cannot be identical, and he does so by exploring the differences between Karl Barth and Friedrich Schleiermacher on the matter. Barth holds that the doctrine of creation requires not a timeless but an absolute beginning for the world. A timeless beginning for the world implies the world's absolute dependence on God in a way that ignores God's actual relationship with the world, manifested in God's gracious decree.[12] Gunton is wary that a timeless act of creation abstracts time from the world,[13] thus diminishing the world's importance as the place of God's ongoing action, and so finds much of value in Barth's position. The act of creation posits something other than God in existence, and the doctrine of providence proclaims God's co-existence alongside the world to care and provide for it.[14] Conversely, Schleiermacher fuses providence and the act of creation,[15] and so lapses into pantheism, for he cannot accommodate the idea of particular divine action in his theology, nor can he do justice to the concept of the relative independence of the world.[16]

Schleiermacher's conflation of creation and providence leads Gunton to observe that unless carefully phrased, any account of divine agency has the potential to deny the world's freedom.[17] This is especially true for those accounts of providence that privilege divine foreknowledge over divine action, for if God knows all timelessly or in advance, it is likely that all is determined in some way. Thomas Aquinas' treatment of providence emphasizes a voluntaristic form of divine action: God is the first cause of a hierarchy of lesser, secondary causes,[18] and so the governor and sustainer of all things. While appreciating these aspects, Gunton nonetheless faults Aquinas for his lack of 'direct christological reference', which poses two difficulties for a viable doctrine of creation: the lingering presence of the idea of the eternity of matter, and the displacement of God's two hands by secondary causes and angels in mediating God's action.[19] Gunton attends to Aquinas no further here, but notes that the place given to causes in his treatment of providence eventually gave way, by the late medieval period, to discussion of divine omniscience and determinism: 'If God knows everything, can there be human freedom and cosmic contingency?'[20] In response, Gunton cautiously suggests that God knows what will happen similarly to a poet, who intuits the whole of a sonnet at once.[21]

Analogies aside, Gunton contends that only a fully trinitarian concept of mediation can do justice to the various issues prompted by creation and providence. Jesus Christ demonstrates that God's determination of the creature establishes its freedom; indeed, as the supreme instance of God's free interaction with the world, the incarnation is the foundation for understanding the relation between God and the world.[22] This Christological accent notwithstanding, the Spirit is in no way absent. Creation is God's project,[23] and Gunton implies here that it is the Spirit's responsibility providentially to guarantee the project's completion. Providence centres on God's action rather than on God's (fore)knowledge. Consequently, the Spirit produces appropriate distance for creatures freely to act in relation to God, without being forced to act in particular ways.[24] The Spirit ensures 'less deterministic' divine action, and so God 'enables something to move from an uncompleted or unsatisfactory present to a completion that is destined, but not fully determined, in advance'.[25] Gunton now makes clear the importance of mediation by God's two hands:

The Spirit, by relating the world – or worldly particulars – to God through Christ releases them to be what they have been created to be. As a form of enabling personal action, providential action, the Spirit's action is that which liberates things and people to be themselves, as, paradigmatically, the Spirit's leading enabled the human Jesus to be truly himself in relation to God the Father and the world.[26]

Thus God's two hands together steer the world to its appointed end. For this reason, notions of progress or evolutionary theory ought not to be feared or elevated beyond their status.[27] Gunton is confident that evolution as a process poses no threat for Christian belief unless it becomes an alternative to divine providence. Darwinism as a hypostatized form of evolutionary theory is Newtonianism focused on the biological level, 'a catapulting of the God of deism into time', similarly presupposing the universe as 'closed'.[28] Instead, it is the Spirit who moves creation forwards: not in the sense of progress, but towards its eschatological perfection.[29] Evolution may or may not prove to be the process by which the Spirit perfects all things. In fact, as the Spirit of the crucified Son of God, the Spirit may choose to perfect creation as much through 'the severely handicapped', for example, as through the development of 'advanced' life forms. Also, the Spirit who raised Jesus *from the dead* radically changes the idea of 'progress', suggesting that the transformation of all things occurs first by taking what is usually perceived as a step backwards.[30]

These musings lead Gunton to suggest that the apparent wastefulness of the evolutionary process and the suffering it generates is, in fact, not necessarily as profligate or as cruel as it seems. If each species is valuable in itself and is allotted its time, then it is difficult to accept that a species' extinction is genuinely a waste.[31] Nonetheless, Gunton recognizes that a world in need of eschatological perfecting accommodates not just evolutionary 'waste', but also real evil. Mortality is not the issue, for space–time limitations are proper to the creature; more pernicious is death proper, death under the curse, death apart from the redemption secured by the death of Jesus, the mediator of creation.[32] Gunton concludes that 'the death and resurrection of Jesus is the model for all providential action, as those acts which enable the world to become itself by action within, and over against, its fallen structures'.[33]

Given the Christological orientation of divine action, Gunton sounds two warnings against the contemporary enthusiasm for all things scientific. First, the doctrine of providence cannot be held hostage by the latest scientific models, for these may change as knowledge is furthered; divine revelation must always have priority.[34] Secondly, the aforementioned contemporary enthusiasm may also diminish in time: 'If pollution is as serious as some of the prophets of doom protest, there may be a revulsion against science which changes the whole balance of our culture.'[35] Where a belief in God's providence colours everyday perception of the world, there must be a corresponding concern to develop a theology of providence that allows both for God's sovereign ordering and determination of all things, and for the genuine reality and integrity of all things that God's action towards them guarantees. This is best achieved, Gunton suggests, by focusing on creation as action and not providence as foreknowledge, for this latter notion is too often a bedfellow of determinism.[36] For Gunton, 'analogies of making', such as the composer or the poet, express capably what takes place through trinitarian mediation, and so serve the articulation of the doctrine of providence far better than sight imagery.[37] As playwrights devise characters that self-develop according to the internal logic and structure of the play,[38] so does God bring the world into existence and allow its inhabitants the necessary freedom for them to be what God wants for them.[39]

Providence, for Gunton, is therefore organized around two models: first, the Son gives structure to the world; and secondly, the Spirit grants space to the world for it to develop within but not apart from the Son's structuring action. This is demonstrated supremely in the incarnation, where the Son becomes human so that the world can be moved towards its eschatological perfection by the Spirit. Thus God is said to order all things,[40] though Gunton is keen to stress that this ordering, even this divine determining, is not deterministic, due to the Spirit's own action. By relating each created thing to the Father through the incarnate Son, the Spirit makes it possible for actions and events 'to become what they will be. In that sense', Gunton notes, 'all providence is particular'.[41]

Gunton ends his chapter on providence with the following definition: providence is

> that activity, mediated by the two hands of God, which at once upholds the creation against its utter dissolution and provides for its redemption by the election of Israel and the incarnation of the one through whom all things were made and are upheld, and to whom, as the head of the church (Colossians 1:18), in the Spirit all things move.[42]

### *2.2 Assessment*

While not devoid of fascinating ideas, Gunton's treatment of providence here is somewhat disjointed, suggesting more that he was still thinking through the issues raised by the doctrine – and particularly that of mediation – than offering a substantial contribution to future conversations. The surest indication of this is the winding route Gunton takes from Schleiermacher's conflation of creation and providence to the cautious affirmation of the

analogy of God as a poet or composer.[43] Gunton connects Schleiermacher
to John Calvin merely to link the foregoing discussion to a fleeting analysis
of the deterministic implications of providence conceived in terms of
divine foreknowledge – and this via an ultimately unnecessary statement of
Aquinas' position. This is not to suggest that Gunton's comments here are
valueless, but that the unevenness of the steps from one to the other in the
passage as a whole does not make for easy progress.

More significant is the possibility of an implied theological determinism.
Throughout *The Triune Creator*, Gunton repeatedly commends the idea of
creation as God's project. On this account, the world as originally created
contains within itself the possibility of eschatological perfecting by the Holy
Spirit, who enables each creature to become what God wills to make of it.
Given the world's fallen state, this enablement takes the form of redemption
from sin and evil, which itself is made possible by the faithful action of
Jesus, God's incarnate Son. Redemption is not the world's return to an
original state of absolute perfection, but its Spirit-inspired movement in
Jesus Christ towards a greater end. The question that must now be asked
is this: if redemption is the Spirit-inspired, Christ-structured movement of
creation towards a greater end than its beginning, is the fallenness of the
world *necessary* to implement the eschatological perfecting of creation? It is
a question that must be asked simply because in an earlier discussion of the
notion of creation as divine project, Gunton appears explicitly to link the
completion of God's project with the redemption achieved only as a logical
consequence of the Fall.[44]

The possibility that the world's fallenness is divinely ordained reveals
Gunton's ambivalence on the issue of determinism. It is clear that Gunton
wishes to avoid deterministic views of divine action: the Spirit gives freedom,
and pneumatology provides the necessary safeguards to ensure that God acts
sovereignly in a world that has its own integrity and freedom. What is not so
clear is how pneumatology provides these safeguards,[45] and how Gunton's
insistence that God may be said nonetheless to determine things escapes
charges of determinism proper. Gunton appears to use 'determination' and
its cognates to connote the divine establishment of creaturely limitations:
that each creature shall be what it is and not another; that each creature shall
have its proper time; and so on.[46] Such an account of divine determination
ostensibly leaves room for positing genuine creaturely freedom, in much
the same way as genes determine a person's form and even predispositions
without negating that person's freedom.[47] Genes do not dictate when
a person marries, for example; but determinism proper holds that one
particular person marries another particular person at a particular time in
a particular place, and that these particularities are unavoidable, given all
antecedent factors.

This rigidity is not what Gunton desires to advance, but neither does he sufficiently explain how his own take on divine determination avoids actual divine determinism, not least because of his insistence that the Spirit relates all particulars to the Father through Christ. God sets the times at which, for example, the man Adolf Hitler would live; the country in which he would be born; the socio-political circumstances under which he would mature to adulthood; and so on. There need be no similar divine determination, on Gunton's account, to elevate Hitler to the position of Germany's Führer, or, indeed, to force him to adopt the nefarious policies he did. Yet if the Spirit related to Hitler in *all* his particularity, that is, at each moment of his life, in each circumstance he faced and in each decision he made; if the Spirit worked to enable Hitler to become what God intended for him – precisely how is the charge evaded that Hitler did become that which God had planned for him to be; that the Second World War was a direct consequence of the Spirit's particular relation to him; that by extension, the same Spirit applies to all other particulars in such a way that divine determinism, and not merely divine determination, is the only logical framework in which to explicate the doctrine of providence?[48]

If this type of reasoning is genuinely fostered by Gunton's position, then it must be possible to state that the Fall as a particular event is also covered by the divine ordering of all things. Gunton's favoured analogy for illuminating God's providential ordering, that of the artisan, is of limited value here: even if it be true that the plot and characters do develop according to the play's intrinsic logic, they cannot do so without the playwright's penmanship. As an analogy, likening God to a playwright has its merits; but within the context of the Spirit's particularizing each act or event to be what God intends for it, it wears a dangerously deterministic sheen that cannot be overcome by Gunton's insistence that pneumatology provides the appropriate space necessary for the created order to be itself.

The positive notes sounded in Gunton's treatment of providence centre around his attempt to account for the matter in terms not simply of divine action, but of the action of the triune God of Christian confession. There is an explicit role for the Spirit to play in relation to the incarnate Son, though the Father's role is not explicated to the same extent or depth.[49] Moreover, Gunton emphasizes the eschatological accents of providence that depict all things heading towards a certain end; providence is not merely the execution of some eternal decree.[50] Finally, Gunton's confidence that the world has genuine freedom and integrity in relation to the triune God is commendable and surely correct, despite Gunton's failure adequately to clarify these in relation to the sovereign determination of the triune God.

## 3.1 *Synopsis of* The Christian Faith

In *The Triune Creator*, Gunton's treatment of providence appears towards the end of the volume, following an analysis of creation themes that emphasizes the priority of understanding God as Father, Son and Holy Spirit in the development of a theology of creation. This priority lends itself to an account of providence in terms of divine action rather than those of the divine will or foreknowledge, which are less open to elucidation in explicitly trinitarian language. Nonetheless, the discussion is self-contained and can be appreciated without appeal to preceding or subsequent chapters. Conversely, the position of his chapter on providence near the beginning of *The Christian Faith* suggests Gunton's fresh recognition that the doctrine of providence is not merely a series of issues pertaining to the relation between divine action and creaturely reality. Providence, along with the doctrine of creation, constitutes the framework within which God's ongoing relation to the world is explored.[51] Thus Gunton conceptualizes providence not just *in terms of* divine action, but *as* divine action.

Many of the themes encountered in *The Triune Creator* appear once more in *The Christian Faith*'s opening chapter on the doctrine of creation. The world that God has brought into existence, to which God has granted its own relative independence and ability to self-develop, nonetheless allows for God's own action.[52] This is cast as trinitarian mediation:[53] The incarnation of the Word of God in the man Jesus of Nazareth reveals God's freedom to act within the world, while the Holy Spirit, who raises Jesus from the dead, demonstrates God's freedom over against the world.[54] Gunton notes that although divine action is accommodated to the world's structures, an event such as the resurrection of Jesus proves that God, at times, interrupts the normal passage of time eschatologically to act in order to make the world into that which God intends.[55] Thus God's power to act is not a matter of impersonal divine will, for divine action can only be understood with reference to the Son and the Spirit – God's 'two hands', which delineate precisely how God's power in relation to the world must be conceived.[56]

From here, Gunton turns his attention to the theology of providence proper. While the world has its relative independence, nonetheless it depends on God at all times for its continued existence. This concept of divine conservation has suffered from the portrayal of the universe as a mechanism, for there is no need on this account even to allude to God's ongoing sustaining of the world. The point for Gunton is not that alternatives to divine conservation are possible to construct, but that the world is not merely conserved as such a mechanistic conception of reality intimates. Creation is not to remain what it is; it is to be perfected through divine and human action.[57] A notion of providence pictured solely as conservation does not take into consideration the fact that God also moves the world forward and does so through God's own involvement in its affairs.[58]

This conviction is often challenged by those who focus on the level of mundane causation. David Hume, for example, argued that genuine causes, divine or otherwise, are impossible to discern. All that can be stated is that the human mind makes connections between things that appear to happen regularly in certain ways.[59] Nonetheless, the modern scientific intellect continues to probe the world to ascertain why things act as they do. The place of providence in a cultural climate that privileges the scientific thus remains a live issue for those wishing to address matters of divine action. Yet the scriptural witness to providence cannot be excluded, and, indeed, must inform contemporary debate, not least because the scriptural authors sought faithfully to testify to divine presence in a world where God frequently appeared absent. These authors' voices must be heard.[60]

If matters scientific form the most immediate context for explicating the doctrine of providence today, then the Christian doctrine of providence proper found its first cogent expression in dialogue with the thought of its own time, particularly that of the Gnostics and the Stoics. For the former, the material world was shaped by a lesser god, the demiurge, and so considered an inferior artefact. Salvation for the Gnostics meant extraction from the material order to the spiritual realm. Gunton's analysis of Origen's theology of providence indicates the latter's similarity to the Gnostics, in so far as he diminishes the importance of the material order by positing the consummation of all things as a return to the original beginning of timeless perfection.[61] In contrast, Gunton commends Irenaeus' theology of providence for its insistence that the sphere of divine action is indeed the material world. On this account, salvation is achieved by Jesus' recapitulation of the life of Adam, the former's obedience reversing the damage caused by the latter's disobedience.[62] Irenaeus' eschatology, contra Origen, emphasizes that the world in Christ is moving towards maturity, for God is concerned not to negate that which is already established, but to perfect it.[63]

Gunton does not dwell so much on Stoic thought as such,[64] but notes especially its peculiarly modern manifestation in the genetic determinism of certain contemporary biologists.[65] Stoic and neo-Darwinian accounts of reality are instances of 'monistic providence',[66] for each school holds that the world is driven by one thing, or one kind of thing, alone: an all-encompassing causal nexus (for the Stoics), or genes (for the neo-Darwinians). Monistic providence is not the only form open for consideration; Gunton notes that there is a dualistic providence,[67] stemming from René Descartes and Immanuel Kant, which posits the material as subordinate to the non-material. While the body, for example, is subject to outside determination, the mind remains free. On this account, providence equates to progress, where reason and will dictate how the future will unfold, usually for the betterment of the human race.[68] Neither monistic nor dualistic providence satisfies Gunton as an adequate description of providence. The impersonal forces of monistic providence are not guaranteed to move the world towards perfection; and dualistic providence similarly appears to negate the need for divine action, with the fate of the world in the hands of humanity.[69] Given these misconceptions, Gunton suspects that the notion of providence painted in Scripture was never truly appreciated before it was displaced by the modern ideas of progress and neo-Darwinianism.[70]

Scripture depicts God sustaining the world in existence and steering it through direct personal involvement.[71] Without divine conservation, the world would simply disintegrate; without God's interaction with creatures, the world cannot attain the end that God intends for it. Gunton offers an account of Genesis 1–2, explaining that divine providence is seen first in the command to humanity to complete the world, which was created for maturity; and secondly, in God's provision of a partner for Adam, so that he has appropriate support. Together, Adam and Eve are to ensure that the world continues on the path to perfection; or, as Gunton phrases it, 'the good world waits for its human inhabitants to make it more able truly to praise its creator'.[72]

The event of the Fall means that providence is conceived as the divine conservation of the world that finds its reorientation towards perfection through redemption. This notion is found, for example, in the tale of Cain, which demonstrates God's ongoing care for the fallen by preventing the consequences of sin from reaching their full potential.[73] Similarly, the story of the flood, at first an account of chaos intruding into God's good creation,[74] shows God promising that the dread effect of fallenness and sin will never again be allowed to reign.[75] For Gunton, these scriptural texts, coming so early in the canon, reveal providence as thoroughly different from those statements that describe the same in terms of the world's continuous amelioration through mechanistic or biological processes.[76] Providence is not a matter of impersonal forces, but of God's dealings with particulars in creaturely time and space.

This providential particularity finds its expression primarily in the election of Abraham.[77] From this divine act of calling and the resulting human act of obedience, divine providence is exercised over the world through genuine relationship with God's covenant people, finding its ultimate fulfilment in the life of Jesus of Nazareth.[78] In Jesus, 'God's providence becomes particular in a decisive and personal way', for he is the 'concrete realization in person of God's providential dealings with his people'.[79] Jews and Gentiles alike are united in Jesus as, through him, God's eschatological purposes are accomplished and disclosed – even though it has too often been claimed that the Jews no longer retain their status as God's covenant people.[80] Moreover, as these particularities of divine providence find summation in the life of Jesus, Gunton is convinced that the notion of election ought not to be restricted to matters of the eternal fate of human individuals. God elects particular persons and communities for the sake of the whole world, and the salvation of humanity implements the restoration of the natural order.[81]

Thus the gospel indicates God's ongoing activity in the world. Modern scientific theories appear to support this claim, for it is increasingly recognized that the universe is not a closed mechanistic order and so, Gunton reasons, must be open to the possibility of divine action.[82] The mundane regularities that shape everyday existence derive meaning from within 'a broader eschatological purpose'.[83] God's eschatological action may be discerned in past and present events, which, given the preceding discussion, finds paradigmatic expression in the life, death and resurrected life of Jesus. Here, Gunton offers a definition of providence: 'God's providence is his action both within and alongside the structures of the world he has created so as to both uphold and shape the direction of things according to their proper season.'[84]

Such a conception of providence points to the continuous vivacity of a world energized and styled by God's two hands.[85] Christ is the basis of the world's unity, for in him all things cohere; and each creature is enabled by the Spirit to become that which God intends for it. The Spirit's action here is a particularizing, not a compelling, of all things, for it is the world itself, in all its variety, that must mature to perfection in response to the Spirit's prompts. At times, the Spirit's action is forceful: the world is presently distorted by sin, and the Spirit's eschatological action, realized definitively in Jesus, violates the fallen structures of the world in order to liberate it and reorient it towards its proper destiny. 'Both the ministry and cross of Jesus presuppose a world so at loggerheads with its destiny that only the personal and active presence of the creation's mediator can effect its redemption.'[86]

It is true that evil persists; but Gunton believes that it does so through God's mercy, whereby the wicked are given time to repent. God's continued involvement in creaturely affairs, particularly God's action manifest in Jesus' death and resurrection, moves God's project to its eschatological completion so that, in the end, all things are truly reconciled to God.[87] Thus providence is 'conservation in eschatological perspective',[88] as God's purposes for all things – human and non-human alike – come to fruition in their own time and space, as a result of Jesus' reinstatement of the world's true orientation towards eschatological perfection. Gunton concludes, 'Here, in what this man does in obedience to the Father and in what the Spirit makes actual through him, is providence not only in action, but in constitutive and definitive action.'[89]

### *3.2 Assessment*

In contrast to the chapter on providence in *The Triune Creator*, Gunton's treatment of the same in *The Christian Faith* is less a series of connected ideas than it is an indication of the shape future accounts of providence could adopt. This is not Gunton's stated aim but an implied consequence of his account. As noted earlier, providence, along with the doctrine of creation, constitutes the framework within which God's ongoing relation to the world is explored. Although his discussion appears mainly to support the possibility and, indeed, actuality of ceaseless divine action in a world increasingly defined by the sciences, Gunton's most significant contribution to the doctrine of providence here is in fact his equation of providence with divine action: the action of the Son and the Spirit, the Father's two hands. The constructive attempt in *The Christian Faith* to depict divine providential activity using explicitly trinitarian conceptuality thus means that Gunton ties the pertinent doctrinal issues to the scriptural themes of creation, election, redemption and eschatological perfection in a way seldom attempted.

In his concern to engage with the sciences, Gunton especially targets mechanistic philosophy and neo-Darwinian thought, for both are monistic, secularized forms of providence that presume the world to be closed to divine action. The notion of the universe as a mechanism is carefully scrutinized, particularly its tendency to explain things in causal categories. Causal language is ambivalent and so needs accurate qualification if it is to be transposed to a more conceptual level and employed for articulating matters concerning providence. That Gunton moves effortlessly from evaluating causality to a strong affirmation of the scriptural witness to God's action[89] suggests his mistrust of letting anything other than the scriptural narrative dictate the content of the doctrine of providence.

This is not to say that Gunton rejects the idea of mundane causation, for such may contribute to the world's integrity as a reality distinct from God, in so far as things happen with regularity and according to particular patterns. Nonetheless, the divinely established stability of the world is due to God's continual conservation, demonstrating God's concern to ensure that the project of creation reaches its intended climax. The world, in all its glorious physicality, matters; and Gunton's contrast of Irenaeus and Origen in the context of providence indicates that God's project finds its completion not in the world's rejection, but through its reorientation, in Jesus Christ, to its true destiny. Election is thus an important element in Gunton's theology of providence, for it reveals that God's providence is exercised primarily by choosing to work with particular persons and communities. Although, in principle, God could unleash a storm of untethered divine power to accomplish the divine ends, in reality God's power is tempered by acts of election, whereby God elects to accommodate divine action to the structures of the world through interaction with certain inhabitants, and supremely in the incarnation of the Son by the Spirit. Moreover, the emphasis on election assigns a status to the entire scriptural narrative – rather than individual scriptural texts – that is seldom recognized in discussions of providence. It is Scripture, not the sciences or certain metaphysical presuppositions, that must shape and continue to shape the doctrine, otherwise justice cannot be done to the doctrine's eschatological orientation.

This assessment of Gunton's chapter on providence in *The Christian Faith* suggests that it is a marked improvement on that found in *The Triune Creator*. As noted earlier, the discussion here implies the shape future accounts of providence could adopt, whereas Gunton's previous sustained engagement with the doctrine simply explored the live issues before closing with a definition. To repeat, there providence is

> that activity, mediated by the two hands of God, which at once upholds the creation against its utter dissolution and provides for its redemption by the election of Israel and the incarnation of the one through whom all things were made and are upheld, and to whom, as the head of the church . . ., in the Spirit all things move.[91]

Note that providence is *an activity mediated by* God's two hands, rather than *the action of* God's two hands, which is Gunton's predominant portrayal of providence in *The Christian Faith*. The question must be asked: is providence *an* action of God or *the* action of God?[92] Also, in the earlier definition, Gunton simply introduces the notion of election – the election of Israel and, in Christ, the Church – to a discussion that previously neglected it, centring as it did on the proper mediation of divine action in contrast to secularized conceptions of providence. However, the inclusion of this important theme in *The Christian Faith*'s chapter on providence suggests that, having earlier discussed the pertinent issues concerning providence, Gunton is now more confident to shape the doctrine's content in such a way that it determines the content of Christian doctrine as a whole. If Gunton truly does equate providence with divine action, it is unsurprising that the doctrine of providence assumes such an elevated status.

## 4. Concluding observations

Earlier, I stated that the aim of this chapter is to identify insights in Gunton's theology that could help to develop a contemporary account of divine providence. To conclude, I shall delineate precisely what I think are these insights.

First, Gunton's equation of providence with divine action means that he prioritizes the providential action of the triune God over unitarianly conceived accounts of the divine will and issues of foreknowledge, which tend to dominate accounts of the doctrine. Both Thomas Aquinas and John Calvin, for example, focus on God's will as the cause of all that happens,[93] without necessitating the explication of providence through the apprehension of God as Father, Son and Holy Spirit. This leads to a theological determinism that is difficult to reconcile with notions of creaturely freedom. By equating providence and divine action, Gunton shifts attention from the problems concerning the compatibility of voluntaristic divine action, divine foreknowledge and creaturely freedom by concentrating on what God has done, what God is doing, and what – on the basis of God's past and present action – God will do. The question of how God acts in the world remains, but this does not entail moving determinism or foreknowledge to centre stage.

This means, secondly, that it is necessary to take seriously the scriptural presentation of God's action in the world. Scripture does not explain God's action as such but continually affirms its reality by testifying to various divine acts of election.[94] These acts find their ultimate expression in the incarnation of God's Son, by whom God redeems that which is fallen and restores its original momentum to eschatological perfection. On this account, the doctrine of providence is a series of positive statements about God's relation to creatures as attested in Scripture, not a set of abstract propositions about how God acts in the world. Gunton's achievement is thus to allow Scripture genuinely to determine the content of the doctrine of providence and its underlying metaphysical commitments. In practice, this means that providence is less concerned with divine omnipotence than it is with divine faithfulness, which demonstrates God's commitment to a world estranged to sustain and redeem it.

Moreover, Scripture's emphasis on God's acts of election indicates the importance of the particularity of divine action: God elects to act towards and alongside each and every creature, for the Spirit relates all things to the Father through the Son. This third insight impacts on the notion of divine determination that permeates Gunton's accounts of providence. To speak of a creature's determination is to speak of its limitations, or, less negatively, its particularity; that is, its need to be temporally and spatially located. Gunton's illuminating discussion of evolutionary theory in the context of the doctrine of providence thus lays foundations for a fuller treatment of what it means to be *created* and, given the divinely established particularities of creaturely existence, what it means for God's creatures to be free and not blindly determined. My conviction is that for reasons already expressed,[95] Gunton insufficiently distances the idea of determination from determinism proper; and while such distance could prove impossible to achieve, the greater idea that the Spirit relates all things, all *particularities*, to the Father through Christ is an insight too significant to lose.

These three insights – that providence equates to the action of the triune God; that the doctrine of providence and its underlying metaphysical commitments must be determined by the scriptural presentation of God's action; and that God acts specifically in relation to each particular creature – are easily stated, easily affirmed but not so easily explicated, at least with Gunton's acuity and consistency. Gunton's insights, if steadily maintained, are radical in their implications and so crucial, I believe, for developing a contemporary account of divine providence.[96]

## Notes

1  Two recent studies of note that focus on the action of the triune God are Charles M. Wood, *The Question of Providence* (Louisville: Westminster John Knox Press, 2008), and Allan Coppedge, *The God Who is Triune: Revisioning the Christian Doctrine of God* (Downers Grove: InterVarsity Press, 2007), pp. 289–328.
2  Colin E. Gunton, *The Triune Creator: A Historical and Systematic Study* (Edinburgh: Edinburgh University Press, 1998), pp. 175–192; *The Christian Faith: An Introduction to Christian Doctrine* (Oxford: Blackwell, 2002), pp. 20–37.
3  Gunton, *The Triune Creator*, pp. 9–13.
4  Gunton, *The Triune Creator*, p. 55.
5  While Gunton credits Irenaeus of Lyons with the 'two hands' imagery, it is possible that Theophilus of Antioch's own use of the same antedates Irenaeus, or that they shared a common tradition. See Theophilus, *Apology to Autolycus*, 2.18. (I am grateful for Graham Gould's guidance on this point.)
6  Gunton borrows this phrase from Basil of Caesarea, *On the Holy Spirit*, 15.38.
7  Gunton, *The Triune Creator*, p. 10.
8  Gunton, *The Triune Creator*, pp. 175–76. Cf. Colin E. Gunton, *The Promise of Trinitarian Theology*, 2nd edn. (Edinburgh: T&T Clark, 1997; 1st edn. 1991), p. 153.
9  The distinction between general and particular providence is the distinction between God's sustaining and directing of the world, and God's restoration of the world in acts of redemption.
10  Gunton, *The Triune Creator*, pp. 176–77. That God in Christ reorients the world to its eschatological perfection presupposes that something primal happened – the traditional doctrine of the Fall – to make the world deviate from its path. Gunton appears reticent to speculate about the precise nature of this fall, but accepts that a world created good and with the capacity to develop is always threatened by a self-movement away from the path to its intended perfection. Gunton, *The Triune Creator*, pp. 55–56. Providence is thus God's ordering of that which, due to sin, is disordered. Cf. Hans Schaeffer, *Createdness and Ethics: The Doctrine of Creation and Theological Ethics in the*

*Theology of Colin E. Gunton and Oswald Bayer* (Berlin: De Gruyter, 2006), pp. 237–38.

11 Gunton, *The Triune Creator*, pp. 177–78. Creation is 'a project – that is to say, it is made to go somewhere . . .. Creation is that which God enables to exist in time, and is in and through time to bring to its completion, rather like an artist completing a work of art'. Gunton, *The Triune Creator*, p. 12. Cf. Gunton, *The Promise of Trinitarian Theology*, pp. 180–84.

12 Karl Barth, *Church Dogmatics* (13 vols.), edited by G.W. Bromiley and T.F. Torrance (Edinburgh: T&T Clark, 1957–1975), III/1, p. 60.

13 Cf. Colin E. Gunton, *Father, Son and Holy Spirit: Toward a Fully Trinitarian Theology* (London: T&T Clark, 2003), p. 141.

14 Gunton, *The Triune Creator*, pp. 178–79.

15 Friedrich Schleiermacher, *The Christian Faith*, 2nd edn., ed. H.R. Mackintosh and J.S. Stewart (Edinburgh: T&T Clark, 1928), p. 146.

16 Gunton, *The Triune Creator*, pp. 156, 180. Gunton notes that this is most likely due to Schleiermacher's captivity to the Newtonian philosophy of his day, which depicted the universe as 'closed'.

17 Gunton, *The Triune Creator*, p. 181. Gunton elsewhere discusses the notion of freedom at length. See Colin E. Gunton, 'God, Grace and Freedom', in Colin E. Gunton (ed.), *God and Freedom: Essays in Historical and Systematic Theology* (Edinburgh: T&T Clark, 1995), pp. 119–33. Cf. Hans Schaeffer, *Createdness and Ethics: The Doctrine of Creation and Theological Ethics in the Theology of Colin E. Gunton and Oswald Bayer* (Berlin and New York: Walter de Gruyter, 2006), pp. 58–62.

18 Thomas Aquinas, *Summa Theologiae*, 1.22.3. It is important to note that God is not the first cause *in* a hierarchy of secondary causes, for this would make God merely the supreme being among many. For Aquinas, God's essence is identical to God's existence, which makes God *sui generis*. Aquinas, *Summa Theologiae*, 1.3.4.

19 Gunton, *The Triune Creator*, p. 181. Cf. Aquinas, *Summa Theologiae*, 1.104.4; 1.104.2; 1.110.1–1.112.1.

20 Gunton, *The Triune Creator*, p. 182.

21 Gunton, *The Triune Creator*, p. 182. Gunton here follows Alexander Brodie's analysis of John Ireland.

22 Gunton, *The Triune Creator*, p. 183.

23 See above, n. 11.

24 Gunton, *The Triune Creator*, pp. 183–84.

25 Gunton, *The Triune Creator*, p. 184.

26 Gunton, *The Triune Creator*, p. 184.

27 Gunton, *The Triune Creator*, pp. 184, 188–89.

28 Gunton, *The Triune Creator*, p. 186.

29 Gunton, *The Triune Creator*, p. 187.

30 Gunton, *The Triune Creator*, p. 188.

31 Gunton, *The Triune Creator*, p. 189.

32 Gunton, *The Triune Creator*, pp. 189–90.

33 Gunton, *The Triune Creator*, p. 190.

34 Gunton, *The Triune Creator*, p. 190.

35 Gunton, *The Triune Creator*, p. 191.

36 Gunton, *The Triune Creator*, p. 191.

37  Gunton, *The Triune Creator*, pp. 191–92.

38  Cf. Gunton, *The Christian Faith*, p. 64.

39  Gunton, *The Triune Creator*, p. 192.

40  Gunton demonstrates here a certain kinship with Aquinas, who similarly presented God as ordering all things to their appointed end. See, for example, Aquinas, *Summa Theologiae*, 1.22.1.

41  Gunton, *The Triune Creator*, p. 192.

42  Gunton, *The Triune Creator*, p. 192.

43  Gunton, *The Triune Creator*, pp. 180–82.

44  Gunton, *The Triune Creator*, p. 12. Elsewhere, Gunton appears to deny that God intended the Fall; see, for example, Gunton, *The Christian Faith*, p. 64.

45  In other writings, there are potentially fruitful links between the life-giving action of the Spirit and the freedom brought by the Spirit. See, for example, Colin Gunton, 'The Spirit Moved Over the Face of the Waters: The Holy Spirit and the Created Order', *International Journal of Systematic Theology* 4:2 (2002), pp. 192–94.

46  In his sermon on 'Time and Providence', Gunton affirms God's total sovereignty over a person's lifespan, commenting that each person is given sufficient time to do all that God requires from that person. Colin E. Gunton, *Theology Through Preaching: Sermons for Brentwood* (Edinburgh: T&T Clark, 2001), pp. 43–48.

47  This, of course, is itself a matter for debate!

48  It is likely that Gunton would argue that God merely permitted Hitler's actions without willing them. Where human actions are permitted, they 'disrupt the purposes of creation and impede its perfecting'. Conversely, human actions that take place according to God's will 'have their model and basis in the life of Jesus', and so conform to the Spirit's movement. These are authentically human actions in a strong sense and participate in the Spirit's perfecting activity. Gunton is certain that God's determination of the human will is not to the creature's detriment, for 'he does it through the Spirit'. Gunton, *Father, Son and Holy Spirit*, pp. 160–62; quotations from p. 161 and p. 162.

49  Elsewhere, Gunton argues that all divine action is that of the Father, which is 'all equally brought about by his two hands, the Son and the Spirit'. Gunton, *Father, Son and Holy Spirit*, p. 80.

50  Cf. *The Westminster Confession of Faith*, 3.1; 5.1–2.

51  Gunton, *The Christian Faith*, p. x.

52  Gunton, *The Christian Faith*, pp. 7–8.

53  Gunton also provides in this chapter a clear definition of what he means by mediation: 'Mediation denotes the way we understand one form of action – God's action – to take shape in and in relation to that which is not God; the way, that is, by which the actions of one who is creator take form in a world that is of an entirely different order from God, because he made it to be so.' Gunton, *The Christian Faith*, p. 5.

54  Gunton, *The Christian Faith*, p. 10.

55  Gunton, *The Christian Faith*, pp. 16, 19.

56  Gunton, *The Christian Faith*, p. 18.

57  Gunton, *The Christian Faith*, p. 20.

58  Gunton, *The Christian Faith*, p. 21.

59  David Hume, *An Enquiry Concerning Human Understanding*, 7.6, pp. 21–25.

Gunton discusses Hume's position on hidden causes along with those of John Locke and George Berkeley. Gunton, *The Christian Faith*, pp. 21–22.

60  Gunton, *The Christian Faith*, p. 23.

61  Origen, *On First Principles*, 1.6.1–2.

62  Irenaeus, *Against the Heresies*, 3.18.1.

63  Gunton, *The Christian Faith*, pp. 24–25.

64  Gunton simply notes the Stoics' pantheism and determinism, and their concern to clarify the notion of human freedom in a fixed universe.

65  Gunton, *The Christian Faith*, pp. 25–26.

66  Gunton, *The Christian Faith*, p. 27.

67  Gunton himself does not use the phrase 'dualistic providence'.

68  Gunton, *The Christian Faith*, pp. 26–27.

69  Gunton, *The Christian Faith*, pp. 27–28.

70  Gunton, *The Christian Faith*, p. 28.

71  Gunton, *The Christian Faith*, p. 28.

72  Gunton, *The Christian Faith*, p. 29.

73  Does Gunton here imply that the consequences of sin and fallenness experienced now are lessened somehow by God's providential action? If so, this seems quite a speculative assertion.

74  Cf. Gunton, *The Triune Creator*, p. 18; 'Water', in Leland Ryken *et al.*, *Dictionary of Biblical Imagery* (Leicester: InterVarsity Press, 1998), pp. 929–32.

75  Gunton, *The Christian Faith*, p. 29.

76  Gunton, *The Christian Faith*, pp. 29–30.

77  Again, Gunton espouses a view similar to Aquinas, who held that predestination is a corollary of providence, and not vice versa. See Aquinas, *Summa Theologiae*, 1.23.1.

78  Gunton, *The Christian Faith*, pp. 30–31.

79  Gunton, *The Christian Faith*, p. 31.

80  Gunton, *The Christian Faith*, p. 31.

81  Gunton, *The Christian Faith*, pp. 31–33. Cf. Colin Gunton, 'Election and Ecclesiology in the Post-Constantinian Church', *Scottish Journal of Theology* 53:2 (2000), pp. 219–20.

82  Gunton, *The Christian Faith*, pp. 33–34.

83  Gunton, *The Christian Faith*, p. 34.

84  Gunton, *The Christian Faith*, p. 34.

85  Gunton, *The Christian Faith*, pp. 34–35.

86  Gunton, *The Christian Faith*, p. 35.

87  Gunton, *The Christian Faith*, pp. 35–36.

88  Gunton, *The Christian Faith*, p. 36.

89  Gunton, *The Christian Faith*, p. 37.

90  Gunton, *The Christian Faith*, pp. 21–23.

91  Gunton, *The Triune Creator*, p. 192.

92  Early in *The Triune Creator*, Gunton does appear to make providence *an* activity of God, along with conservation, preservation (I am not sure why Gunton distinguishes between these) and redemption; see Gunton, *The Triune Creator*, p. 10. In the definition of providence here under discussion, Gunton includes conservation, redemption and election within the concept of providence. These observations add weight to my claim that Gunton's account of providence in *The Triune Creator* is disjointed.

93 Aquinas, *Summa Theologiae*, 1.19.4; John Calvin, *Institutes*, 1.18.2. For Gunton's critique of Calvin's theology of providence, see Colin E. Gunton, 'The End of Causality? The Reformers and their Predecessors', in Colin E. Gunton (ed.), *The Doctrine of Creation: Essays in Dogmatics, History and Philosophy* (Edinburgh: T&T Clark, 1997), pp. 72–76.

94 Cf. Gunton, *Father, Son and Holy Spirit*, pp. 159–60.

95 See above, 2.2.

96 For an attempt to build on Gunton's insights, see my *Providence Made Flesh: Divine Presence as a Framework for a Theology of Providence* (Milton Keynes: Paternoster, 2009), where I seek to lay a foundation for the doctrine of providence based on the scriptural concept of divine presence realized in Jesus Christ's Spirit-enabled obedience to his Father.

Chapter 11

COLIN GUNTON AND THE THEOLOGICAL
ORIGIN OF MODERNITY

Brad Green

As doctoral students, a never-ending question seemed to follow us from seminar to seminar: what is the nature of 'modernity'? We quickly learned that there were a constellation of main characters and usual suspects – Descartes, Locke, Hume, Kant, *et al.*, and a number of issues whirling about – autonomy, a disinterest in the past, the quest for certainty, etc. We were reading Alasdair McIntyre and Stephen Toulmin avidly but I was not really satisfied with their accounts. Then I stumbled upon Colin Gunton's *The One, the Three and the Many*, his 1992 Bampton Lectures.[1] Here was what I had been looking for – a *theological* account of the nature of modernity.

In *The One, the Three and the Many*, Gunton offers a theologically informed reading, critique and analysis of the nature and origin of modernity. For Gunton, modernity constitutes – at times – a rejection of an inadequate portrayal of the Christian faith, a construal that was *perhaps worthy of rejection*. Of course, this is undoubtedly part of the picture. However, in this chapter, I want to argue that a properly Christian approach to the intellectual life and to notions such as perception and cognition (key to Gunton's understanding of modernity) must work with a more theologically and biblically informed view of such things. By recourse to such figures as St Paul, Augustine, Hugh of St Victor, John Calvin and Pascal, I will argue that our *prior alienation* as fallen persons contributes to the constellation of issues known as 'modernity'. That is to say, it is not simply the case that the modern Enlightenment – an understandable reaction to bad theology in Gunton's view – leads to alienation. Instead, poor thinking is rooted in our fallen state and this – not poor theology – leads to modernity.

The chapter will proceed as follows. First, the chapter summarizes Gunton's general understanding of the nature and origin of modernity, giving attention mainly to two works, *The One, the Three and the Many: God,*

*Creation and the Culture of Modernity*, and *Enlightenment and Alienation: An Essay Toward a Trinitarian Theology*. Second, the chapter attempts to criticize Gunton's understanding by offering a different account of the nature of modernity. While I agree with much in Gunton's account, I suspect that the quotation by William Morris with which Gunton begins *The One, the Three and the Many* – 'Modernism began and continues to *deny* Christ'[2] – is underplayed. Only by extending and deepening what is at the heart of this statement, can modernity be properly understood as fundamentally and integrally rooted in the denial of the lordship of Christ. Ultimately, however, my positive proposal seeks – on the whole – to *supplement* Gunton, rather than simply to *supplant* his work in this area.

### Colin Gunton and the nature of modernity

Gunton's understanding and explication of modernity is a recurring theme in his writing, although it takes centre stage in *The One, the Three and the Many* and *Enlightenment and Alienation*. We will allow the basic structure of Gunton's *The One, the Three and the Many* to structure our summary of Gunton's understanding. In this book Gunton diagnoses the key elements of modernity under four main headings: (1) the one and the many, (2) particularity, (3) relationality and (4) meaning and truth.[3] These four themes are developed in part one, 'The Displacement of God'. At the outset, Gunton writes: 'For all of its unifying vision, the era of Christendom was dearly bought, that is to say, at the expense of certain dimensions of the Christian gospel which became effectively submerged.' Modernity is 'in need of the healing light of the gospel of the Son of God, made incarnate by the Holy Spirit for the perfecting of the creation'.[4] Gunton notes that while *all* cultures are ultimately in need of such healing, there is nonetheless something distinctive or unique about the modern era. The modern era 'is unlike some in that the distinctive features of its plight derive from its rejection of that gospel, albeit for some understandable reasons'. For Gunton, something more than the 'mere denunciation' of modernity is therefore necessary: 'Christianity is indeed offensive to the natural human mind; and yet it is often made offensive by its representatives for the wrong reasons.'[5] Gunton's overarching concern therefore is 'to aid a process of healing the fragmentation which is so much a feature of our world' by constructing a better account of the gospel.[6]

For Gunton, it is clear that certain theological construals – particularly those of the Western church – have, in a sense, been an impetus for the development of modernity. Central here is the doctrine of creation, and a chief concern of Gunton's is the poor way this doctrine has developed.

To wit: 'There is a relation between the way the doctrine of creation was formulated in the West and the shape that modern culture has taken.'[7] Indeed, 'modernity, in its greatness and pathos, has a queer and what could be called dialectical relation to that most central and neglected of Christian doctrines'.[8] Also central to Gunton is the advancement of a more properly trinitarian conception of God. He writes:

> [A]n account of relationality that gives due weight to both one and many, to both particular and universal, to both otherness and relation, is to be derived from the one place where they can satisfactorily be based, a conception of God who is both one and three, whose being consists in a relationality that derives from the otherness-in-relation of Father, Son and Spirit.[9]

By attending to God as properly trinitarian, we will be helped in overcoming – at least to a degree – our modern malaise, a malaise which is due in part to a somewhat justifiable rejection of inadequate theological construals. Let us now turn to the first of Gunton's four key themes that constitute his understanding of modernity – the issue of the 'one and the many' – to see how his diagnosis plays itself out in detail.

## The one and the many

Gunton takes the perennial philosophical problem of the one and the many as the key theme of chapter 1 of *The One, the Three and the Many* (and it can be argued that this theme underpins Gunton's overarching theological program). The Christian tradition – at least in the West – has tended (due largely to influences like Augustine) to conceive of God fundamentally as a unity, or as 'one'. In the modern era there has been a general rejection of this overemphasis on the oneness and unity of God, in that the modern era has recoiled at the seemingly oppressive nature of such a deity. Gunton writes that 'for the most part the Western theological tradition has preferred Parmenides to Heraclitus in its search for a focus of unity. The God of most Western philosophy is single, simple and unchanging. And that is the problem'.[10]

## Particularity

The second key theme Gunton treats is the issue of particularity. Modernity – legitimately reacting against certain strands in the Western tradition – has displaced God, and thus there is 'no God to give things space in which to be', and 'we lose the space between one another and between ourselves and the world of particulars without which we are not truly what we are'.[11]

Interestingly, in this chapter on *particularity* the heart of the issue is still *displacement*. And it is a displacement linked to the elevation of the human will, an elevation and ultimately a perversion of a proper understanding of humanity that does not give full attention to the createdness and fallenness of man – and of the confusion that results from failing to come to terms with humanity's createdness and fallenness. Gunton writes: 'When any human activity becomes the realm of pure will, of a putative creation out of nothing, the problems of particularity and freedom are exacerbated, not solved.'[12] Without the reality of the triune God of the Christian faith, 'particularity' is increasingly difficult to account for, understand and affirm.

## Relationality

From the 'displacement of God' (chapter 1) to 'particularity' (chapter 2) Gunton moves to 'relationality' (chapter 3), though he is still tracing out the implications of the displacement of God, and of how best to make sense of particularity. For the question of 'relationality' is the question of 'how particular things and persons are understood to be related to one another'.[13] Gunton sees the question of *relationality* as integrally linked to a proper understanding of *time*. Because of the development in the West of a poor theological understanding of time – where time is, for example, simply the stage upon which redemption occurs – there is pressure to give less than full weight to the importance of particulars and hence of the nature of the relations of particulars. This is a true crisis: 'Modern culture is marked by a pathological inability to live in the present, while at the same time, as in the consumer culture, it is unable to live anywhere but in the present.'[14] Thus, because we are unable theologically to construe a proper understanding of the present, we are thereby unable to properly understand the nature of the relationality of particulars.

## Meaning and truth

The fourth chapter deals with the issues of meaning and truth. The key issue is still the displacement of God, and all that flows from that. As Gunton writes, 'Because God no longer features as the one who provides the coordinates by which life's various activities are related, the fragmentation so characteristic of Western experience follows in the train of the developments we have followed'.[15] Kant looms large in Gunton's account, and in two main areas. First, for Kant 'the basis of meaning was shifted from "referral and self-referral to a transcendent dimension" to self-referral alone'.[16] Second, the will for Kant was 'conceived in abstraction from any foundation in other aspects of the person or in its broader environment'.[17] The result of these two components of Kant's thought was 'a radical disruption of the relation of the transcendental realms of truth, goodness and beauty, and so also of the unity of thought and culture'.[18] And thus, modernity continues to struggle to properly construe the reality of meaning and truth.

## Gunton and the healing of modernity

### Establishing meaning and truth

Having traced Gunton's understanding of the dilemma in some detail, we now move to Gunton's understanding of the way ahead – Gunton's 'solution' to the vexing issues of modernity, we might say. Gunton states his overarching goal for the second main part of *The One, the Three and the Many* by saying that the Christian theologian must 'seek for ways to rehabilitate or reinvigorate the concept of truth, without, however, ignoring the genuine weaknesses of that against which much modern thought has reacted'.[19] Gunton therefore seeks 'a renewed theological vision of truth that does justice to the concerns of modernity and offers a way forward that is free of some of the weaknesses of the Western tradition'.[20] Ultimately, for Gunton the key problems that he has elucidated are an inadequate theology of creation and the modern displacement of God. The 'answer' is to be found in a proper construal and understanding of creation rooted in the fully trinitarian God, for in such a theological vision we have a more robustly Christian and proper way of thinking about and construing particularity, relationality and meaning and truth.

Gunton turns to Coleridge to borrow the notion of 'idea'. 'Ideas' are realities which, when contemplated, give rise to other insights. Gunton suggests that the Trinity is the 'idea of ideas', and that through contemplation upon this 'idea of ideas', *transcendentals* are generated. The transcendentals which emerge as we reflect upon the Trinity can shed light on the key issues of the first part of *The One, the Three and the Many*: relationality, particularity, temporality and 'the status and relationship of the three great transcendentals of truth, goodness, and beauty'.[21]

### The recovery of relationality

In the sixth chapter, the second of his 'solution' chapters, Gunton deals with relationality. Essentially, Gunton suggests that 'perichoresis' may be one of the 'open transcendentals' of which he has been speaking. Gunton has raised the question of time and space (and the fact that we are temporal and spatial beings) and asks if perhaps humanity and all of reality can be understood in a 'perichoretic' way. He writes, 'If things can be so understood, if to be temporal and spatial is to echo in some way, however faintly, the being of God, may we not find in this concept a way of holding things together that modernity so signally lacks'.[22] Indeed, 'If God is God, he is the source of all being, meaning and truth. It would seem reasonable to suppose that all being, meaning and truth is, even as created and distinct from God, in some way marked by its relatedness to its creator'.[23]

## *The importance of the particular*

Gunton then considers the question of particularity (chapter 7). Granted, Gunton notes, Christianity is a faith rooted in particulars – the *particular* nation of Israel and the *particular* person Jesus Christ. And modernity – with its various homogenizing forces – mitigates against particularity. What is needed? '[A] theology giving central place to particularity is precisely what the modern age needs.'[24]

The heart of this chapter is the explication of the transcendental of *hypostasis*, defined by Gunton as 'substantial particular'.[25] And it is in the recovery of such a transcendental (or in the insights generated by reflection upon such a transcendental) that we might begin to heal our age from the homogenizing forces of modernity: 'It is by developing the practical implications of such a transcendentality that the threatened and incipient homogenization of culture and reality can be counteracted.'[26] In simple terms, 'All particulars are formed by their relationship to God the creator and redeemer and to each other'.[27]

## *Back to the one and the many*

In the final chapter of *The One, the Three and the Many*, Gunton brings his argument to a close and seeks one final transcendental, this time in the context of the question of the one and the many – the question which has been nearby throughout the volume. This final transcendental is 'relationality', above all as seen in God as a 'unity of persons in relation', that provides the root of a proper way of construing and understanding humanity's place in the world, and how properly to think of God, human beings, and the rest of the created order. To wit: 'the created world, as that which is what it distinctively is by virtue of its createdness, reflects in different ways the being of God in communion'.[28] As Gunton writes, 'The theology of the Trinity as dynamic personal order of giving and receiving is, in the idea of sociality that it suggests, the key to the matter of transcendentality that we are seeking'.[29]

## *Colin Gunton and modernity: appreciation and critique*

I want to suggest that while Gunton's critique of the nature and modernity is at many points brilliant and illuminating, it might be strengthened. There are two key pillars or tendencies in Gunton's construal that I want to critique. These two tendencies are (1) the tendency to construe our modern quandary mainly in terms of improper theological construals or constructs (particularly certain intellectual missteps or errors), and (2) the tendency to see our alienation as flowing from rather than contributing to the various intellectual errors and missteps that developed in the modern era. These two tendencies are clearly intertwined. In terms of the first tendency, Gunton sees modernity chiefly in terms of certain intellectual developments – for example overemphasizing the *one* in relationship to the *many*. In terms of the second tendency, Gunton argues that certain missteps (e.g. emphasizing the one over the many) has engendered modern alienation (and again the modern person's tendency to reject certain theological construals is often seen by Gunton as justified or at the least understandable due to the poor nature of much of Western Christendom). I will suggest that because Gunton's analysis of the nature and origin of modernity is somewhat flawed, likewise Gunton's suggestions for what provides healing in the light of modernity indeed may be flawed.

Let me put my goals as simply possible. Gunton sees modernity generally in terms of getting the ideas or concepts *wrong*, and then naturally tends to see the healing of modernity as primarily a matter of getting the ideas or concepts *right*. To wit, modernity has tended to get the idea of God terribly wrong, and hence the healing of modernity is primarily concerned with the formulation of a better idea of God. I want to change things a bit and suggest that modernity does indeed include certain intellectual developments (like getting the idea of God wrong), but that more attention should be given to the cognitive and noetic effects of human sinfulness, and how mistaken intellectual developments should be seen *at least in part* as rooted in the reality of human sinfulness. But if modernity's problem is at least in part due to, in Paul's terms, the suppression of the knowledge of God (Romans 1), or 'disordered loves' (Augustine), or the eyes of the heart being in need of cleansing (Hugh of St Victor), or our corrupted knowledge (Calvin), or our moral decadence (Pascal), then we will be forced to think about the path to the healing of modernity's ills in a different way as well. To that extent I am in agreement with Stephen N. Williams: 'Gunton wrongly appraises the texture of modernity and hence, to change the figure, approaches the healing task with the wrong implements.'[30]

## *The centrality of Scripture*

I will initially take my cue from Paul. Paul writes that the wrath of God is being 'revealed against all ungodliness and unrighteousness of men, who by their unrighteousness suppress the truth' (1.18).[31] Paul teaches that the created order reveals certain things about this God, and that this revelation has been given to all persons. And importantly, it is *not* simply the case that man knows *that* there is God. Rather, man truly knows *certain things* about this God, or better put, man *knows* God, although not necessarily salvifically. Thus, what can be known about God '*is plain to them*', for God '*has shown it to them*' (1.19). And what really is it that man knows? Strikingly, Paul contends that man actually knows God's 'invisible attributes, namely, his eternal power and divine nature' (1.20). These attributes have been 'clearly perceived' (1.20), and persons 'knew God' (1.21). But this knowledge has been suppressed (1.18), and Paul recounts a long line of results of such suppression, which both leads to and/or is constituted by not honouring God (1.21): the darkening of the heart (1.21), futile thinking (1.21), idolatry (1.22-23), sexual perversion (1.24-27), a debased mind (1.28), being filled with a long list of other sins (1.28-32) and ultimately to approving those who practice such sins (1.32).

All persons – despite their protestations to the contrary – believe in God, if not salvifically. Sadly, all persons suppress this knowledge, and this suppression can lead to the horrific consequences outlined in Romans 1. For Paul our intellectual lives are integrally related to, shaped by, and informed by, our spiritual state. Or rather, our acts of knowledge (or the acts of suppressing knowledge) are inherently and inescapably *moral* and *wilful* and *spiritual* acts. Thus, for Paul mankind is 'without excuse' when he suppresses the knowledge of God (1.20). Whereas Paul sees sinful humanity as recoiling from the truth, Gunton often sees humanity as recoiling from poor theological constructs. But perhaps more importantly, whereas Paul sees human knowing as fundamentally moral and wilful, and as bent toward rebellion, Gunton seems rarely to approach the act of human knowing and thinking with such a Pauline trajectory. Gunton's tendency, at least it seems to me, is to construe the intellectual developments of modernity as consisting of two main strands: (1) the traditional developments of which students of modern thought are aware – i.e. the usual figures such as Hume, Kant, Locke, Berkeley, Hegel, etc. – and Gunton often gives fascinating interpretations of such figures; (2) a second strand in which modern persons naturally (intuitively?) reject the onerous and ill-conceived theological construals – construals almost always associated with the Western theological tradition. But attention is generally *not* given to the notion that the intellectual development of modernity might fundamentally and inextricably be bound up with a fallen tendency to resist the truth of God, a tendency outlined explicitly by Paul in Romans 1.[32]

On reading Paul, it appears that there is an inextricable link between the state of our hearts and our knowing process or intellectual life. Stephen N. Williams summarizes his understanding of the link between one's own spiritual state and knowing something: 'if his [i.e. Jesus'] claims are true, the disposition of the heart is relevant to discerning them as such. Those convinced of the fact of divine reconciliation should thereby be convinced that intellectual conviction is not attained in a kind of spiritual vacuum. One must have bared one's soul, even reckoned oneself as some kind of sinner.'[33] To be fair to Gunton it should be noted that at times he argues in a way very similar to how I am arguing here. For example, in *The Actuality of Atonement* Gunton – referencing Kierkegaard – writes: 'authentic Christianity is intrinsically offensive. Its very particularity, and even more its centering of doctrines of God and salvation on the figure of a crucified teacher in such a way that the teacher becomes the teaching, is an offence to the intellect and moral sense of the "natural" person.' Indeed, 'It offends the moral sense also that human redemption should come as sheer gift in so unattractive a packaging.'[34] Later in the same work Gunton can speak of the Enlightenment's 'demonic human self-confidence and lack of a doctrine of sin'.[35] I suspect that a fuller fleshing-out of these insights over Gunton's corpus would have resulted in a somewhat different understanding of modernity.

Stephen N. Williams also insightfully argues that Gunton may have difficulty accounting for certain events in the life of Jesus. Particularly, do we not read in the gospels that it is the fuller and further revelation of the Son and the Holy Spirit that elicits such violent opposition from certain Jewish leaders (e.g. the parable of the tenant, where the landowner's *son* is murdered by the current tenants)? That is, it is further revelation of the persons of Son and Spirit that lead to violent rebellion. It is not a *misunderstanding* of the nature of God that elicits a vigorous response. Rather, it is the *true and proper* understanding of Son and Spirit that elicits a violent response. As Williams notes, 'According to the New Testament presentation of matters, the more clearly the divine nature and ways are presented, the more manifestly the rebel will breaks the cover of its concealment'.[36] Thus, a biblical anthropology reveals that in our fallen state our human tendency is not to gravitate toward better theological construals *or* to resist poor theological construals. Rather, the more fully God reveals himself, the fallen sinner's mode is to resist such revelation.

Indeed, we often get things 'wrong' because at some fundamental level we *choose* or *want* to get things wrong – an unsettling notion indeed. Our problem is that we simply do not see things the way they are. Gunton writes of the Enlightenment: 'in a number of ways it has at the same time prevented us from seeing things as they are'.[37] This is getting at the heart of the matter. We *do* have a problem seeing things as 'they are'. But the problem is not simply the Enlightenment. It is probably better to say – with Paul, Augustine, Hugh of St Victor, Calvin, Pascal, *et al.* – that our problem in seeing things as 'they are' is rooted in disordered loves and a will and heart that is 'bent'. And *then* the Enlightenment might be said to be both (1) a manifestation of such disordered loves, and (2) an exacerbation and furthering of such disordered loves in a particular time and place.

We might turn to any number of places in Scripture for similar testimony. In Colossians 1.20 the non-Christian is spoken of as being hostile to God in *mind,* and in Ephesians 2.3 Paul speaks of the *thoughts* of the sinful nature. Romans 12.2 commands persons to be 'transformed by the renewing of your *mind*'. Ephesians 4.23 speaks of being made new 'in the attitude of your *mind*'. Indeed, Paul can speak of his mission partly in terms of destroying 'arguments' and 'lofty opinions' and of taking 'every thought captive to the *obedience* of Christ' (2 Cor. 10.5). Biblically, even the demonic realm *recognizes* the Son and his divine status – and resists and recoils (Mk 1.24 ff.). Interestingly, key to Jesus' critique of certain Jewish leaders was his teaching that it was because of their love of receiving glory from each other that they were unable to believe (Jn 5.44). And their failure to recognize the reality and lordship of Jesus was due to a prior and apparently consistent failure to believe what God had spoken through Moses. In short, resistance to the revelation of God at one point in redemptive history was integrally related to a resistance of the (fuller) revelation of God at a later point in redemptive history (Jn 5.46-47). Indeed, Jesus was rejected by some because they *loved* darkness (Jn 3.19). In short, Scripture consistently links our ability to know with our desires and loves, and with the state of our hearts, and the reality of sin shapes and mitigates and twists our ability to know.

## *Lessons from the tradition*

Not surprisingly, we find similar insights into the nature of the knowing or thinking process in Augustine. Augustine contends that in both knowledge of the created order and in the knowledge of God sin plays a large part. In his *Confessions*, Augustine affirms that creation is indeed beautiful – objectively beautiful. But, when some people look at creation they do not really 'see' the beauty that is there.[38] But how can that be? Is it beautiful to some and not to others? Not at all. Some persons do not see the beauty *that is really there* because of disordered loves. Their disordered loves prevent such persons from actually seeing reality.[39] In terms of seeing God, Augustine can argue in *On the Trinity* – against certain Neo-Platonists – that our destiny as Christians is to see the triune God one day face to face, and in order to see this God our minds must be purified and transformed by the gospel.[40] In short, the beatific vision is a vision that is only attainable by travelling through a bloody cross. As Earl Muller has written in summarizing Augustine's argument: '*there can be no intellectus* [understanding] *apart from the concrete sacrificial act of Christ*'.[41] Muller continues: Augustine '*refuses to deal with anything above the human mind without first purifying his mind in the sacrifice of Christ, the only way for sinful humans to obtain the eternal*'.[42] And, as Augustine writes in *The Teacher*, Christ is the 'Teacher' who illumines the human mind in *every* act of knowing, showing the knower – among other things – how a particular word refers to a particular thing. In short, for Augustine, to know or understand God or the created order is to know with a mind that has been transformed by the gospel.

Hugh of St Victor (d. 1141), similarly wrestled with the nature of human knowing, as seen particularly in his *Didascalicon*. Thus, referencing Socrates, Hugh can write: 'the eye of the heart must be cleansed by the study of virtue, so that it may thereafter see clearly for the investigation of truth in the theoretical arts'.[43] It is appropriate that Hugh has been dubbed the 'other Augustine' (*alter Augustinus*) for he – like Augustine – is concerned to think about the intellectual life in relationship to the work of Christ. All of the arts are linked ultimately to (and subservient to) 'divine wisdom'. In such divine wisdom consists 'knowledge of truth and love of virtue; and this is the true restoration of man'.[44] Restoration, for Hugh, is brought about by atonement, and restoration consists of 'knowledge of truth and love of virtue'.

Knowledge was central to the nature and method of John Calvin's theology. He structured the first two books of his *Institutes* around two key 'knowledge' issues: (1) the knowledge of God the Creator, and (2) the knowledge of God the Redeemer. Additionally, he opens the *Institutes* with the *duplex cognitio* ('two-fold knowledge'): knowledge of God and knowledge of the self. For Calvin to know God is to honour him,[45] and real and true knowledge of God is a gift from him.[46] Indeed, knowledge of God has been implanted in every person. Sadly, all persons 'degenerate' from this true knowledge.[47] Thus, instead of apprehending God 'as he offers himself', persons imagine God 'as they have fashioned him in their own presumptions'.[48] This implanted knowledge goes to waste, and therefore Scripture is necessary to give us a fuller knowledge of God,[49] the knowledge of which should primarily be sought in God's *works*, not in his 'essence' *per se*.[50] Apart from Scripture our minds are like 'labyrinths' leading to falsehoods. Thus, for Calvin, we should locate our cognitive errors, weaknesses and missteps (generally) in our fallen state. We should *then* seek to tease out the repercussions and consequences of these various intellectual developments – and it is this latter step that Gunton does so brilliantly. But I suspect he starts in the wrong place by not giving necessary attention – as do Augustine, Hugh and Calvin – to the fact that our cognitive and intellectual missteps and errors are first and foremost rooted in human sinfulness and fallenness. To quote Stephen Williams again: 'The theology of the Reformers themselves consistently reminds us that the biblical drama is about the tragedy of a world alienated and loved in spiritual rebellion, root of our cognitive dysfunction'.[51] Knowing or thinking are acts that are inextricably moral and wilful – and are bound up with who we are as sinful and fallen beings.

Finally, we turn to Pascal. In some senses Pascal gives us some of the most provocative insights. Pascal repeatedly spoke of the intellectual life as inextricably a part of our moral lives. For example, he wrote: 'The greatness of wisdom, which is nothing if it does not come from God, is invisible to carnal and intellectual people. They are three orders differing in kind'.[52] Indeed, Pascal expresses *concern* for 'those who seek God apart from Christ'.[53] Pascal also writes:

> Not only do we only know God through Jesus Christ, but we only know ourselves through Jesus Christ; we only know life and death through Jesus Christ. Apart from Jesus Christ we cannot know the meaning of our life or our death, of God or of ourselves. Thus without Scripture, whose only object is Christ, we know nothing, and can see nothing but obscurity and confusion in the nature of God and in nature itself.[54]

Even Friedrich Nietzsche quotes Pascal on the relationship between our moral decay and our inability to know the truth: 'Our inability to know the truth is the consequence of our corruption, our moral decay'.[55] For Pascal it is our moral rebellion and fallenness that hinder and prohibit our knowing the truth. Indeed, 'Those who do not love truth excuse themselves on the grounds that it is disputed and that very many people deny it. Thus their error is solely due to the fact that they love neither truth nor charity, so they have no excuse'.[56] We are again in the land of Paul, Augustine, Hugh and Calvin, and it is this anthropology and understanding of sin that could inform and strengthen Gunton's understanding of modernity.

## *The nature of the (fallen) human mind and heart*

By not attending sufficiently to what I will call a biblical-Pauline anthropology or understanding of sin, it might also be the case that Gunton is prone to abstraction. Here again Stephen Williams is helpful. The problem with Gunton's proposal, as Williams sees it, is that Gunton's schema is 'excessively abstract'.[57] As Williams notes, for Gunton the problem is not the *will* or the *clash* of wills but the *belief* that the will is primary. In short, the problem is an intellectual one, a cognitive error, of getting certain concepts right. And Williams can conclude, 'getting such *concepts* of particularity right does not take us far in the healing of culture'.[58]

Yet Gunton wrote that 'the triune God is the one who, as creator and sustainer of a real world of which we are a part, *makes it possible for us to know our world*'.[59] But what has happened now that man has rebelled against his maker? It is our spiritual rebellion, *and how this rebellion affects our thinking and knowing process* that seems to me to be underplayed in Gunton's work. Gunton appropriately turns to Michael Polanyi, and approvingly quotes Polanyi on Augustine: 'In the fourth century A.D. St. Augustine brought the history of Greek philosophy to a close by inaugurating for the first time a post-critical philosophy. He taught that all knowledge was a gift of grace, for which we must strive under the guidance of antecedent belief . . .'[60] Exactly. But this Augustinian/Polanyian insight does not appear to have been traced out consistently in Gunton's understanding of modernity. Knowledge is *indeed* a gift, and it certainly *is* the case that we must 'strive' in our 'antecedent belief'. But what if 'antecedent belief' is missing? That is, what if the knower does not have such belief? The Augustinian approach (echoed here by Polanyi) is that – of course – of faith seeking understanding. But does not a fully Augustinian (and Pauline/biblical) view of knowing lead us to the conclusion that just as knowledge is a *gift* of a merciful and good God, so too unbelief and spiritual rebellion hamper, distort and prohibit the knowing process amongst those persons who have not bowed their knees to Jesus?

One could hardly find a better summary of the modern spirit as when Gunton summarizes Kant: 'It is inappropriate for the human individual to receive instructions from anyone or anything outside his or her own reason'.[61] This is also a good summary of the (fallen) human tendency to reject instruction or wisdom from outside the self, including instruction or wisdom of a divine kind. Although Gunton does not move in the direction (generally) that this chapter is seeking to go, he does *raise* the question I am trying to ask. Gunton writes: 'The Enlightenment's programme is to replace God with the individual as the source of all authority'. And Gunton continues, 'We must now move on to an examination of some of the reasons why it thought this to be necessary'.[62] On a traditional Christian understanding, the idea that a person would resist receiving 'instructions from anyone or anything outside his or her own reason' points to a deep and real spiritual problem – the reality of rebellion and pride. But while Gunton certainly would *not* deny human sinfulness, the Pauline trajectory I am trying to outline in this chapter does not appear to be central to his diagnosis of modernity.

As we have noted, Gunton's tendency is to affirm the propriety of certain modern rejections of poor Western theological construals – particularly those that highlight the *oneness* or the *power* of God. But Gunton's cautious concession to the propriety of rebellion against such an all-powerful God seems odd: 'God does appear to be an authoritarian power against which revolt may seem to be an appropriate reaction'.[63] This concession seems a bit out of balance. Gunton suggests that it is understandable that persons – including Sartre – would resist inadequate ways in which divine omnipotence has been construed in much of Christian theology. But is *that* the best way to understand what Sartre – in this particular example – was rebelling against? When we look at Scripture, is poor theology what people tend to resist? Is not the pattern in Scripture a long, sad story of resisting what is *true*? And resisting *that which one knows – at some fundamental level – to be true*? Perhaps we could read Gunton charitably here as someone simply trying to concede weaknesses in the history of Christian theological work. Perhaps. But the pattern in Gunton's work is often one of attributing resistance to the God of Abraham, Isaac and Jacob to rightful wariness of poor theological constructs, rather than a stubborn or wicked or deceitful heart.

Interestingly, Gunton at one point suggests that Adam, 'as representative alienated man, did aspire to a kind of Kantian and Sartrian autonomy and self-assertion'.[64] That is, in attempting to live 'autonomously', Adam was rebelling against God. Here Gunton begins to sound something like a traditional Reformed theologian – almost like a Cornelius Van Til. But Gunton does not linger here long. I wish he had, for in coming to terms with the nature of man's desire for autonomy we certainly gain insight into at least one of the driving forces of modernity: a spiritual and moral rebellion whereby man seeks to live and think on his own terms, without worshipping and honouring the God who has created us and who supplies even the possibility of life and thought.

## Conclusion

There is indeed no end to the making of books, and many of these have attempted to explore the nature of the so-called 'modern' and 'post-modern' worlds. Gunton served the Christian community well by encouraging her members to think theologically about the nature of our age. Certainly any *Christian* account of modernity and post-modernity must face head-on one of the central marks of the modern age: the desire to displace the God of Holy Scripture. If one's account attempts to dodge that issue, it can scarcely be called Christian. I have tried to show that greater attention to a Christian understanding of the knowing and intellectual life might both (1) make recourse to many of Gunton's brilliant insights, but (2) go higher up and farther in by giving greater attention to the realities of sin and the way in which the fallen knower and thinker inevitably resists the truth of God, and suppresses what one knows to be true – whether in this or in any other age.

## Notes

1   Colin E. Gunton, *The One, the Three and the Many: God, Creation and the Culture of Modernity* (Cambridge: Cambridge University Press, 1993). I have been learning from Gunton since first discovering this book. My doctoral dissertation at Baylor University (Waco, TX), 'Colin Gunton and the Failure of Augustine: An Exposition and Analysis of the Theology of Colin Gunton in Light of Augustine's De Trinitate', explores Gunton's generally negative assessment of Augustine. The thesis of this chapter picks up, in a sense, where my dissertation left off.

2   Gunton, *The One, the Three and the Many*, p. 1. Gunton is quoting Peter Fuller, *Theoria, Art, and the Absence of Grace* (London: Chatto and Windus, 1988), p. 130.

3   Gunton, *The One, the Three and the Many*, p. 129. The first four chapters of *The One, the Three and the Many* offer a diagnosis of modernity, and then the fifth through eighth chapters offer a theological response to modernity. It should be noted that chapters 1 through 4, and chapters 5 through 8 form a chiasm: chapter 5 responds to chapter 4, chapter 6 to chapter 3, chapter 7 to chapter 2, and chapter 8 to chapter 1.

4   Gunton, *The One, the Three and the Many*, p. 1.

5   Gunton, *The One, the Three and the Many*, p. 1.

6   Gunton, *The One, the Three and the Many*, p. 7. This language is common in Gunton's work. For example, Gunton writes in *Enlightenment and Alienation*: 'an understanding of God as triune enables us to develop an account of the way things are, an account of the intelligibility and rationality of God and of the world as it depends upon, and is given to us to be known, by him', and to point to 'possibilities in Christian theology for illuminating and healing our modern existence'. Colin E. Gunton, *Enlightenment and Alienation: An Essay Toward a Trinitarian Theology* (Eugene, OR: Wipf and Stock, 2006), p. 53.

7   Gunton, *The One, the Three and the Many*, p. 3.

8   Gunton, *The One, the Three and the Many*, p. 4.

9   Gunton, *The One, the Three and the Many*, pp. 6–7.

10   Gunton, *The One, the Three and the Many*, p. 24.

11   Gunton, *The One, the Three and the Many*, p. 71.

12   Gunton, *The One, the Three and the Many*, pp. 72–73.

13   Gunton, *The One, the Three and the Many*, p. 74.

14   Gunton, *The One, the Three and the Many*, p. 99.

15   Gunton, *The One, the Three and the Many*, p. 116.

16   Gunton, *The One, the Three and the Many*, pp. 116–17.

17   Gunton, *The One, the Three and the Many*, p. 117.

18   Gunton, *The One, the Three and the Many*, p. 117

19 Gunton, *The One, the Three and the Many*, p. 129.
20 Gunton, *The One, the Three and the Many*, p. 130.
21 Gunton, *The One, the Three and the Many*, p. 150.
22 Gunton, *The One, the Three and the Many*, pp. 165–66.
23 Gunton, *The One, the Three and the Many*, pp. 166–67.
24 Gunton, *The One, the Three and the Many*, p. 181.
25 Gunton, *The One, the Three and the Many*, p. 203.
26 Gunton, *The One, the Three and the Many*, p. 203.
27 Gunton, *The One, the Three and the Many*, p. 207.
28 Gunton, *The One, the Three and the Many*, p. 217.
29 Gunton, *The One, the Three and the Many*, p. 225.
30 Stephen N. Williams, *Revelation and Reconciliation: A Window on Modernity* (Cambridge: Cambridge University Press, 1995), p. 172.
31 Unless otherwise noted, all scriptural references in English are from the *English Standard Version*.
32 Gunton at times inches in the direction I am suggesting. For example in the loss of the particular to various homogenizing influences modern culture is 'confusing the creature and the creator, and will destroy itself' (*The One, the Three and the Many*, p. 203). Gunton here is referencing Romans 1, and *that* is the right direction.
33 Williams, *Revelation and Reconciliation*, p. 146.
34 Colin E. Gunton, *The Actuality of Atonement: A Study of Metaphor, Rationality and the Christian Tradition* (Grand Rapids, MI: William B. Eerdmans Publishing Company, 1989), p. 24.
35 Gunton, *The Actuality of Atonement*, p. 176.
36 Williams, *Revelation and Reconciliation*, p. 170.
37 Gunton, *Enlightenment and Alienation*, p. 112.
38 Augustine, *Confessions*, II.vi.12. Cf. *Confessions*, II.iv.9; X.vi.9.
39 Augustine, *Confessions*, X.vi.10.
40 Augustine argues along these lines in Books IV and XIII of *On the Trinity*. Gunton spends time both in *The One, the Three and the Many* and *Enlightenment and Alienation* on the notion of vision. Thus, in *The One, the Three and the Many* he writes: 'Thus it is that with the eyes given us by the doctrine of the Spirit we are enabled to see that substance is a kind of transcendental'. Fair enough, but might it not be better to speak of the 'eyes given us by the Spirit' *himself*?
41 Earl C. Muller, 'Rhetorical and Theological Issues in the Structuring of Augustine's *De Trinitate*' in *Studia Patristica* XXVII, edited by Elizabeth A. Livingstone (Leuven: Peeters, 1993), p. 359.
42 Ibid., p. 362.
43 Hugh of St. Victor, *Didascalicon*, translated by Jerome Taylor (New York: Columbia University Press, 1991), 'Appendix A: Division of the Contents of Philosophy', p. 154.
44 Hugh of St. Victor, *On the Sacraments of the Christian Faith*, translated by Roy J. Deferrari (Eugene, OR: Wipf and Stock, 2007), Prologue. 6, pp. 5–6.
45 John Calvin, *Institutes of the Christian Religion*, edited by John T. McNeil and translated by Ford Lewis Battles (Philadelphia: The Westminster Press, 1960), I.I.1.
46 Calvin, *Institutes of the Christian Religion*, I.I.1.

47  Calvin, *Institutes of the Christian Religion*, I.IV.1.
48  Calvin, *Institutes of the Christian Religion*, I.IV.1.
49  Calvin, *Institutes of the Christian Religion*, I.IV.1.
50  Calvin, *Institutes of the Christian Religion*, I.V.9.
51  Williams, *Revelation and Reconciliation*, p. 173.
52  Blaise Pascal, *Pensèes*, translated by A.J. Krailsheimer (Harmondsworth: Penguin Books, 1966), p. 308.
53  Pascal, *Pensèes*, p. 449.
54  Pascal, *Pensèes*, p. 417. Emphasis mine. I was led to this Pascal quote through the provocative book by James R. Peters, *The Logic of the Heart: Augustine, Pascal, and the Rationality of Faith* (Grand Rapids, MI: Baker Academic, 2009), p. 161.
55  Friedrich Nietzsche, *The Will to Power*, translated by Walter Kaufmann and R.J. Hollingdale (New York: Vintage Books, 1968), I.83.
56  Pascal, B. *Pensèes,* p. 176.
57  Williams, *Revelation and Reconciliation*, p. 171.
58  Williams, *Revelation and Reconciliation*, p. 171.
59  Gunton, *Enlightenment and Alienation*, p. 52. Emphasis mine.
60  Gunton, *Enlightenment and Alienation*, p. 51. Gunton is quoting Michael Polanyi, *Personal Knowledge: Toward a Post-Critical Philosophy* (Chicago: University of Chicago Press, 1974), p. 266.
61  Gunton, *Enlightenment and Alienation*, p. 61.
62  Gunton, *Enlightenment and Alienation*, p. 63.
63  Gunton, *Enlightenment and Alienation*, p. 65.
64  Gunton, *Enlightenment and Alienation*, p. 95.

# Chapter 12

## THE SHAPE OF COLIN GUNTON'S THEOLOGY. ON THE WAY TOWARDS A FULLY TRINITARIAN THEOLOGY

### Christoph Schwöbel

The title of this chapter seems rather 'shapeless'. We associate shape with the physical forms of material objects, but can it also be applied to a theology? What I have in mind is the configuration of theological themes and theses, reflecting various influences, from inside and outside theology, which have come together in Colin Gunton's career to form a structured whole of connected theological insights, combining positions he shared with others with his own particular emphases. Over the years, the development of Gunton's theology has been shaped by his conversations with his teachers and his colleagues, by new reading, which often resulted from these conversations, and by the inspirations that came from his doctoral students. He consciously sought to integrate these insights in his attempt to work out his own theology.

However, originality in matters theological was not one of Gunton's aims. In fact, he was convinced that whenever a theologian claimed too much originality he or she was in danger of deviating from the teaching of the Church or, more seriously still, from the gospel, thus losing touch with the very basis of Christian theology. His theological work was therefore consciously conducted on the basis of scriptural exegesis and by constantly referring back to the creeds of the Church, which, for Gunton, somehow paradoxically, seemed like an unplumbed mine of theological wisdom. Further, Gunton's theology was consciously located in the Church as a communion of people whose life has been shaped in a particular way as a response to the presence of the triune God in their lives, liberating them for the proclamation of the gospel, the celebration of God's presence in word and sacraments, and for the 'reasonable worship' (Romans 12.1), which includes theology.

The integration of these different influences occurred with increasing intensity under the heading of Trinitarian theology, which, for Gunton, defines definitively that which makes Christian theology *Christian* and that which makes it *theology*. It makes theology theology because God can only be known if God gives himself to be known in the way the Father relates to us through the Son in the Spirit. Since this relationship is focused in Christ as the Son who knows the Father and makes the Father known in the Spirit it deserves the name 'Christian', which refers back to Jesus the Christ, his life, death and resurrection, and forward to his coming in glory. The shaping of Gunton's theology can therefore most appropriately be described as the process by which he brought all these different theological influences, ecclesial experiences and interpretations of our situation into the framework of a trinitarian understanding of God as the comprehensive frame for understanding God in a Christian theological sense.

The formation of Gunton's theology can in this manner be understood as a way 'toward a fully Trinitarian theology'.[1] In this chapter, we will look at a number of significant stages along this way, hoping to describe, almost in a morphological sense, the shape of Gunton's theology.

## 1. Starting at the centre

It is not often the case that a young theologian writing his doctoral thesis immediately hits upon the theme that becomes the main topic of his work from then on. With Gunton, however, such was the case when he started, first under the direction of Robert Jenson, at that time Lutheran World Federation exchange professor at Oxford, then under the supervision of John Marsh and John Macquarrie, on his comparative analysis of the doctrine of God in Charles Hartshorne and Karl Barth. This work, which was eventually published as *Becoming and Being*,[2] clearly addresses some of the chief issues and raises some of the guiding questions that shaped Gunton's further theological thinking.

In comparison with Hartshorne, Barth's theology is presented under the heading 'Barth's Trinitarian theology' and it is observed: 'The account of the Trinity in fact takes the place long taken by natural theology . . . Its function is at least partly *hermeneutical*.'[3] Gunton accepts Jüngel's point that this is not a hermeneutics of signification, but a hermeneutics of revelation, and this points to the 'roots' of the doctrine of the Trinity: God acts in historical events as God is.

> The doctrine of the Trinity has true roots in the biblical witness to revelation not in textual evidence of references to the Father, Son, and Spirit, but in the Bible's understanding of the historical events in which God is God. That is the basic insight on which all depends.[4]

The hermeneutics of revelation, as Gunton reconstructs Barth, and the doctrine of the Trinity are mutually constitutive, so that the latter is an *a posteriori* rational reconstruction, taking seriously that this is the way in which God wants to be known in relation to us as he is in himself. If, however, this mode of knowledge reflects the way God is, God's involvement in history must be seen as part of God's being which leads to a distancing from classical metaphysics which is no less radical than Hartshorne's attempt. The primary aim is therefore to clarify the nature of this involvement and its consequences on an epistemological *and* ontological level.

Epistemologically, Gunton criticizes Hartshorne's understanding of God in that it presupposes an 'analogy to hold timelessly between God and that to which he is eminently related, i.e. the world'.[5] This is the corollary of the view that divine relativity in Hartshorne leaves no room ontologically for genuine divine action over against the world, or as the heading of the last chapter of the book puts it rather provocatively: 'Receptivity is not enough.'[6] The principal aim is thus to maintain the language of *divine* agency – God's being in his act – while making sense of the language of God's freedom, love and grace. As a result, the trinitarian conditions for establishing such appear as a constant sub-theme in *Becoming and Being*.

It is in this context that Barth is also decisively criticized. The orientation to the past, noticeable in such concepts as that of 'divine self-repetition', is analysed by Gunton with Jenson as being due to 'the neglect of the third person of the Trinity': 'If the goal of history in the Holy Spirit is totally subordinate to its origin in the Father, the tendency of a theology will be [to] locate its centre of gravity in the (possibly timeless) past.'[7] This is identified as a 'platonic element . . . in Barth's doctrine of God',[8] which, given the 'tendency to define eternity in opposition to time', leads to 'a negation of the historical orientation of the understanding of revelation'.[9] The result of this dualistic tendency forms the background for the re-appropriation and reinterpretation of the doctrine of analogy. Gunton can say of Barth: '. . . he fails to carry his programme through, and ends up with a doctrine of analogy that collapses into timelessness.'[10] This again points not only to neglect of the Spirit and the Spirit's eschatological work but shows itself also in 'Barth's apparent lack of interest in the historical figure of Jesus',[11] so that a gulf opens between history and eternity which contradicts Barth's conjunction of the event of revelation and the doctrine of the Trinity.

In spite of these criticisms, the conclusion of *Becoming and Being* is a celebration of Barth's theological achievement and a commitment to follow Barth's approach in order to develop a theological rationality grounded in God's trinitarian self-revelation. The Hartshornian alternative is dismissed scathingly, but not without sympathy for its theological motivations.

Thus, the comparison between Hartshorne and Barth has a clear lesson for theology:

> It shows clearly that the theology that wishes to stand on the intellectual feet of a philosophy is likely to remain a cripple. Moreover, it demonstrates the lunacy of so much as taking seriously the rationalist dogma that philosophical abstractions are more intellectually appropriate than personal analogies when speaking of God. It makes clear the choice either that the Christian doctrine of the incarnation be relativized and shown to be no more than a pictorial ('mythological') expression of what the philosopher can say better – though, it must be noted, always with a very different meaning – or that the rationalist dogma be itself overcome by the Word's becoming flesh in Jesus of Nazareth.[12]

Strong words, especially coming from someone who was lecturer in philosophy of religion at King's College London at the time of publication of the book![13] Yet, more importantly, the statement contains a commitment, a theological programme *in nuce*. If we have to make a choice between seeing the incarnation as the illustration of some otherwise established philosophical principle or having faith that Jesus Christ is the Word made flesh, it is not enough to show that this event overcomes rationalist dogma. It must also serve as the foundation of a theological rationality – and Gunton insists throughout that Barth is a rational theologian! – that, while anchoring rationality in the revelation of the triune God, also shows that this rationality offers an illuminative account of ourselves and the world in which we live. That is, it implies demonstrating the rationality of 'the belief that certain events, described, remembered, and promised in the biblical books, are correctly attributable to the agency of God and are such as to *illumine consistently both human life and the world in which they happen*'.[14] The doctrine of the Trinity, the argument suggests, would have to safeguard the correct attribution of the events witnessed in Scripture to God's agency *and* illumine our life and the world we live in. It thus serves as a conceptual reconstruction of God's self-identification and of God's self-interpretation in his relationship to the world that illumines the reality we experience, because it is the decisive factor in shaping this reality. It is here that Gunton locates Barth's 'partial failure':

> Barth's partial failure . . . lies in his not being Trinitarian enough at a crucial point in his argument. The third person of the Trinity, whatever additional functions he may have, is the mode of being of the one God by whose activity is anticipated the future redemption of man and the whole created order of which he is a part . . . It is our need to be open always to the 'things that are

coming' (John xvi: 13) – another explicit reference to the Spirit – that ensures the openness and provisionality of our ways of speaking about God. For if the meaningful activity of God is already completed in past – or timeless – eternity, the outworking of divine decision has all the necessity of a timeless concept, and our theology becomes the quest . . . for timeless truths. The lesson of Barth's doctrine of the Trinity is that if God and also the creature are to have the freedom proper to their natures, the conception of God as triune, and fully triune, is going to be instrumental in ensuring it. Above all it acts to preclude the making absolute in any conceptual structure the relation between God and the creature.[15]

With hindsight one can detect crucial elements here that were later fully developed in Gunton's theology: the emphasis on the Spirit and the Spirit's eschatological action, the rejection of an eternity located – to phrase it as *prima facie* contradiction – in an eternal act in the past, and the concern to correlate divine and human freedom as part of a Trinitarian theology that sees God as 'fully triune'. However, there are also elements that were to be corrected in the further shaping of Gunton's theology, and explicitly spelt out in the 'Epilogue' to the second edition.[16] Chief among those is the tacit acquiescence to Barth's interpretation of the concept of 'person' as 'mode of being' (later identified as one of the main reasons why Barth's theology could not be 'trinitarian enough') and the argument from divine and human freedom to the Trinity (instead of from the personal communion of the Trinity to the freedom of God and humans).

## 2. Overcoming alienating dualisms

The attempt at developing a theological rationality based on the incarnation led Gunton, not surprisingly, to Christology. In *Yesterday and Today. A Study of Continuities in Christology*,[17] he launched a consistent attack on the assumption of discontinuities, above all, the discontinuity between past and present, between the contingent and the necessary, between history and reason, the material and the spiritual, time and eternity and the transcendent and the immanent. These discontinuities betray underlying metaphysical dualisms, with dualism defined as 'a metaphysic . . . which conceives two realities as either opposites or contradictions of each other'.[18] As Gunton sees it, this must seriously distort the duality that we find in the New Testament, which, 'for all its diversity of expression . . . portrays Christ as one in whom the work and presence of God are given through the medium of a human being' so that 'both the eternal God and his historical self-presentation, are given together'.[19] Christology's task therefore is to find conceptual means to express this reality. However, it founders in this endeavour if it uncritically accepts the dualisms which dominate contemporary thought, both yesterday and today.

Gunton argues that 'post-Kantian dualism and the dualistic thinking of the Greeks . . . are one and the same intellectual phenomenon'.[20] The Greek dualism was a dualism 'from above' insisting on the utter transcendence of God as the eternal principle of being beyond temporal being, most clearly expressed in the axiom of impassibility. The dualism of our culture, one which has reigned since the Enlightenment, is described as a 'dualism from below, seeing the world as a closed and self-sufficient system with no possibility for or need of reference beyond it' and therefore 'always near to a collapse into a monism which makes the immanent the *only* real'.[21] Both, however, have the same effect of being unable to conceive in Christ the personal union of the transcendent God and a human being in which neither God's divinity nor the authentic character of humanity is compromised. For Gunton, the underlying similarity of a dualistic metaphysic is the 'fountainhead of the Christological schizophrenia of the West' and has produced a situation where 'contemporary problems are so often mirror images of those that so exercised the Fathers'.[22] There is thus a negative continuity between patristic times and the modern situation documented by the persistence of a dualistic worldview in different guises that, if it is allowed to have a normative function as an obligatory form of thought, will be destructive for the Christological content. This, however, raises the question of a possible alternative: 'is it possible that the content may be strong enough to create its own form from the materials available in contemporary thought?'[23]

There is, however, also a positive continuity from the Christology of the Fathers to contemporary thought, not so much in theology, Gunton suggests, but in the philosophy of music (suggesting new ways of understanding time) and in the philosophy of science (conceiving new forms of relating word and object).[24] The inspirations taken from Zuckerkandl's philosophy of music and Polanyi's epistemology both have the same point: they question epistemologies that appear wedded to dualistic ontologies. If time is not to be identified with decay and the gradual disappearance of everything into the void of meaninglessness, but, from a musical point of view, gains a positive significance as a conveyor of lasting meaning, and if rationality is not focused on necessary truths or on empirical data but allows for the significance of the contingent, not in a distanced relationship but as a form of indwelling, the central claims of classical Christology no longer seem to be impediments of rationality to be expressed only paradoxically, but as pointers to a new form of rationality that has been liberated from dualistic ontologies and reductionist epistemologies.

> At the centre of things is the self-actualization of God in time, the self-differentiation through love of the eternal to become temporal for us. The link between eternal and temporal is not ideal but actual. Something happens in time which compels interpretation as the actuality of the eternal. God, as the creator of the temporal order through his outgoing Word, not only gives temporal and spatial form to what is other than himself (creation), but takes it also. He becomes flesh. This means that the eternal love of God locates itself in time and space, and so becomes datable.[25]

These arguments, as the result of consistent considerations of the claims of Christology, suffice to understand 'Jesus as the temporal logic of the eternal God',[26] which is the pivotal statement of the book. These sentences are also the ones where Gunton comes closest to an explicitly trinitarian reflection. However, these statements do little more than raise the question of the relationship between Christology and the doctrine of the Trinity: what is it in the constitution of the being of God that allows for God's involvement with the temporal and the spatial without falling into the trap of either denying the significance of the eternal being or of the temporal self-presentation of God in Jesus?

In its subtitle 'An Essay Towards a Trinitarian Theology', *Enlightenment and Alienation*, published two years after the Christological study and in many ways its companion piece, takes up the emphasis on the Trinity already hinted at in *Becoming and Being*.[27] Emerging from teaching a course on the history of modern philosophy at King's College, Gunton engages the great philosophers of the Western tradition – particularly those who have contributed to what is known by its rather self-congratulatory name as the Enlightenment – in a conversation about the making of modernity and its implications for Christian theology. In the three parts of the book, 'Seeing and Believing', 'Thinking and Acting' and 'Reading and Understanding', Gunton analyses the effects of central aspects of the Enlightenment under the heading of 'alienation'. This suggests that the after-effects of the Enlightenment are in danger of turning us into strangers in relation to the world around us and in relation to one another. '(E)xcess of light can blind',[28] and this shows itself as much with regard to our understanding of perception and autonomous freedom as with regard to our dealing with the task of interpreting Scripture.

Against this effect it is argued, with the help of a veritable choir of 'dissenting voices'[29] counting Berkeley, Coleridge and Michael Polanyi as its most prominent members, that theological reflection can help – as it is expressed with a phrase borrowed from Stewart Sutherland – 'to establish possibilities' for a different way of perceiving the world and ourselves by reviving theological resources often discredited by their Enlightenment critics. In this sense the aim of the book is 'to make connections between apparently disparate phenomena in our culture and to draw attention to theological resources which appear at once to speak to and to transcend current ways of looking at the problem'.[30] The proposal made has a tentative character, as Gunton explains in the summary of the first part of the book on perception, but it appeals to another enlightenment:

> . . . among all the possibilities for our understanding of perception, the overtly theological is but one. But in its favour is a claim that is 'saves the phenomena' better than alternative accounts. Whether it is the true account cannot be solved on grounds internal to the discussion of perception. This, too, requires some form of antecedent faith in the light of which we are able to understand what kind of problem or area of enquiry is facing us.[31]

The argument runs like this. If all our understanding follows the pattern of *fides quaerens intellectum* – as in different ways Berkeley, Coleridge and, above all, Polanyi seem to suggest – we may ask *which* faith offers a better way of understanding ourselves and the world. Faith in the triune God may in fact throw a better light on our interaction with the world than seeing ourselves as the recipients of sense data leaving imprints on the *tabula rasa* of our passive minds, leaning towards a materialistic faith, or as the active epistemic synthesizers of knowledge whose activity constitutes the objects they know.

In following the logic of faith in the triune God, Gunton argues that the 'Fatherhood of God' implies 'that he has created us within the world yet in a relationship that also transcends it'[32] so that our knowledge of the world mediated concretely through our senses is part of being created in the image of God. If we affirm, following the same logic, that the world was created through the Son 'we can understand that the world is other than God, and therefore we exist as separate and free beings'.[33] Furthermore, applying belief in God the Holy Spirit to these epistemological issues we understand that our capacity to know the world and our ability to exercise created freedom 'are the gift of the Holy Spirit, so that we understand both that our knowledge is necessarily partial and that its limitedness is not a defect'.[34] This is, in effect, 'an attempt to reverse the traditional order of so-called natural' and "revealed" theology' which – Gunton claims – points to the right sort of enlightenment:

> It attempts to see nature – an aspect of our relation to the created world – in the light of an understanding of God in such a way that there is mutual illumination, from God to the world and, in direct correspondence, from the world to God.[35]

A similar argument is developed with regard to human freedom. Here the argument goes beyond the economic Trinity and, following Coleridge, engages the immanent Trinity. Over against a view of mechanical determinism on the one hand and a view of human freedom as autonomously creative freedom on the other, an account of freedom in relationship is presented as an implication of the doctrine of the Trinity:

> For it says that God is eternally a God in relationship. However difficult it is to give a clear account of such a reality, it is an implication of the way God must be seen to be if we take with full seriousness his activity as Son and as Spirit. In turn, the eternal relatedness of God gives form and meaning to our human reality as beings in relation to each other. It is here that God can be understood as the ground of our acting according to the laws of our being. This was Samuel Taylor Coleridge's point: that a God who is not a bare unity but a unity within and by means of an interrelatedness of 'persons' can ground an understanding of a correspondingly free humanity. In this case, human life is conceived not as the play of impersonal and mechanistic forces, not as the impotent assertion of a false divinity, not as a collection of isolated atomic individuals, but as a community where the law of our being is worked out, however stumblingly and inadequately.[36]

If we try to assess the implications of *Yesterday and Today* and *Enlightenment and Alienation* for the shaping of Gunton's theology, we see with the benefit of hindsight that the shape is still somewhat in flux. After starting at the centre of the doctrine of God, from the critical analysis of Barth's Trinitarian theology that was deemed to be 'not Trinitarian enough', both books engage the two central questions being raised in connection with the doctrine of the Trinity: God's self-identification and God's self-interpretation. While the Christological study is centrally concerned with establishing God's self-identification in Jesus of Nazareth by showing 'the belief that certain events, described, remembered, and promised in the biblical books, are correctly attributable to the agency of God',[37] the constructive suggestions remain still very tentative, mainly based on analogies from the philosophies of music and science. Notable is the absence of explicitly Trinitarian reflections, most obvious in the lack of any considerations of the role of the Spirit in Christology – a lack which Geoffrey Nuttall noted at the time when the book was published, as Colin Gunton himself recounts.[38] *Enlightenment and Alienation*, however, is not so much concerned with understanding the manner of God's triune self-identification but with God's Trinitarian self-interpretation by means of which Trinitarian thought can help 'to *illumine consistently both human life and the world in which they happen*'[39] (to quote the second half of the programmatic statement from *Becoming and*

*Being*). However the shape of the doctrine of the Trinity is still relatively undeveloped. There is clear awareness, mostly expressed with reference to Coleridge, that the economic and the immanent Trinity form an inextricable relationship, but how exactly this relationship is to be understood is still a relatively open question.

It is also remarkable that at this stage Gunton was as yet relatively unsure of the right conceptuality for the doctrine of the Trinity. In the lengthy quotation above, the word 'persons' is still used in quotation marks, as if to indicate that the word is still a stand-in for a more appropriate understanding. In some sense we can say of Gunton's view in *Enlightenment and Alienation* what he says there himself about Coleridge's doctrine of the Trinity: '. . . it is easier to see what function the doctrine performed for him than precisely how it is to be expounded.'[40] In effect, the shape of Trinitarian theology was still on the way to being clearly sketched. However, the two 'missing links', to change the metaphor, that we have noticed – an appropriate understanding of the 'person' and an adequate account of the being and status of the Spirit in relation to Christ and the Father, and so in the Trinity – were soon to be added when Gunton was appointed to the chair in Christian Doctrine at King's College London in 1984. And, with these two elements in place, the relationship of the immanent and the economic Trinity could be more clearly described.

### 3. Persons and the Spirit

Gunton's inaugural lecture at King's, 'The One, the Three and the Many',[41] contains the central insights concerning the trinitarian understanding of the concept of personhood which could bind together the exposition of the doctrine of the Trinity and its function. Over against an intellectualist and individualist understanding of the person as *res cogitans* in Descartes and against the programmatic surrender of the concept of personal identity in Derek Parfit's work, Gunton appeals to John Macmurray's approach in *Persons in Relation*. Starting from the negation of a dualism of body and mind, Macmurray focused on the notion of personal agency and extended that to a view of persons in relation. '*As persons we are only what we are in relation to other persons*'[42] is how Colin Gunton summarizes Macmurray's crucial insight, before tracing this view back through Sir William Hamilton, Coleridge, Calvin, Richard of St Victor to the Cappadocians in their interpretation by John Zizioulas. Furthermore, Gunton asserts, in sharp contradiction to Feuerbach, that, historically and systematically, the theological and, more specifically, Trinitarian concept of personhood is prior to the anthropological: '. . . anthropology stems from theology, and not the other way around.'[43] In the Cappadocians' view of the persons in the Trinity, the concept of the person first acquires the logical priority, which, in the twentieth century, philosophers like Macmurray and Strawson claimed for it, but it does so because it is embedded in a new ontology which breaks both the identification of person and substance and the treatment of personhood as a particular attribute of some sorts of substances. Furthermore, the Cappadocian suggestion makes a sharp distinction between the person and the individual by understanding the personal particularity of the three as being constituted in their relational communion and their unity as a communion constituted in their relations and not in some underlying divine substance. The upshot of this is that the 'one' and the 'many' are mutually constitutive in the divine three.

> In God, that is to say, there is no ultimate breach between the 'one' and the 'many' because of the part played by the person conceived relationally. Accordingly, there is 'a reality of communion in which each particular is affirmed as unique and irreplaceable by the others.'[44]

What are the consequences of adopting this view of trinitarian personhood and of the relationship of being persons in communion in the Trinity and in human communities? In his inaugural lecture Gunton pointed to a third way of human community organisation between the Scylla of individualism and the Charybdis of collectivism, careful to avoid a relapse into forms of personalism which focus on the relationship between a self and an other. Identity, otherness and communion require at least three in created communities, and in God the three persons form a perfect communion. This emphasis, for which Richard of St Victor and Samuel Taylor Coleridge are the chief witnesses, has many implications both in anthropology and in theology where the personhood of the third person, the Holy Spirit, had for Gunton a crucial significance.

The theology of the Holy Spirit therefore developed alongside the exposition of the doctrine of the Trinity as persons in communion, and it forms a constitutive part of it, perhaps that part which distinguishes Gunton's Trinitarian theology most clearly from that of his most frequent conversation partners, like Robert Jenson and John Zizioulas. Gunton's theology of the Holy Spirit can be seen in Christological and ecclesiological connections, contexts where lack of attention to the role of the Spirit has in his view led to most problematical results: to a reductive view of the humanity of Christ and to a view of the Church which in its essential structures is defined on an exclusively Christological pattern as a historical institution of salvation, lacking a foundation of freedom in communion. The Christological problem can be seen in the often repeated charge that a Christology 'from above', following the movement of Alexandrian Christologies, result in a docetic view of the humanity of Christ. But there is a mirror image of that charge in that Christologies which try to do justice to the human nature often tend to produce a stereotype of a static idealized humanity which leaves little room for the historical reality of Jesus the first-century Jew and does not seem to have much in common with the humanity we know, always embedded in its concrete particularity, always becoming, fragmentary, characterized by susceptibility to temptation and self-deception, if not downright fallenness.

In his treatment of these questions in Christology, Gunton characteristically inspired, and was inspired by, the research of two of his doctoral students: by Alan Spence's research on John Owen[45] and Graham MacFarlane's work on Edward Irving.[46] Gunton phrases the central question in this way: '[H]ow can it be conceived that the Word became flesh without ceasing to be Word but, equally, without depriving the historical person of Christ of real humanity?'[47] According to Gunton, there can only be a satisfactory answer – that is 'an incarnational Christology which will yet do full justice to the historical particularity of Jesus and the detailed lineaments of his story'[48] – if the incarnation is firmly placed within a Trinitarian context and worked out in terms of Jesus the incarnate Word's relationship with God the Father in the Spirit, and, through the Spirit perfecting the work of the Father in the incarnate Son, to us and the whole of humankind.

A possible way for such a Trinitarian view of the incarnation is pointed out by John Owen's dictum: 'The only singular and immediate act of the person of the Son on the human nature was the assumption of it into subsistence with himself.'[49] This excludes any view of the Word employing his body like a mere tool, and creates the space for a fully Trinitarian view of the incarnation as an expression of the eternal will of the triune God to establish communion with his creation through Jesus. The way the incarnate Son relates to God the Father and to other human beings in all the different aspects of his ministry must be exercised in the Spirit. This is the view that is further developed by Irving, whether he built on Owen or not. In the incarnation, by the will of the Father and through the Holy Spirit, the Word becomes incarnate by assuming our fallen human nature and relates to the Father, to other human beings and to the world of nature, in the Spirit. His humanity is ours – 'the unassumed is the unhealed' – but in and through this humanity he does not fall prey to the gravity of fallenness in virtue of the enlivening, directing and supporting power of the Spirit, bringing in Christ the eschatological perfection to humanity that is God's will for his human creatures. This implies that the Spirit is not to be conceived as a 'substantial possession' but 'as a personal other in free relation to Jesus',[50] granting that freedom from the restrictions of fallenness that characterises Jesus' whole ministry.

Does this still leave room for a statement of the full divinity of Christ and of his full and unrestricted humanity? Gunton's answer is in the affirmative, provided we see it as a logical and theological implication of the doctrine of the Trinity that Christ as the incarnate Son is not 'conceived as divine *in the same way* as the Father',[51] but, we might add, in a way appropriate to the Son in his communion with the Father and the Spirit.

> He is divine, we might say, according to his own hypostasis, a hypostasis having its shape by virtue of its relations to Father and Spirit, but having its distinctive shape manifested by self-giving, obedience, *kenosis*. That is the reason why the humanity of Jesus is not foreign to but an expression of the deity of the Son, in all of what I have called its lineaments . . . It is as human that Jesus expresses the divinity of the eternal Son and so makes known the Father.[52]

This trinitarian explication of the incarnation has an important implication. The personal union of divinity and humanity in Christ is in this way not focused exclusively on the act of the incarnation or on the cross or on the resurrection but encompasses the whole of what Gunton called 'the career' of Jesus Christ – his conception, birth, baptism, life, ministry, suffering, death, resurrection and ascension. The totality of Christ's actions and passion, enveloped by his origin in God the Father and directed towards the Holy Spirit's eschatological perfection of the communion of creation with the communion of the triune God, therefore becomes the material of the Trinitarian explication of Christology. In each aspect of this 'career' the three persons of the Trinity act together and relate to one another, undivided, but in each aspect in different constellations, each person's contribution according to his hypostatic particularity.

Similar points as in Christology are made with regard to ecclesiology, again building on some of Owen's insights but developing them within a Cappadocian framework. This is most clearly seen in Gunton's Congregational Lecture from 1988, 'The Transcendent Lord. The Spirit and the Church in Calvinist and Cappadocian [Thought]'.[53] The ecclesiological reflections start with the claim that it would be possible 'to write a history of the Church as the story of the misappropriation of the doctrine of the Holy Spirit'.[54] The symptoms of such misappropriations extend from an extreme clericalism (identifying the bearers of ecclesiastical authority with the bearers of the Spirit) to extreme individualism (seeing the private judgement of individuals absolutely sanctioned by the illumination of the Spirit). The different forms of misappropriation all document the same mistake: '. . . we have confused, what we, the Church, have done with the action of the Spirit.'[55] A more appropriate understanding of the action and the person of the Spirit needs to accompany repentance for such confusions.

In contrast to much of the tradition, Gunton maintains that the action of the Spirit is misconstrued if it is understood as an immanent force. The biblical witnesses point to the transcendence of the Spirit, the Spirit's 'over-againstness', which the later Eastern tradition correctly saw as an expression of the personal particularity of the Spirit in his relation with the persons of the Father and the Son, and in relation to the created order. While John Owen is to be credited with rooting the Spirit's transcendence in the Spirit's personal being, the Trinitarian relationship in which this person exists to the Father and the Son was, in Gunton's estimation, not equally observed so that it obscured the way in which the Spirit is also the creator of the community of those sanctified by the Spirit. The understanding of the Spirit should therefore

> give a central place to his being the transcendent and free Lord who creates community by bringing men and women to the Father through Jesus Christ and so in relation with one another. The Spirit is not some inner fuel, compulsion or qualification – in fact he is nothing impersonal at all – but the free Lord who as our *other* liberates us for community.[56]

On the basis of this understanding of the person and work of the Spirit, the constitution of the Church is understood as his work, whereas the institution of the Church, its establishment as a historical reality, is the work of Christ. Here the Cappadocian insight is helpful: the Spirit is the perfecting cause in God's Trinitarian action and anticipates creation's eschatological fulfilment by liberating it from fixed structures rooted in the past and from any claim to absolute perfection by an institution.

> In the economy, the Son represents God's immanence in history: he becomes flesh, history. The Spirit, contrary to what is often assumed, is God's transcendence. He is God's *eschatological otherness* from the world, God freeing the created world for its true destiny – and so, to use Basil's phrase, its perfecting cause.[57]

When these statements are added to those concerning the role of the Spirit in relation to Christ, we have a fairly complete description of the Spirit's role in the Trinitarian economy. The Spirit is the transcendent Lord who – as the perfecting cause of all God's works – liberates the creature from bondage to anything penultimate which claims ultimacy, frees the creature from slavery to anything relative that assumes absoluteness and does so by confronting the creature with the anticipation of its eschatological goal. This liberation is a liberation for community in history, for being part of the community

of the Church that constantly transcends itself because it is only a witness
– and, as such, a foretaste – of the perfected communion of the triune God
with his redeemed and transformed creation.

How, then, does this help to determine the Spirit's particular place in
the immanent Trinity? It is in this connection that Gunton seeks to expand
Augustine's understanding of the Trinity as love.[58] This is but one aspect of a
much wider and often radical criticism of the effects of Augustine's theology
in the Western church,[59] but, with regard to Augustine's interpretation of the
Spirit as the link of love (*vinculum amoris*) between the Father and the Son,
Gunton is surely right that love returned in an inward cycle leads to such
tensions with the outward direction of the Spirit in the divine economy that
'the immanent Trinity is in effect conceived in terms contradictory of the
economy'.[60] In effect, it produces an image of love 'as self-involved rather
than as oriented outwards'.[61] Here, therefore, Richard of St Victor serves as a
better guide for understanding the love between two as perfected only when
it turns outward towards a third, and is, in this way, 'a love intrinsically
oriented to community'.[62] Corresponding to the eschatological dynamic of
the Spirit in the economy, the Spirit is therefore described as the 'dynamic
of divine love', the one whose being is 'to perfect the love of Father and Son
by moving it beyond itself'.[63]

The distinctive elements of Gunton's Trinitarian theology are now to
hand. The constructive appropriation of the Cappadocian conception
of the Trinity in which the personal particularity of the Father, the Son
and the Spirit is constituted in their internal relationships and determines
their relationship to what is not God in all its economic richness, *and* the
special emphasis on the work of the Spirit with regard to Christology and
ecclesiology, combine to shape Gunton's thought. The early criticism of
Barth – for 'not being Trinitarian enough' by neglecting the person and
agency of the Spirit – has been positively and constructively followed
through. Likewise, Barth's deficient conceptual description of Father, Son
and Spirit, which led him to misplace the personal by ascribing it to the one
God instead of the three persons, is remedied.[64] Similarly, the account of
the Trinity as persons in communion with the central concepts of person,
otherness and relation and an understanding of the unity of the divine being
as relationally constituted, serves to keep the self-identification of God and
God's self-interpretation through the Trinitarian economy together. Thus
Coleridge's deficiency of having much to say about the function of the
doctrine of the Trinity for our understanding of the world while remaining
relatively opaque about the conceptual explication of the doctrine itself
is also overcome. If God is Trinitarian in all aspects of his being and if
God is Trinitarian in the specific way of being as a communion of persons
constituted in their particularity and otherness through their relations,

then all relationships between God and the world must be interpreted in trinitarian terms.

For Gunton, this conclusion means that negative theology cannot be given priority. The apophatic element functions only *within* the understanding of the Trinity that we gain from the economy and does not hint at something *beyond* the self-identification of God. This is one reason why Gunton refused to speak of the Father as the cause of the communion of the Trinity, as Zizioulas did. Whatever priority is afforded to the Father, it must not detract from the fact that all three persons are together the cause of the communion in which they exist in relations of mutual and reciprocal communion. Thus the Father is what he is not only because he begets the Son, but also because the Son responds in the way made known in his obedience as incarnate, and so can be understood to be the one who shares in the constitution of the being of God by means of his eternal response of obedience and love. Similarly, the movement of the Spirit can be argued to be constitutive of the being of God the Father in that it is the Spirit who ensures that the love of Father and Son is not simply mutual love but moves outward so that creation and redemption are indeed free acts of God but as acts grounded in his being as *love*. Beyond this, however, it would be better to preserve an element of reserve: God's unknowableness prevents us from further inquiry into the *cause* of his being who and what he is.[65]

The emphasis on the Spirit as the transcendent Lord, which is an implication of his inner trinitarian personhood, also points to an equally important element. As transcendent, the Spirit respects, so to speak, the otherness of the world and the created freedom of God's human creatures not by overwhelming the creation but by engaging it in such a way that it can find its true destiny, not as an infusion of divine power but as a personal gift. Although the Spirit, as the perfecting cause in whom every divine act is completed, performs this task because of his eternal personal particularity as the 'dynamic of divine love', he draws the creature into communion with God in such a way that the destiny of the world is fulfilled and its otherness finds its true meaning in communion with God. The otherness built into the understanding of the Trinity, in its immanent as well as in its economic sense, is that element which, for Gunton, excludes any form of straightforward participationist metaphysics with its attached forms of *analogia entis*. Though it has to be affirmed that the destiny of the human person is to be included in the communion with the triune God, this can only occur through the mediation of the Trinitarian economy because the otherness granted to the world is its creaturely dignity. This emphasis on otherness and mediation is a central implication of Gunton's theology.[66]

### 4. Integration as mediation: on the way toward a fully Trinitarian theology

With *The Promise of Trinitarian Theology*, the shape of Gunton's theology was defined in its principal outlines. The rapid succession of books that followed this seminal work are simply ways of refining his approach to Trinitarian theology. On the one hand, there is the application of the rule that if God's being is Trinitarian in the specific way described, then every form of divine action must in some way be understood as an expression of God's being. For Gunton, this expression of God's Trinitarian being in his trinitarian acts cannot be short-circuited by concepts like that of divine 'self-communication', which for him could not be rescued from their emanationist implications. Doing Trinitarian theology means working patiently through the ordered richness of the divine economy, spelling out and testing its relationships to the immanent Trinity. In effect, the particularities and specificities of the divine economy must not be circumvented – though its referential centre is the being and action of the God it witnesses to – in favour of some sort of underlying Trinitarian principle. The concrete engagement of the Father with the world he created through his 'two hands', the Son and the Spirit – probably the most often quoted reference to Irenaeus in Gunton's work – must not be reduced to a philosophico-theological principle.

On the other hand, the process of inquiring into the specific Trinitarian shape of every *locus* of Christian dogmatics also reflects back on the doctrine of the immanent Trinity, enriching and modifying it. The Trinitarian integration of Christian doctrine – and even of Christian theology as a whole – depends on the mutual shaping of what can be said about the immanent Trinity on the basis of the Trinitarian economy and *vice versa*. However, this mutual shaping can only occur if the two are understood to be distinguished in their relationship *and* related in their distinction. Any other way – either divorcing the one from the other or simply identifying them – would do away with the mediation that constitutes salvation history. In effect, it would assume a stance of the eschatological completion of the economy, which was always Gunton's main objection to Hegel. Such a stance would exercise a dictatorship of closure on the activity of doing theology. Theology could no longer be understood as engagement with the trinitarian God as living reality who has not yet come to the end of his ways with the world, and would therefore destroy the openness and provisionality of theological concepts. For Gunton, the transcendence of the Spirit in the divine economy is a safeguard against such forms of theologizing.

The integration of all theological doctrines into the 'frame' of Trinitarian theology must therefore be an open integration, which can only be an anticipation of the glory of eschatological perfection if it insists on the fragmentary character of believing as distinguished from the beatific vision which in Gunton's theology could only be envisaged as a synaesthetic experience. This is perhaps most clearly demonstrated by his most elegant book, *The One, The Three and the Many*, the 1992 Bampton Lectures, which bears the subtitle *God, Creation and the Culture of Modernity*. The subtitle, however, is slightly misleading. Whereas all of Gunton's earlier books were concerned with the effects of modernity on Christian theology and the ambivalence of the Enlightenment and its successors, this one takes up the sensibilities of post-modernity and reflects them in a trinitarian framework. This is evident in the way that both post-modern particularity and plurality are taken up in a trinitarian fashion so as to steer a course between the formal universalism of the Enlightenment and the relativistic particularism of post-modernity, while, at the same time, questioning the underlying assumptions which might be just as problematical whether they are affirmed or denied. In his 'Epilogue' to the second edition of *Yesterday and Today*, Gunton reflected on the complexities of the situation as defined by 'modernity's premature and Procrustean attempt to mould all claims for meaning and truth into the bed of a particular kind of rationality' and the post-modern suggestion 'that there can be no truth at all, or at best only the assertion of local truths which are simply asserted against others on the grounds that they are not subject to rational comparison'.[67] Looked at from a theological perspective the verdict is as clear as it is negative:

> Theologically speaking, however, postmodernism is a denial of the doctrine of creation, which holds, among other things, that because God has created the universe it is a universe in the sense of a single reality, and one, as 'very good', is understood to be a place for universal human culture, involving a quest for goodness, truth and beauty.[68]

However, there is something more to be said, and it must underline the particular *veri* of post-modern thought:

> The relevance of Christology to this, and of it to Christology, is that postmodernism's celebration of the rights of the *particular* is liberating, to the extent that the person of Christ cannot be subsumed under the kind of extraneous conceptions of reality which was the original intention of this book to contest. Jesus of Nazareth is, after all, a particular, and his very particularity is an offence to the modernist view which maintains that the only truth worthy of its name is to be found in universal rational truths . . . But it is also an offence to postmodernism's refusal of any narrative or claim which affects to encompass a universal truth. What postmodernism . . .

cannot countenance is the assertion that because Jesus is also God, his claim and his reign are universal.[69]

The Bampton Lectures address this problem as one of the many dualisms that are mirrored in the debate between modernism and post-modernism. In its elegant chiastic structure, the problems of particularity and universality, time and eternity and the one and the many are related in such a way that the questions raised by the 'displacement of God' (part one) are answered – albeit provisionally and tentatively – in an attempt at 'rethinking createdness' (part two) from a trinitarian perspective and in a trinitarian structure. The problem of the particular and the universal is reflected pneumatologically, the question of relatedness finds a Christological response and the overarching issue of the one and the many leads to the heart of the whole doctrine of the Trinity which provides the framework for relating truth, goodness and beauty.

The theory of open transcendentals is at the heart of the proposal, a highly original development of suggestions and allusions made by Coleridge.

> An open transcendental is a notion, in some way basic to the human thinking process, which empowers a continuing and in principle unfinished exploration of the universal marks of being. The quest is indeed a universal one, to find concepts which do succeed in some way or other in representing or echoing the universal marks of being.[70]

What if – and this is Gunton's question – transcendentals are generated neither from a primordial but abstract Unity, nor from an irreducible plurality that ultimately produces a view of an atomistic, unrelated multiverse, but are generated from the Trinity in which the one and the many, the particular and universal and the relationship between temporality and eternity are mediated in the communion of persons which God is and as which he relates dynamically to that which is not God? Gunton is careful in upholding Coleridge's distinction between the Trinity as the 'Idea Idearum' and the transcendental power of ideas, however. The Trinity is not a transcendental. Assuming that would merely lead to a Neoplatonic scheme of the 'great chain' of being, redefined in Trinitarian fashion. The Trinity, however, generates transcendentals by what the three persons are in relation to one another when this God creates in love and freedom. The open transcendentals are the way in which otherness and relation and the immanent and the economic Trinity can be seen as related.

> In the case of God, the transcendentals are functions of the eternal and free relations of the persons, each of whom has, in inseparable relation to the

others, his particular manner of being and acting . . . In turn, the doctrine of God derived from the economy enables us to see that the creation bears in different ways the marks of its making, so that the transcendentals qualify people and things, too, in a way appropriate to what they are. In sum, the transcendentals are functions of the finitely free relations of persons and of the contingent relations of things.

The open transcendentals are therefore not a parallel structure to the divine economy. They are, so to speak, the inner logic of the divine economy – and that is the burden of the argument that particularity and perichoresis, otherness, relation and community are ultimately to be understood *theologically*. If they are simply the logic in which the economy is worked out, they cannot be read off the way things go as static patterns. There is no naked transcendentality; it is always clothed in the particular circumstances of nature, history and culture. Furthermore, there is no straightforward top-down transcendentality. Rather, the transcendentals can only be grasped in their dynamic, goal-directed actualization. This process, which comprises the whole of the not yet completed divine economy, gives a special place to created persons in enabling cooperation with the triune God in achieving the perfection of the non-personal creation, and that is the cultural unity grasped in the relationship of truth, goodness and beauty.

> Ontologically, the creature is ordered to the completion of its particular end in space and time; ontically, it is caught up in a history and dynamic that would subvert its orderedness. Redemption thus means the redirection of the particular to its own end and not a re-creation. The distinctive feature of created persons is their mediating function in the achievement of perfection by the rest of creation. They are called to forms of action, in science, ethics and art – in a word, to culture – which enable to take place the sacrifice of praise, which is the free offering of all things, perfected, to their creator. Theologically put: the created world becomes truly itself – moves towards its completion – when through Christ and the Spirit, it is presented perfect before the throne of the Father. The sacrifice of praise which is the due human response to both creation and redemption takes the form of that culture which enables both personal and non-personal worlds to realize their true being.[71]

It has to be borne in mind that the theory of open transcendentals is not a novel proposal introduced on the open market of philosophical ideas and theories. It is Gunton's suggestion of how the relationship of the immanent and the economic affects our understanding of the world that can only be adequately grasped if it is understood in relation – in *this* relation, he suggests

– to the triune God. For all its intricate engagement with philosophical ideas, old and new, and with cultural theories, modern and post-modern, *The One, the Three and the Many* has no other subject matter, and indeed no other doctrinal proposal to offer, than *The Triune Creator*[72] which was published a few years later.

On the way to a fully Trinitarian theology? The Bampton Lectures explore the full scope of the relationships between the triune God and the world the Father creates through the Son in the Spirit in a theology of the culture of createdness. A fully Trinitarian theology in this sense is one that covers the full scope of the relationship between God and the world, just as Gunton's *The Christian Faith. An Introduction to Christian Doctrine*[73] is intended to show that this framework can indeed be successfully applied to the whole of Christian doctrine. His following books, like *Intellect and Action*, *Act and Being* and, indeed, *Father, Son and Holy Spirit*, do not expand the scope of this Trinitarian theology. Rather, they are concerned with developing its internal structure, and with applying the insights that define the outline of Trinitarian theology to the particular questions found within the areas comprised by that outline. For Gunton, a fully Trinitarian theology is one where the Trinity shapes both reference and meaning, extension and intension, of the being and act of the triune God in relation to the world the Father, Son and Spirit create, redeem and perfect.

## 5. *The shape and style of Colin Gunton's fully Trinitarian theology*

What then is the shape of Colin Gunton's theology? It would amount to literalizing a metaphor – and so taking it too far – to suggest that a theology, which aims at being fully Trinitarian, must, of necessity, have a three-dimensional shape so that its dimensions correspond to the trinitarian being of God. Facile though it may be, it is nevertheless informative to reflect for a moment on the shape of three-dimensional objects in space. Gunton had always criticized theology's taking up of the spatial imagery of popular religious imagination to characterize a particular style of doing theology. The metaphors 'from above' and 'from below', criticized in *Yesterday and Today*, are but one example of the misguided imposition of the measurements of created spaces to the relationship of God and the world. 'Above' stands for a divine initiative of the outgoing of the triune love that God *is* in order to relate to a created other. This divine initiative, however, takes a form which really engages the 'below' so that it cannot be described simply in terms of created reality, be it an ideal of humanity in Jesus Christ. Rather, the divine initiative leads to the incarnation, a real coming into flesh, a real acting in history, a real death on the cross, so that the reality of the incarnation must be construed as the real presence of the triune God on the plane of history. And it is not only the superficial spatial imagery of *height* but also of *length* that is transformed by Trinitarian theology. There is no simple contrast of the beginning and the end, as the opposition of protological and eschatological modes of theological thinking would suggest. The presence of the end of God's will for communion with his creation is, so to speak, there before the beginning of the length of created time so that the end is really to be understood as the completion of the distance the triune God has to go to achieve the end of his creation which is at the same time the destiny by which the creation comes to be itself. The story of Jesus is therefore both the recapitulation of an earlier segment of salvation history but in such a way that it represents the end of the line for all contradiction and resistance to God's will of love. Through all this, the dimension of *depth* points to an intricate patterning, creating rational order out of the contingencies of worldly events. In this way the superficial notion of space is subverted and no longer made to refer to the measurements of three-dimensional objects but to the space that is created by letting the other be the other in a relationship of unbreakable *koinonia* in which the Trinity exists and in which we shall be included without losing our own space, our otherness, by being swallowed up into the divine life.

What do such illustrations – admittedly rather superficial – say about the shape of a theology? One important point is that theology must be concerned with an interrelatedness that has clear contours and presents a recognizable shape, although this shape will not be perfected and finished as long as we do theology *in via* and not *in patria*. In that sense the shape of a theology, and surely that of Colin Gunton's theology, is like a sculpture. In an article with the characteristic title 'Anselm of Canterbury, Samuel Taylor Coleridge and the Possibility of an English Systematic Theology',[74] Gunton again recommends Coleridge as an example of doing systematic theology. The reason he gives is: 'Coleridge wanted to see things whole'.[75] What better way is there to express the driving force behind the activity of a sculptor and, indeed, of a systematic theologian trying to mould the shape of theology? Seeing things whole was for Coleridge and Gunton an unavoidably theological task bound up with a desire for truth that can only be satisfied by God as the ground of wholeness. Again, Gunton refers to Coleridge: 'What Coleridge saw, and saw clearly, is that in all thought there is choice of divinity to be made.'[76] Not surprisingly, Coleridge is recommended for conceiving wholeness and truth in patterns of interrelatedness that are grounded in the Trinity.

> Coleridge's point is that only a God conceived trinitarianly – that is, in terms of his personal otherness to and free relation with the world – is consistent

with a universe that is a fit place for human beings to live their lives. It is such a concern for the interrelatedness of things, of world and life, of theology and ethics, that founds the necessity for being systematic in theology, for thinking things together.[77]

Here, however, the analogy of the activity of doing systematic theology and giving form to a sculpture – a task that is inherently critical since it involves chipping away at whatever destroys the form and prevents its wholeness – must be expanded through an analogy that focuses on the texture of the shape of theology. Theology is the forming of an ordered pattern of particulars, combining repetition and novelty, a notion of textured shape created from interrelated particulars which is much closer to a quilt than a sculpture. This suggests that the activity of a systematic theologian 'with a concern for the interrelatedness of things' is more like the work of a quilter. Or, indeed, could it be that both these forms of shaping – seeing things whole and expressing their particularity and interrelatedness by forming patterns of particulars – come together in the activity of a gardener? Whichever we prefer, the Coleridgean quest for truth as a form of the quest for God contains an element that carries our reflection beyond integrated coherence, or, rather, sees the coherence as one that is rooted in its correspondence to the subject matter – although this correspondence may be one that can only be grasped provisionally now and awaits its eschatological 'fit'. It is furthermore not a correspondence of immediacy, as if word and their object could be isomorphically related. '. . . it is a correspondence which depends not so much on a naïve view of the relation of words and the world, as on a reality *already mediated through language*.'[78] The materials of systematic theology which through the activity of the theologians give their theology a particular shape – Scripture, the creeds, the tradition of life and thought of the Church in its interaction with other communities and beliefs – are therefore to be regarded as 'mediation' in a strict theological sense, witnessing to the work of the Son and Spirit who mediate the work of God the Father. Therefore, systematic theology cannot be done in abstraction from these mediations because this is the way in which the subject matter of theology, the triune God, gives himself.

With this claim, we move from the shape of Colin Gunton's theology – which is always relative to its subject matter, given in its manifold mediations – to the way in which systematic theology takes shape.

Systematic theology takes shape in the world as the discipline concerned to engage with the reality and implications of the economy of divine action in creation, reconciliation and redemption as it is recorded in Scripture. By indwelling the biblical words and the writings of the tradition, it seeks –

again in the *koinonia* of the body of Christ and in dependence on the Spirit – both to *integrate* the various elements of the economy without depriving them of the mystery of their many-sidedness and use that economic action as the basis for a doctrine of God.[79]

It is this understanding of how systematic theology takes shape in the world that determines the shape and the style of Colin Gunton's theology: its particular form of communication, systematic without presenting a system constructed *more geometrico*; historical without reducing the truth claims of the historical authors in a historicist manner; and in constant touch with the practical task of thinking and living theology in the Church – and always conversational in character. In his reflections on the possibility of an English systematic theology Gunton asks: 'What are the strengths in the English tradition?' And he answers: 'Historical studies and a concern for practicalities'[80] – and supplements this in a footnote by a hint that in this tradition, more than in some others, theology can be done as a collaborative enterprise, as a conversation, or, as he sometimes put it, in *koinonia* style. It is therefore fitting that the shape and style of Colin Gunton's theology invites further conversation with his thought.

## Notes

1 This is the subtitle of Colin Gunton's last book *Father, Son and Holy Spirit* (London/New York: T&T Clark, 2003).
2 Colin E. Gunton, *Becoming and Being. The Doctrine of God in Charles Hartshorne and Karl Barth* (Oxford: Oxford University Press 1978, 2nd ed.: London: SCM Press, 2001).
3 Gunton, *Becoming and Being*, p. 186.
4 Gunton, *Becoming and Being*, p. 135.
5 Gunton, *Becoming and Being*, p. 144.
6 Gunton, *Becoming and Being*, p. 215.
7 Gunton, *Becoming and Being*, p. 182.
8 Gunton, *Becoming and Being*, p. 183.
9 Ibid.
10 Gunton, *Becoming and Being*, p. 184.
11 Gunton, *Becoming and Being*, p. 185.
12 Gunton, *Becoming and Being*, p. 222.
13 It is not surprising that statements like these created, for those who defended or at least toyed with the idea of a philosophical foundation for theology, the impression that Gunton was a Barthian *simpliciter*. However, those who could perhaps be described as Barthians *simpliciter* were quite suspicious of Gunton's sharp criticisms of Karl Barth in *Becoming and Being*.
14 Gunton, *Becoming and Being*, p. 219.
15 Gunton, *Becoming and Being*, pp. 218 ff.

16 The 'Epilogue' (2001) concentrates on three areas of discussion where Gunton states how his theology had changed since 1978: 'The Person and the Trinity', 'Pneumatological Considerations' and 'Analogy and Attribute'.
17 Colin E. Gunton, *Yesterday and Today. A Study of Continuities in Christology* (2nd edn.: London: SPCK, 1997).
18 Gunton, *Yesterday and Today*, p. 86.
19 Ibid.
20 Gunton, *Yesterday and Today*, p. 87.
21 Gunton, *Yesterday and Today*, p. 97.
22 Gunton, *Yesterday and Today*, p. 95. This sharp diagnosis applies not only to the doctrine of the person of Christ but has wider implications: 'In Christology ... the outcome has been such dualisms as those of the Jesus of history and the Christ of faith; in soteriology, the suffering Jesus has often been divorced from the forgiving God; and in political thought the power of God has been understood in abstraction from the cross of Jesus.'
23 Gunton, *Yesterday and Today*, p. 101.
24 Above all, of course, there is the continuity that is located in the Church, and centrally in the celebration of the Eucharist. In the 'Epilogue' Gunton cites with approval J.S. Whale's observation that '[n]ot one Lord's day has ever passed without this showing of the Lord's death by the Lord's people' (J.S. Whale, *Victor and Victim: The Christian Doctrine of Redemption*. [Cambridge: Cambridge University Press, 1960], p. 135).
25 Gunton, *Yesterday and Today*, p. 134.
26 Gunton, *Yesterday and Today*, p. 208.
27 Colin E. Gunton, *Enlightenment and Alienation. An Essay Towards a Trinitarian Theology* (Basingstoke: Marshall Morgan & Scott, 1985).
28 Gunton, *Enlightenment and Alienation*, p. 2.
29 The title of Chapter 3.
30 Gunton, *Enlightenment and Alienation*, p. 92.
31 Gunton, *Enlightenment and Alienation*, p. 52.
32 Gunton, *Enlightenment and Alienation*, p. 53.
33 Ibid.
34 Gunton, *Enlightenment and Alienation*, p. 54.
35 Gunton, *Enlightenment and Alienation*, p. 52.
36 Gunton, *Enlightenment and Alienation*, p. 107.
37 Gunton, *Becoming and Being*, p. 219.
38 Cf. the 'Epilogue' to the second edition.
39 Ibid.
40 Gunton, *Enlightenment and Alienation*, p. 87.
41 Here quoted in the version published in: Colin E. Gunton, *The Promise of Trinitarian Theology* (Edinburgh: T&T Clark, 1991).
42 Gunton, *The Promise of Trinitarian Theology*, p. 90.
43 Gunton, *The Promise of Trinitarian Theology*, p. 93.
44 Gunton, *The Promise of Trinitarian Theology*, p. 97. The quotation in the quotation is, of course, from John Zizioulas. Gunton quotes from the paper 'The Ontology of Personhood' which was originally prepared for the British Council of Churches' (BCC) Study Commission on Trinitarian Doctrine Today, later published in: Christoph Schwöbel and Colin E. Gunton (eds), *Persons, Divine and Human* (Edinburgh: T&T Clark, 1991), pp. 33–46, 41. Gunton

and Zizioulas worked together in this Study Commission from 1983 to 1988. From 1986 Bishop John was a regular visiting professor at the Department of Christian Doctrine and History (as it then was) at King's College each summer term. The Report of the BCC Study Commission, *The Forgotten Trinity*, published 1989, marks an important stage in the renaissance of Trinitarian theology in Britain. At an ecumenical theological conference in 2001 the then Bishop of Monmouth and Archbishop of Wales, Rowan Williams, remarked to me in conversation: 'That was when John Zizioulas became the English Pope.'

45 Cf. Alan Spence, 'Inspiration and Incarnation: John Owen and the Coherence of Christology', *King's Theological Review* 12 (1989), pp. 52–55 and: 'Christ's Humanity and Ours: John Owen', in: Christoph Schwöbel and Colin E. Gunton, *Persons, Divine and Human* (Edinburgh: T&T Clark, 1991), pp. 74–97. Cf. also the monograph: *Incarnation and Inspiration: John Owen and the Coherence of Christology* (London: Continuum – T&T Clark, 2007).

46 Graham MacFarlane, *Christ and the Spirit. The Doctrine of the Incarnation According to Edward Irving* (Carlisle: Paternoster Press, 1996).

47 Colin E. Gunton, 'Two Dogmas Revisited: Edward Irving's Christology' (1988), now in Colin E. Gunton, *Theology Through the Theologians* (Edinburgh: T&T Clark, 1996), pp. 151–68, 154.

48 Gunton, 'Two dogmas', p. 153.

49 John Owen, *A Discourse Concerning the Holy Spirit* Works III. (Edinburgh: T&T Clark, 1862. First published in London, 1674), pp. 160 f., quoted in: 'Two Dogmas', p. 168.

50 Gunton, 'Two Dogmas', p. 163.

51 Gunton, 'Two Dogmas', p. 167.

52 Ibid.

53 Colin E. Gunton, 'The Transcendent Lord. The Spirit and the Church in Calvinist and Cappadocian [Thought]', Congregational Lecture, London: Congregational Memorial Hall Trust, 1988. Here quoted from the version published as 'The Church. John Owen and John Zizioulas on the Church', in: Gunton, *Theology through the Theologians*, pp. 187–205.

54 Gunton, 'The Transcendent Lord', p. 187.

55 Ibid.

56 Gunton, 'The Transcendent Lord', p. 194.

57 Gunton, 'The Transcendent Lord', p. 199.

58 Cf. 'God the Holy Spirit: Augustine and his Successors', in Gunton, *Theology Through the Theologians*, pp. 105–28. The chapter was originally written for a planned collection of essays to be written by the group that had collaborated in *On Being the Church* (Edinburgh: T&T Clark, 1989) – Colin Gunton, Dan Hardy, David Ford, Werner Jeanrond, Richard Roberts and myself – which, however, never came to be.

59 Cf. especially the much criticized chapter 3 of *The Promise of Trinitarian Theology*: 'Augustine, the Trinity and the Theological Crisis of the West', pp. 31–57. Not all the elements that Gunton attributes to the influence of Augustine can be traced back to Augustine himself. Rather, 'Augustine' and 'Augustinian' are for Gunton red flags indicating difficulties and problems in the Western tradition that call for new doctrinal elucidation. Conversely, not all insights Gunton develops from the Cappadocians can be traced back to their own writings in their own contexts and in their own systematizations.

Rather, referring to 'Cappadocia' is a way of marking the starting point from which doctrinal reconstruction can successfully commence, most of all with regard to the ontology of the person, but being enriched in the course of its development by insights some of which were still beyond the horizon for the historical Cappadocians. As he himself mentions in *The Promise of Trinitarian Theology*, p. 174, Gunton originally wanted to call that book *Homage to Cappadocia*, echoing George Orwell's *Homage to Catalonia* of 1938, and could barely be persuaded to adopt the present title. However, even after *The Promise of Trinitarian Theology*, he would eventually wonder whether the title might not serve as a rather splendid title for another collection of essays.

60 Gunton, 'God the Holy Spirit', p. 124.
61 Gunton, 'God the Holy Spirit', p. 126.
62 Gunton, 'God the Holy Spirit', p. 127.
63 Ibid.
64 Gunton, *The Promise of Trinitarian Theology*, p. 164: 'This means that we must reject the claim of Barth and other modern theologians that personality is a function of the one God, made known, in Barth's terminology, in three modes of being. The objection to Barth's development is not that it is modalist . . . It rather fails to reclaim the relational view of the person from the ravages of modern individualism.'
65 Gunton, *The Promise of Trinitarian Theology*, p. 165.
66 And one in which he remained in critical conversation with his teacher and friend Robert Jenson; cf. especially 'Immanence and Otherness. Divine Sovereignty and Human Freedom in the Theology of Robert W. Jenson', now in *The Promise of Trinitarian Theology*, pp. 122–41, and: 'Creation and Mediation in the Theology of Robert W. Jenson. An Encounter and a Convergence', now in *Father, Son and Holy Spirit. Essays Toward a Fully Trinitarian Theology*, pp. 93–106.
67 Colin E. Gunton, *Yesterday and Today: A Study of Continuities in Christology*, 2nd edn. (London: SPCK 1997), p. 216.
68 Ibid.
69 Ibid.
70 Gunton, *The One, the Three and the Many*, p. 142.
71 Gunton, *The One, the Three and the Many*, p. 230.
72 Colin E. Gunton, *The Triune Creator: A Historical and Systematic Study* (Edinburgh: Edinburgh University Press, 1998).
73 Colin E. Gunton, *The Christian Faith. An Introduction to Christian Doctrine* (Oxford: Blackwell, 2002).
74 Now chapter 1 in: Gunton, *Theology Through the Theologians*, pp. 1–18.
75 Gunton, *Theology Through the Theologians*, p. 10.
76 Gunton, *Theology Through the Theologians*, p. 13.
77 Ibid.
78 'A Rose by any other Name? From "Christian Doctrine" to "Systematic Theology"' (1999), p.42, now in: Colin E. Gunton, *Intellect and Action. Elucidations of Christian Theology and the Life of Faith* (Edinburgh: T&T Clark, 2000), pp. 19–45.
79 Gunton, *Intellect and Action*, p. 43.
80 Gunton, *Theology Through the Theologians*, p. 17.

# INDEX

Barth, Karl (*continued*)
  and Schleiermacher 147
  theology of 22, 27, 183, 186
beatific vision 175, 199
belief, antecedent 177
Berkeley, George 37, 162, 172, 188–9
Brentwood 100

Cain 155
Calvin, John 108–9, 138, 151, 159, 165,
  171, 174–6, 180
Catholicism 109
causation, mundane 154, 157
Christ
  begetting of 14–15, 58, 79
  career of 194
  and the Church 3, 15–16, 104–5, 107,
    109, 111
  cosmic 101
  and creaturely ontology 92
  death of 132–3, 135, 139, 141, 149
  divinity of 26, 55, 58–9, 70, 194
  encounters with demonic forces 136
  and the Eucharist 108–10
  humanity of 2–4, 25–6, 28, 55, 62,
    69–72, 94, 102, 110, 118–19, 192–4
  and knowledge 175–6
  miracles of 70
  as moral exemplar 131–2
  personal agency of 54–5
  priesthood of 5, 25–6, 105, 117, 125,
    138
  and providence 155–6
  resurrection of 70, 153
  as second Adam 118–19, 126–7, 154
  status in Trinity 13–15
  theology of 3, 28
  two natures of 52–3, 56, 61, 107–9
  ubiquity of 110
  unity of person of 50–3, 61, 107
Christology
  from above 192–3
  in Barth 26
  classical 28, 34, 187
  and communion of attributes 15

and doctrine of creation 80
duality in 55–7, 61–2
of Forsyth 53
Gunton's 3–4, 34, 52, 54, 59, 70, 109,
  193
Holy Spirit in 23, 69, 188, 190
language in 3
modern 61
and ontology 5
post-metaphysical 72
and postmodernism 199–200
Reformed 28
Church
  importance for Gunton 100–1, 103–4
  as a sacrament 109, 111–12
clericalism 104, 141, 194
Coleridge, Samuel Taylor
  and community 192
  concept of ideas 89, 169
  Gunton's interest in xii, 38, 78, 188–9,
    203
  on the Trinity 74, 190–1, 196, 200
collectivism 75, 192
  36, 71, 80, 102, 107
communion
  of attributes 15
  and food 125
  with God 197, 203
  in Gunton 116
  and mediation 2, 74, 91
  and particularity 74–5, 77
  rupture of 124
  triune 13, 74–7, 79, 196–7
community
  Christian 101, 178
  of the Church 195–6
  organisation of 192
confession, nature of 27
Congregationalism 101, 104, 141
contingency 86, 148
covenant 26, 91, 139–40
creation
  and Christ 118
  as divine project 147, 151
  goal of 122, 125

CPSIA information can be obtained at www.ICGtesting.com
Printed in the USA
LVOW100742010912

296977LV00004B/14/P